INDEX
ON CENSORSHIP

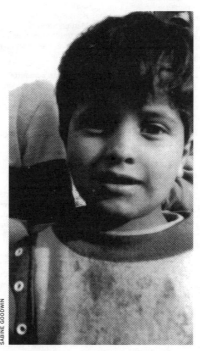

SABINE GOODWIN

Unrecognised Palestine

INDEX ON CENSORSHIP 1/2 1994

Index on Censorship (ISSN 0306-4220) is published
bimonthly by a non-profit-making company: Writers
& Scholars International Ltd, Lancaster House,
33 Islington High Street, London N1 9LH
Phone: 071-278 2313 Fax: 071-278 1878

Second class postage (US subscribers only) paid at
Irvington, New Jersey. Postmaster: send US address
changes to Index on Censorship c/o Virgin Mailing
& Distribution, 10 Camptown Road, Irvington, NJ
07111

Subscriptions 1994 (6 issues p.a.): £30 (overseas
£36 or US$48). Students £23/US$35

STEPHEN SPENDER

Silence falls

It is fitting that with this Spring number *Index on Censorship* should be completely renewed. For we have moved into an entirely different world from that which existed in 1968 when I received a letter from Pavel Litvinov, then in Moscow, in response to one I had sent him. Pavel asked me to set up a committee in England to consider what action we might take to diffuse worldwide knowledge of censorship wherever this happened — not only in that part of the world dominated by the Soviet Union, he insisted, but all over the world wherever there was censorship. He cited Greece (this was the era of the Colonels) and South Africa as examples.

In those days, because of the vast areas subjected to direction from Moscow, censorship, though happening to a greater or less extent all over the world, had a monolithic look. Today we live in an era of fragmentation and censorship is liable to be local. It is liable to be one of the phenomena connected with ethnic conflicts in which one group aware of itself as a people shuts itself off from other groups — the Serbs from the Croats, the Croats from the Muslims.

Fragmentation may not lead directly to overt censorship. Yet it is in itself a concentration on particular points of view which inhibits wider, more general, points of view from being expressed. At the end of this century there is the danger of our entering an extensively fragmented world, particularly in areas where old centres of power have broken up.

The opposite of censorship is self-expression, which we call literature. And one result of the present period of fragmentation through which we are living seems to be the disappearance of the literature which previously attained a kind of notoriety through its being banned or smuggled out of the countries where it was banned. Nations are released from tyranny, but instead of there following an upsurge of creativity there falls a silence.

Reporting on censorship was, and still doubtless is, the main task of *Index*. But recent circumstances suggest that as well as being concerned with what is negative, *Index* should be concerned with the positive: the state of the culture in certain countries: that is not only whether freedom is being suppressed there, but to what effect it is being used.

EDITORIAL

Whose rights, whose freedom?

Sixty-one years ago this week, a torchlight parade of students marched to a square in Berlin on *Unter den Linden* and made a bonfire of some 20,000 books, among them some of the great works of nineteenth and twentieth century thought and literature. In the words of a student proclamation, any book was condemned to the flames 'which acts subversively on our future or strikes at the root of our thought, our home and the driving forces of our people'. The book burning, that abiding metaphor for censorship that would light the way to the Holocaust, had begun.

Today we see the revival of nationalism (another infantile disorder, as Danilo Kis said), the decay of the social and economic fabric and the return of private affluence and public squalor. The void left by the fall of communism has not been filled by parliamentary democracy or thriving economies. In the search for a social and economic identity in the new states, the temptation to assert identity by intolerance has led to xenophobia, racism and anti-semitism.

As we go to press, daily reports confirm the rise of the New Right, with its excluding hate speech, across Europe. This dramatises one of the most difficult debates about censorship. The new *Index* faces a world where the conviction that freedom of expression is a fundamental human right is challenged 'not only', as Ronald Dworkin says, 'by freedom's oldest enemies but also by new enemies who claim to speak for justice, not tyranny', who point to the need to protect other values, including freedom from racial hatred.

Dworkin is convinced that the right of free expression is an inalienable one, and that the right of some people to say despicable and harmful things is the price we all must pay. Umberto Eco, however, believes we must define the limits of tolerance, and to do this we must first know what is intolerable. The extracts from Vladimir Zhirinovsky's *A Last Bid for the South*, with their bizarre echoes from an earlier credo, *Mein Kampf*, and published here in English for the first time, illustrate the dilemma. And our country file, to be a regular feature of the new *Index,* focuses on Egypt, where another version of hate speech, the fundamentalist variety, is growing in intensity.

The amplified power of the modern media has presented more ambiguities. Dubravka Ugresic demonstrates with devastating clarity how media lying became an instigator of the tragic war of intolerance in the Balkans, while in America, where violence on TV has become a perverse art form, Anne Nelson cites evidence of a causal relationship between screen violence and real life violence. How much have we the right to monitor what the media puts out, and where do we draw the line?

These are difficult questions, and there are more, and *Index* must become an arena for debating them. But still censorship remains, beyond question, a central metaphor for many kinds of oppression, and the level at which it operates most revealing of the condition of a country. 'The opposite of censorship', says Stephen Spender,' is self-expression, which we call literature.' *Index* will continue to monitor freedoms suppressed the world over. On the whole the news is not good. 'The contempt of governments for the rights of their citizens seems never to have been higher', says Caroline Moorehead in her overview of the year. Close to home, we don't have much to be proud of either: Matthew d'Ancona, reflecting on the Scott inquiry, tells us 'just how deeply ingrained the habits of secrecy are in the British administrative psyche.' Even the first steps taken by the British government towards greater openness have been compromised for the sake of some military or administrative convenience.

The new, redesigned *Index* will be published six times a year, its pages open to the world's best and best known writers as well as the unknown and marginalised. It will focus not just on the censored but on the silenced, and a new feature, Babel, will carry the voices of those not usually heard. The magazine will continue its tradition of news analysis, highlighting the world's most troubled areas; it will also publish fiction and poetry, reviews, interviews, personal witness and writers' diaries. And it will continue its crucial monitoring of free speech violations in a more comprehensive and accessible Index Index.

The language of oppression, as Toni Morrison said in her Nobel acceptance speech 'does more than represent violence; it is violence: does more than represent the limits of knowledge; it limits knowledge. Whether it is obscuring state language or the faux-language of mindless media: whether it is the proud but calcified language of the academy or the commodity driven language of science: whether it is the malign language of law-without-ethics, or language designed for the estrangement of minorities, hiding its racist plunder in its literary cheek — it must be rejected, altered and exposed. It is the language that drinks blood, laps vulnerabilities, tucks its fascist boots under the crinolines of respectability and patriotism as it moves relentlessly towards the bottom line and the bottomed-out mind.'

Index will fight that language of oppression and publish the language of dissent; be a place for divergent voices to be heard; and defend everywhere the right of the imagination to flourish.   **Ursula Owen**

CONTENTS

Volume 23 (New Series) Nos 1&2 May/June 1994   156/7   ISSN 0306 4220

STEPHEN SPENDER	Silence falls	3
EDITORIAL	Whose rights, whose freedom?	4
RONALD DWORKIN	A new map of censorship	9
SALMAN RUSHDIE	Bosnia on my mind	16
DUBRAVKA UGRESIC	The culture of lies	23
JAMES FENTON	The Exchange	44
UMBERTO ECO	Tolerance and the intolerable	47
PHOTO FEATURE	Nationalism and the new right	57
VLADIMIR ZHIRINOVSKY	A last bid for the south, introduced by Aleksei Venediktov	61
ADEWALE MAJA-PEARCE	Letter from Lagos Living in the last days	72
22 YEARS AGO	Stephen Spender For those not free	78
RONALD HARWOOD	Diary Sanction busting in Belgrade	80
ANNE NELSON	Colours of violence	86
POSY SIMMONDS	Cartoon	92
HUMAN RIGHTS	Caroline Moorehead 1993: What rights?	93

Amnesty Political prisoners; Middle East Watch Algeria; Asia Watch China and Tibet; Helsinki Watch/ Memorial Tajikistan; International Pen Writers in prison; Article 19 Campaigns and partnership

Volume 23 (New Series) Nos 1&2 May/June 1994   156/7   ISSN 0306 4220

FILE ON EGYPT   **Karim Alrawi** Introduction; **Naguib**   **111**
Mahfouz Terminal sickness; **Said al-**
Ashmawi The militants; **EOHR** The
mosque; **Farag Fouda** The heart that
grieves; **Latifa al-Zayyat** A Raid;
Mohamed Mustageb Woman; **Mariam**
Muhamad The press; **EOHR** Press laws;
Gamal el-Ghitani The air we breathe;
Mahmoud el-Lozy Theatre

NEWS ANALYSIS   **Matthew d'Ancona** UK; **Michael Farrell**   **150**
Ireland; **Jeff Rigsby** Belarus; **Vesna**
Bjekic & Ozrenka Radulovic Serbia;
Vesna Roller Croatia: **Alexandrine**
Civard Macedonia; **Nathalie Nougayrede**
Georgia; **Henri Frasque** Chiapas; **Boris**
Adam Vietnam; **Robert Ménard** Turkey

MINORITIES   **Peter Calvert** The indians of Chiapas   **166**

BABEL   **Sabine Goodwin** Unrecognised in Israel   **171**

REVIEWS   **Alberto Manguel** Arabia; **Suzanne**   **182**
Gibson Women; **Doris Lessing** China

WEN YUHONG   The mad city   **192**
JOHN GITTINGS   The truth behind the fiction   **204**

MICHAEL GRADE   The state of the nation   **207**

ROBERT McCRUM   Indifferent death   **214**

LEGAL   **Anthony Burton** Tribute to Bernard   **221**
Simons; **Andrew Kelly** Silent witness

INDEX INDEX   A record of those not free   **228**

CONTRIBUTORS   **254**

CAMERA PRESS

ROMANIA'S REVOLUTION/CAMERA PRESS

Spanning more than a century of news and features and with an archive of more than ten million images, **Camera Press** is one of the world's leading photo agencies. We are pleased to be involved with the relaunch of **Index on Censorship** and hope to continue our support long into the future

RONALD DWORKIN

A new map of censorship

The old order changes yielding place to new — and freedom finds itself in disarray, under attack from new enemies among its old champions

Is freedom of speech a universal human right? Or is it, after all, just one value among others, a value cherished by middle-class intellectuals in Western democracies, but one which other cultures, drawing on different traditions, might well reject as unsuitable for them, and which radical groups within those Western democracies might well challenge as no longer central even there?

Index was founded in the first conviction: that freedom of speech, along with the allied freedoms of conscience and religion, are fundamental human rights that the world community has a responsibility to guard. But that strong conviction is suddenly challenged not only by freedom's oldest enemies — the despots and ruling thieves who fear it — but also by new enemies who claim to speak for justice not tyranny, and who point to other values we respect, including self-determination, equality, and freedom from racial hatred and prejudice, as reasons why the right of free speech should now be demoted to a much lower grade of urgency and importance.

In part, this new hostility reflects reluctance to impose Western values on alien cultures. Free speech may be important within our own secular traditions, some critics say, but it would make no sense to graft it on to very different styles of life. We cannot reasonably ask peoples whose entire social structure and sense of national identity are based on the supreme authority of a particular religion to permit what they believe to be ridicule of that religion within their own borders.

How can we expect people who are committed to a particular faith, as a value transcending all others, to tolerate its open desecration?

Other critics insist that free speech is overvalued even within Western democracies, and particularly within the USA. When the Supreme Court ruled, in the Skokie case, that the Constitution's First Amendment protected neo-Nazis who wanted to carry swastikas through a town of Holocaust survivors in Illinois, many people of good will wondered how justice could require people to accept such a grotesque insult. In the decades since the Skokie decision, moreover, Americans have become even more aware of the malign, chilling force of hate-speech and hate-gesture. That kind of speech seems particularly odious in universities, where it has been directed against women and minority students and fuelled by a backlash against the affirmative-action and other special recruiting programmes such universities adopted to increase the number of such students.

Officials at some of these universities have adopted 'speech codes' to prohibit remarks that are sexist or derogatory of a particular race or religion or sexual orientation; they defend that apparent violation of freedom of speech by insisting that the regulations are necessary to protect the dignity and equal status of all students. Some speech code supporters have taken the opportunity not just to argue for an exception to free speech, however, but to deny its importance in principle. They say that though the right of free speech has been much prized by liberal writers who profit from it, it has proved of little value to the poor and disadvantaged, and has often acted as an excuse for their oppression. One such critic, Stanley Fish, declared that, 'There's no such thing as free speech, and a good thing too.'

But the strongest new attack on freedom of speech, within democracies, has been organised by those feminists who are anxious to outlaw pornography or to make its publishers liable for punitive damages if a rapist or other criminal convinces a jury that pornography made him act as he did. They say that pornography contributes to a general cultural environment in which women are treated only as sexual devices, and subordinated to men in every way. One such American feminist, Catharine MacKinnon, is contemptuous of the objection that such censorship violates an important right; she says that Americans elevate freedom of speech to an absurd level of importance, and that more sensible people, in other parts of the world, recognise that it is to be tolerated only so long as it does not jeopardise more important goals.

Even Tom Stoppard, a distinguished and long-standing Patron of *Index*, has joined in this recent demotion of free speech. Speaking at an anniversary of Khomeni's hideous *fatwa* against Salman Rushdie, Stoppard said that though it was of course outrageous for Iran's priests to suppose that they had a right to order a murder in Britain, it was nevertheless a mistake to regard freedom of speech as a 'fundamental' human right. 'The proscription of writing which seeks to incite race hatred sits as comfortably in the Western liberal conscience,' he said, 'as the proscription against falsely shouting "Fire!" in a crowded theatre.'

Free speech has proved of little value to the poor and disadvantaged, and has often acted as an excuse for their oppression

These are all thoughtful opinions that will strike many people as reasonable. They signal, just for that reason, a new and particularly dangerous threat to free speech, for we are more likely to relax our defence of that freedom when its betrayers are foreign, or when the speech in question seems worthless or even vile. But if we do, then the principle is inevitably weakened, not just in such cases, but generally. So we must try to abstract from the particular challenges to free speech that now dominate the argument, and to return to the wider question I began by asking. Is free speech a universal human right, a right so important that we must work to secure it even in nations where it is unfamiliar and alien? Is it so important that we must tolerate, in its name, despicable and harmful speech in our own society?

I do not mean, by posing that last question, to agree that bad speech has had the malign consequences that have recently been claimed for it. Many of those claims are inflated and some are absurd. But if free speech really is as fundamental as many of its defenders have supposed in the past, we must protect it even if it does have bad consequences, and we must be prepared to explain why. We must explain this, moreover, bearing in mind everything that, if we are right, must be tolerated. It may seem easy to defend the rights to investigative reporters exposing corruption or serious novelists exploring literary and intellectual boundaries. But free speech, if it is a universal right, also protects pornographers hawking pictures of naked women with their legs spread, and bigots sporting swastikas or white hoods and selling hatred.

We must start by recognising that the most famous and honoured defence of free speech — John Stuart Mill's argument in *On Liberty* — cannot support a right with that scope. Mill said that we should tolerate even the speech we hate because truth is most likely to emerge in a free intellectual combat from which no idea has been excluded. People with passionate religious convictions think they already know the truth, however, and they can hardly be expected to have more confidence in Mill's doubtful epistemology than in their own bibles. Nor could Mill's optimism justify, even to us, tolerating everything that those who believe free speech is a basic human right insist should be tolerated. Pornographic images hardly supply 'ideas' to any market place of thought, and history gives us little reason for expecting racist speech to contribute to its own refutation.

If freedom of speech is a basic right, this must be so not in virtue of instrumental arguments, like Mill's, which suppose that liberty is important because of its consequences. It must be so for reasons of basic principle. We can find that basic principle, moreover. We can find it in a condition of human dignity: it is illegitimate for governments to impose a collective or official decision on dissenting individuals, using the coercive powers of the state, unless that decision has been taken in a manner that respects each individual's status as a free and equal member of the community. People who believe in democracy think that it is fair to use the police power to enforce the law if the law has been adopted through democratic political procedures that express the majority's will. But though majoritarian procedures may be a necessary condition of political legitimacy, they are not a sufficient condition. Fair democracy requires what we might call a democratic background: it requires, for example, that every competent adult have a vote in deciding what the majority's will is. And it requires, further, that each citizen have not just a vote but a voice: a majority decision is not fair unless everyone has had a fair opportunity to express his or her attitudes or opinions or fears or tastes or presuppositions or prejudices or ideals, not just in the hope of influencing others, though that hope is crucially important, but also just to confirm his or her standing as a responsible agent in, rather than a passive victim of, collective action. The majority has no right to impose its will on someone who is forbidden to raise a voice in protest or argument or objection before the decision is taken.

That is not the only reason for insisting on freedom of speech as a condition of political legitimacy, but it is a central one. It may be objected that in most democracies that right now has little value for many citizens: ordinary people, with no access to great newspapers or television broadcasts, have little chance to be heard. That is a genuine problem; it may be that genuine free speech requires more than just freedom from legal censorship. But that is hardly an excuse for denying at least that freedom and the dignity it confirms: we must try to find other ways of providing those without money or influence a real chance to make their voices heard.

This argument entails a great deal more than just that governments may not censor formal political speeches or writing. A community's legislation and policy are determined more by its moral and cultural environment — the mix of its people's opinions, prejudices, tastes and attitudes — than by editorial columns or party political broadcasts or stump political speeches. It is as unfair to impose a collective decision on someone who has not been allowed to contribute to that moral environment, by expressing his political or social convictions or tastes or prejudices informally, as on someone whose pamphlets against the decision were destroyed by the police. This is true no matter how offensive the majority takes these convictions or tastes or prejudices to be, nor how reasonable its objection is.

The temptation may be near overwhelming to make exceptions to that principle — to declare that people have no right to pour the filth of pornography or race-hatred into the culture in which we all must live. But we cannot do that without forfeiting our moral title to force such people to bow to the collective judgements that do make their way into the statute books. We may and must protect women and homosexuals and members of minority groups from specific and damaging consequences of sexism, intolerance and racism. We must protect them against unfairness and inequality in employment or education or housing or the criminal process, for example, and we may adopt laws to achieve that protection. But we must not try to intervene further upstream, by forbidding any expression of the attitudes or prejudices that we think nourish such unfairness or inequality, because if we intervene too soon in the process through which collective opinion is formed, we spoil the only democratic justification we have for insisting that everyone obey these laws, even those who hate and resent them.

Someone might now object that my argument shows, at most, only that free speech is essential to a democracy, and therefore does not show that it is a universal human right that may properly be claimed even in non-democratic societies. We may want to reply, to that objection, that democracy is itself a universal human right, and that non-democratic societies are tyrannies. But we need not rely on that claim, because we can distinguish democracy, as a form of political organisation, from the more basic obligation of government to treat all those subject to its dominion with equal concern, as all people whose lives matter. That plainly is a basic human right; and many of the more detailed human rights we all recognise flow from it. And so does a right of free speech. Even in a country ruled by prophets or generals in which ordinary citizens have no real vote, these citizens must nevertheless have the right to speak out, to cry for the attention or to buy the ear of those who will decide their fates, or simply to bear witness, out of self-respect if nothing else, to what they believe to be wicked or unfair. A government that deems them too corrupt or debased or ignoble even to be heard, except on penalty of death or jail, can hardly pretend that it counts their interests as part of its own.

It is tempting, as I said, to think that even if some liberty of speech must be counted a universal right, this right cannot be absolute; that those whose opinions are too threatening or base or contrary to the moral or religious consensus have forfeited any right to the concern on which the right rests. But such a reservation would destroy the principle: it would leave room only for the pointless grant of protection for ideas or tastes or prejudices that those in power approve, or in any case do not fear. We might have the power to silence those we despise, but it would be at the cost of political legitimacy, which is more important than they are.

Any such reservation would also be dangerous. MacKinnon and her allies failed in the USA: the courts held their statute unconstitutional. But they persuaded the Canadian legislature to adopt a severe censorship law, and the law was upheld against constitutional challenge there. As liberals had warned, the first authors to be banned under the new Canadian statute were not those the feminists had in mind. They were, in fact, prominent homosexual and lesbian authors, a radical black feminist accused of stirring up hatred against whites, and, for a time, Andrea Dworkin, MacKinnon's main ally in the feminist censorship movement, herself. Principle is indivisible, and we try to divide it at our peril. When we compromise on freedom because we think our immediate goals more important, we are likely to find that the power to exploit the compromise is not in our own hands after all, but in those of fanatical priests armed with *fatwas* and fanatical moralists with their own brand of hate.

Cairo 1981: Muslim extremists on trial for the murder of Anwar al-Sadat

SALMAN RUSHDIE

Bosnia on my mind

I have never been to Sarajevo, but I feel that I belong to it. There is a Sarajevo of the mind, an imagined Sarajevo whose present ruination and torment exiles us all

It is, in spite of some signs that things may be improving, still impossibly hard to make any sort of statement at all about the situation in Bosnia-Hercegovina. It is possible to read that it was the threat of air strikes that persuaded the Serbs to withdraw their heavy artillery from positions above and around Sarajevo, that it was the Russians who persuaded them, that in fact the Serbs relocated their tanks in civilian areas where air strikes against them would not be possible and from which they could attack Sarajevo just as easily as before, that the Russians and Greeks are backing Nato, that the Russians and Greeks, in defiance of Nato are ganging up with their Orthodox allies the Serbs to ensure the success of Serbian strategy, that now that the Bosnian Croats under Tudjman are willing to form a federation with the 'Muslims' this may provide the basis for a deal with the Bosnian Serbs to preserve some sort of unified state of Bosnia-Hercegovina, that the partition of Bosnia into three mini-states is inevitable and the 'Muslims' must be forced to accept it, that black is white and yes is no and down is up and stop is go and it remains only to join the demented old codgers in James Fenton's *Ballad of the Shrieking Man* and sing:

> *Tramps are mad*
> *And truth is mad*
> *And so are trees and trunks and tracks.*
> *The horror maps have played us true.*
> *The horror moon that slits the clouds*
> *The gun*
> *The goon*
> *The burly sacks*
> *The purple waistcoats of the natterjacks*
> *Have done their bit as you can see*
> *To prise the madness from our sanity.*

It will not do, however, this codger-fashion despair. It will not do to decide, in the saloon bars of our hearts, that they have hated each other for millennia over there, they have been wanting to slaughter each other for centuries, and now the goblins are out of the bottle, the warlords are standing at their roadblocks, let them get on with it. Equally unsatisfactory is the cleaned-up, Newspeak version of the above, which says the Situation Is Complex and there are No Easy Answers and do we really want Our Boys to be embroiled forever in What Is, After All, A Civil War?

It will not do because there is still such a thing as truth, however much the war and the world's politicians may have shredded it. And that truth, for me, lies in the nature and meaning of the city of Sarajevo, where, as Susan Sontag has said, the twentieth century began, and where, with terrible symmetry, it is ending.

I have never been to Sarajevo, but I feel that I belong to it, in a way. I am proud to be an honorary member of the PEN club of ex-Yugoslavian writers, and I hope they will not think me presumptuous if I say that as a result of this newly-forged connection I, too, can claim to be, in some sense, an exile from Sarajevo, even though it is a city I do not know.

There is a Sarajevo of the mind, an imagined Sarajevo whose ruination and torment exiles us all. That Sarajevo represents something like an ideal;

a city in which the values of pluralism, tolerance and coexistence have created a unique and resilient culture. In that Sarajevo there actually exists that secularist Islam for which so many people are fighting elsewhere in the world. The people of that Sarajevo do not define themselves by faith or tribe, but simply, and honourably, as citizens.

If that city is lost, then we are all its refugees. If the culture of Sarajevo dies, then we are all its orphans.

Sarajevo's truth (as opposed to the saloon-bar version) is that the different communities have not been hating each other since the dawn of time, but have been good neighbours, schoolfriends, work-mates and lovers; that in this city miscegenation and intermarriage have been not the exception, but the norm. (And if they were bad neighbours, enemies at school, and rivals at work, and if their marriages failed, it was for the ordinary human reasons of personality and affinity, rather than the 'cleansing' evils of nationalism).

Sarajevo's truth (as opposed to the Newspeak version) is that the city has been the scene not of a civil war but of a war of aggression by the Serbs; that if the Serbs do once and for all cease their bombardments, it will be because they have already seized 'their' quarter of the city, forcing a *de facto* partition on what should have remained united; and that the outside world seems bent on imposing on this hybrid city the 'logic', the 'reality', of ethnicity, and on giving the aggressor the spoils of war.

Sarajevo's truth is that its citizens, who reject definition by religion or confession, who wish to be simply Bosnians, have for their pains been labelled by the outside world as 'Muslims'. It is instructive to imagine how things might have gone in former Yugoslavia if the Bosnians had been Christians and the Serbs had been Muslims, even Muslims 'in name only'. Would Europe have supported a 'Serbian Muslim' carve-up of the defunct state? It's only a guess, but I guess that it would not. Which being true, it must also be true that the 'Muslim' tag is part of the reason for Europe's indifference to Sarajevo's fate.

I have not been to Sarajevo — I have wanted to, but it has thus far proved impossible to arrange — but I have in recent months met three of its many extraordinary citizens: Zdravko Grebo, of the radio station that is the city's voice and conscience, Radio Zid; Haris Pasovic, a man bursting with projects, the man who brought about last year's Sarajevo Film

SEAN SMITH/CAMERA PRESS LONDON

In the graveyards of Sarajevo

Festival — and what an achievement, to stage a festival of over a hundred movies in the midst of such a war!; and Kemal Kurspahic, editor of Sarajevo's battling newspaper *Oslobodjenje*. They taught me a further, simple truth: that to define the people of besieged Sarajevo simply as entities in need of basic supplies would be to visit upon them a second privation: by reducing them to mere statistical victimhood, it would deny them their personalities, their individuality, their idiosyncrasies — in short, their humanity. When UNPROFOR officers limit the number of personal letters that can be carried in or out of the city; when permission for artists to visit the city is refused, as Pasovic can attest it has been, and when Western government spokesmen avow that culture is a luxury in wartime, this denial of Sarajevo's humanity is precisely the crime they are committing.

Grebo, limping from a wound, overwhelmingly impressive in his gentle dignity — seems to embody Sarajevo's spirit; Pasovic, its determination to keep its culture alive. Kurspahic is more melancholy, and a recent essay by his *Oslobodjenje* colleague Zlatko Dizdarevic expresses the city's present mood. 'Sarajevo no longer believes anyone ... Sarajevo has seen everything there is to see till now, and it has felt the worst there is to feel upon its own skin. The results are obvious. Until six or seven months ago, every true Sarajevan needed at least an hour to walk from the Holiday Inn to the cathedral. You had to stop and say hello to so many people, to ask after everyone. Now that same distance takes just 15 minutes because no one stops. No one has anything left to ask anyone.' He tells of a boy whose father was killed, and who now says, 'Last night I dreamt about my father. I dreamt about him on purpose.' 'Somebody will one day have to watch out', Dizdarevic warns, 'for boys from Sarajevo who dream about their murdered fathers on purpose.'

A city, a people, does not have an unlimited supply of spirit, not even this city, this people. Will the secular 'Muslims' of today become vengeful fundamentalists of tomorrow, dreaming on purpose of the dead? So far, by all acccounts, hard-line Islamism has made amazingly small strides in the city, but that's just so far. Will Sarajevo be saved? Sarajevo scarcely believes it will. But the fact remains: that the fight for the survival of the unique culture of Sarajevo is a fight for what matters most to us about our own.

I have just seen a strange short film in which a man driving down the sniper-infested streets of Sarajevo repeats, over and over, like a mantra, my name. *Salman Rushdie, Salman Rushdie, Salman Rushdie; Salman Rushdie; Salman Rushdie, Salman Rushdie; Salman Rushdie, Salman Rushdie, Salman Rushdie.* Is he chanting it to remind him of his danger, or as a kind of spell to keep him safe? I hope it is the latter, and it is in that spirit of sympathetic magic that I have begun to murmur, under my breath, the name of this unknown city of which I declare myself to be an imaginary citizen:

Sarajevo, Sarajevo, Sarajevo,
Sarajevo,
Sarajevo, Sarajevo,
Sarajevo, Sarajevo, Sarajevo,
Sarajevo, Sarajevo,
Sarajevo

© *Salman Rushdie 1994*

SUBSCRIBING TO OUR PRINCIPLES ISN'T ENOUGH.

You should be subscribing to our magazine, too.

Because week in and week out *The Nation* brings you the likes of Katha Pollitt, Alexander Cockburn, Slavenka Drakulić and Christopher Hitchens in every issue.

They're not only some of the best writers around—they do their best work for us.

The Nation.
Since 1865.

DUBRAVKA UGRESIC

The culture of lies

New lies are written over old truths as the people of ex-Yugoslavia are terrorised by war into remembering — and forgetting

People are always shouting that they want to create a better future. It's not true. The future is an apathetic void of no interest to anyone. The past is full of life, eager to irritate us, provoke and insult us, tempt us to destroy or repaint it. The only reason people want to be masters of the future is to change the past. They are fighting for access to the laboratories where photographs are retouched and biographies and histories rewritten.
Milan Kundera. *The Book of Laughter and Forgetting*

I was in a Zagreb hospital recently and happened to come across an acquaintance from Sarajevo. He looked pretty wretched: right leg in plaster, left arm bandaged, a mass of dark bruises...

'My God...' I exclaimed, because I didn't know what else to say.

'I've just come from Sarajevo...' he said.

'My God...' I shook my head. 'So, how did this happen?' I asked. (I couldn't have asked a stupider question).

'I'll tell you, but promise you won't tell anyone...' I nodded, filled with a sense of guilt and deep compassion for my acquaintance from Sarajevo.

'I was sitting in my room, when suddenly — wham — a grenade flew in through the open window...'

'And then?!' I gasped.

'Nothing. It didn't explode... I picked it up... and threw it out of the window, what else could I have done...'

'And then?!'

'Nothing. It exploded and took off the front wall...'

'And then?!'

'Nothing. I peered out through the broken wall of the room and fell, from the second floor... into the street.'

'And then?!'

'Nothing. I smashed myself up...'

My Sarajevo acquaintance had told the truth. But his truth was self-discrediting, for a moment it destroyed the terrible, general truth of the sufferings of the inhabitants of Sarajevo, it sounded like a parody of their real collective suffering. All in all, at that moment I felt betrayed, as though my acquaintance had told me a tasteless joke (looking for sympathy too!). The fact that the unfortunate fellow had barely survived, that he had lived through the terrible fate of his city for a whole year, that, when he did get out, he had told me only the last, personal episode — somehow none of that was able to prevent my slight sense of disappointment. With all those bandages he could have invented a heroic tale. Which, *really*, would have been true!

His situation was like that of all those who tell their *own* truth in these terrible war times. Terrible times are usually Collective times. The Truth is only what may be smoothly built into the picture which the Collective accepts as the Truth. If we add to that a time of general postmodern confusion — then the truth will sound like a lie, a lie like the truth.

In the terrible times of war, apart from the culture of death, the things that come irrepressibly to the surface, like hologram grimaces, are the shapes of parallel lives. In the chaos, an infernal balance is established: suffering masks its parody under a black mourning cloth, tragedy drags farce in its wake, as unhappiness does cynicism, brutality and compassion go everywhere together. Times of great truths are usually deeply permeated with the all-pervading culture of lies.

It seems that this culture of lies is something that the small nations of the Balkans created long ago, learning to live with it and reinforcing it to this day. Lying — just like dying, after all — has become a natural state, a norm of behaviour, liars are normal citizens. And if one really should give any credit to Dobrica Cosic, Serbian writer and failed president of the *false Yugoslavia*, then it must be for his remark: 'Lying is an aspect of our patriotism and confirmation of our innate intelligence.'

What is most astounding, as everyone who has taken part in the negotiations in today's Yugoslavia will tell you, is the unbelievable capacity of people — at all levels — to tell lies. An incredible phenomenon. Just look at how many ceasefires have been broken. And they carried on signing papers with the obvious intention of disregarding them. In ex-Yugoslavia our norms of honour don't exist, it's part of the culture. 'It's so widespread that you won't be at all surprised when you realise that X or Y is a liar, here people live with a culture of lies,' said

Lord Owen on one occasion. Owen himself discredited Western 'norms of honour', if such a thing exists and if that was what was at stake, by signing agreements with liars.

I s this matter of the culture of lies really so simple?

The peoples of (now non-existent) Yugoslavia lived for several decades in their own country, building not only cities, bridges, roads, railways but also a certain complex of values. Built into the foundations of that Yugoslav complex of values were, among other things, 'the ideology and practice of socialism' (today those same ex-Yugoslavs call that 'Communism', 'Tito's regime', 'Communist dictatorship'). It was a practice which to a considerable extent confirmed the earlier break with Stalin (even if the break was carried out on the principle of 'the same medicine': numerous individuals, usually out of a sheer inability to cope with the rapid ideological U-turn, ended up on the Yugoslav Gulag, Goli Otok). Then there was that famous 'Yugoslavism'. This implied a multinational and multicultural community and was reinforced over the years not only by Tito's popular slogans — 'Cherish brotherhood and unity as your most precious possession' — but also by the practice of daily life. (Today those same peoples claim that they lived in a prison of nations, and that it was that idea, the idea of Yugoslavism — not they themselves — which is responsible for the present brutal war.)

Some ten years ago, the nations of now former Yugoslavia wept sincerely at the funeral of their long-lived mummy, Tito. Now those same nations claim unanimously that they lived under the 'repressive boot of a communist dictator'. The more extreme settle their scores with plaster heads of Tito as though they were clay pigeons. And so, belatedly (ten years on!) they are exorcising the ghost of their Communism. The necrophiliac Balkan passion for digging up old bones (and burying new ones!) spares no one: the Serbs threaten the Croats by saying they will dig up Tito's bones, buried in Belgrade, and send them to the Croats.

Today the same national, collective language is used to proclaim their truth by all those who kept silent for 50 years, that is by all those who, in

RINGIER/CAMERA PRESS LONDON

Tito's funeral Yugoslavia 1980: a nation mourned

that same collective language, lived out their multinational togetherness for a full 50 years as their own truth.

Other totalitarian states articulated their dissatisfaction with their regimes in strong intellectual undergrounds, both in the country and abroad. Yugoslavia had virtually no intellectual underground (apart from an insignificant number of dissidents in the early Communist years). After the second world war 'ustashas', 'chetniks', 'collaborators' and 'anticommunists' were driven out of the country (dead or alive); some 20 years later there was an economic migration out of the country, of *Gastarbeiter.* The intellectual emigration was numerically insignificant. If a strong intellectual underground did exist, as everyone swears it did today, then how is it that no one knew about it; and if it didn't exist, how can we believe that the truth which people craved behind the walls of the so-called 'prison of nations' is the one that has now come to the surface? Perhaps the regime, that soft Yugoslav totalitarianism, was not so soft after all, perhaps it was worse than the Albanian or Romanian versions? If that was the case, how come there was so little protest?

At this moment it is an indisputable and statistically verifiable truth that many intellectuals from the former Yugoslavia (writers, directors, philosophers, actors, journalists) are voluntarily joining the ocean of involuntary refugees and knocking on the doors of other countries. What, then, is the truth and what is a lie? Could it be that a new lie is springing up in the place of the old truth? Or is it the other way round?

Terrible times are marked by the rhythm of destruction and construction, chaos and order, rapid demolition and simultaneous building. What was there is destroyed (cities, ideological notions, bridges, criteria, libraries, norms, churches, marriages, monuments, lives, graves, friendships, homes, myths) the old truth is destroyed. What will become the new truth is rapidly built in its place.

In Duga Res, a small town in Croatia, a little wood was planted: 88 trees, for Tito's birthday. Today the inhabitants of Duga Res have cut down the wood: they say they were removing 'the last remnants of the communist regime'. The people who cut the wood down were the same people who planted it.

There is a story going around about the murderer, the Serbian General Mladic, who for more than a year has being turning the innocent city of Sarajevo into a graveyard. It is said that he aimed his guns from the surrounding Sarajevo hills straight at the house of a friend. The story goes on to say that the murderer then telephoned his friend to tell him he was about to blow up his house.

'You've got five minutes to take your albums and get out.'

The Murderer-General meant family photograph albums. Before destroying everything he owned, the General had 'generously' bequeathed his chosen victim life together with the right to memory, life with a few family snapshots.

What is being annihilated with guns, grenades, murders, rape, the displacement of peoples, 'ethnic cleansing', the new ideology supported by the media — is Memory. What is being built on the ruins is the new truth, the one that will one day be the only memory. In that sense, the war on the territory of former Yugoslavia is only a repetition of the old story of disappearance and appearance, the story of human civilization.

Unaccustomed to the culture of scepticism, at this moment the Yugoslav peoples are firmly convinced that they are fighting for the truth. Even if this were not the case, they know that every newly established lie eventually becomes — the truth. And that is why, when the terrible times finally pass, those who survive will not be ashamed. The peoples of the new countries will not be ashamed because of the hundreds of thousands of dead, displaced, unhappy, because of the millions of destroyed lives, because of the destroyed country which they once built together... .Neither the stronger ones, the more brutal, those who attacked, nor the weaker ones, who defended themselves.

Is it possible for the media to provoke war? I permit myself the theory that the war on the territory of Yugoslavia began several years ago with the posterior of a completely innocent Serbian peasant. I still remember his surname: Martinovica. For months the poor man, who was allegedly found in a field with a bottle in his backside, became a topic in many Yugoslav newspapers and TV stations, particularly in Serbia. Some maintained that Martinovica had been raped with a beer bottle by Albanians, others that he was a pervert who had been masturbating with the bottle. Others again affirmed that he had been raped by Serbs so that they could blame the Albanians. Yet others, the most fundamental, calculated on the basis of the nature of the injury, that Martinovica had himself jumped onto the bottle from a nearby tree. His sorrowing and numerous offspring gave statements in their father's favour, teams of doctors disagreed in public about the various possibilities of injury and self-injury. Martinovica spent the whole time in his hospital bed smiling feebly at the anxious TV-viewers. The media made a political spectacle of Martinovica's backside, quite in keeping with the Balkan spirit.

So the case of Martinovica simply confirmed the belief of the Serbian people that the Serbian leader Milosevic's decision — to change the constitution violently and revoke the autonomy of Kosovo and Vojvodina — was more than justified! So the masses became accustomed to participating passionately and collectively in that miserable and tasteless media story. And so they confirmed once again their receptivity to any kind of media manipulation.

After Martinovica there was an abundance of 'evidence', which the Serbian media 'milked' to the full, of 'genocide' carried out against the Serbian minority by Albanians (!); and numerous Serbian women sprang up from somewhere, having been raped by (who else but) Albanians. Justifying themselves by their injured national pride and the national myths served up by the media, Serbian nationalists collectively supported the Serbian repression of the Albanians in Kosovo, or took an active part in it themselves.

And since in these cursed Balkan lands every lie becomes a truth in the end, every spoken word becomes reality, so just a few years later a *male* and, from a psychoanalytical point of view, deeply homosexual war came about, and the war strategy of rape became cruel everyday reality. The women who were to be raped were, of course, completely innocent, their bodies simply serving as a medium for the transmission of male messages.

The media only discovered anew what they knew already: that promiscuity with leaders and power, with their political pretensions and aims, functions perfectly; they also discovered what they may not have known before — the scale of their power! They quivered with satisfaction at the confirmation that a lie very easily becomes legitimate truth; they were astonished at the realisation that in the absence of other information people believe what is available to them, that even despite other information, people believe what they want to believe, their media, in a word: their custom-built myths.

And the infernal media campaign was able to continue. In Serbian newspapers there began to appear articles about the *ustasha* camps during the second world war (and no one could deny their truthfulness, because they existed and in them perished Serbs, Gypsies, Jews and also Croats!). There began to be more and more pictures of the camps on Serbian television. Croats began increasingly to be called criminals, 'ustashas'. Serbian newspapers were full of horrifying stories of 'necklaces of Serbian children's fingers', worn by the Croat 'ustashas', of the 'genocide' which the Croats were again preparing to carry out against the innocent Serbs.

The Serbian media propaganda (orchestrated by the Serbian authorities and the Serbian leader) finally achieved what it had sought: a reaction in the Croatian media. And when the Croatian media also filled with tales of 'necklaces of Croatian children's fingers' worn round their necks by Serbian 'cutthroats' — the preparations were laid for war.

Today, in what is still wartime, no Serbian newspapers can be found in Croatia (and if they could no one would buy them), nor are there Croatian papers in Serbia (and if there were no one would believe them), and television programmes waging a war to the death can only be received with satellite aerials. Which is hardly necessary in any case as the programmes are identical. The Serbs put together information in their interest, the Croats in theirs. Telephone links between Croatia and Serbia have not been functioning for a long time.

Growing out of the worn-out Yugoslav system, following the same old habits, the media have succeeded in legalising lies. From being a political and journalistic way of behaving, lies have developed into a war strategy, and as such have rapidly become established as morally acceptable.

'When the homeland is at stake, I am prepared to lie,' said one Croatian journalist and she attained a high rating on the Croatian journalistic scene. In a completely upside-down system of values, therefore, lies have become not only acceptable but a positively marked way of behaving (we lie in order to defend the homeland, we lie in the name of that homeland, we lie, of course, only temporarily because the homeland is in danger).

The culture of lies is most easily established if we have an opponent who lies more that we do, or who speaks the ancient palindromic language, 'the devil's verse', the one that is read the same backwards and forwards, from left and right. And the weary postmodern outside world, to which the nations doggedly direct 'their truths', tries reluctantly and with difficulty to set up coordinates: both sides lie equally; or one side lies more, the other less; or one side lies, the other tells the truth... . It is only the dead who do not lie, but they have no credibility.

Croatia (which I take here as an example, simply because it is closest to me) establishes its public, political and moral coordinates on the basis of the formula: Murderer and Victim. In this tandem (from the Croatian point of view) Croatia is the victim, which is hard to deny: part of its territory is occupied by Serbs, they have partly (or completely) destroyed some Croatian villages and towns (which have posthumously become symbols of national remembrance, like Vukovar or Dubrovnik!), railway lines and bridges (which have posthumously become symbols of past and the possible future connectedness!). At the same time, of course, the Croats too have destroyed, particularly in Bosnia. This fact has not diminished the collective emotion, fostered passionately by Croatian citizens, government and the media, of being the victim.

This collective experience is in ironic contrast (although no one notices the irony!) with what has become today one of the commonest words in Croatian public, cultural and political life: the word *image*. It is not necessary to emphasise that the word image means: impression, representation... . However, in local usage, this word implies 'the truth about Croatia'. The Croatian media are full of phrases about the fact that 'we must all build a positive image of Croatia in the world' (in this case the word 'world' usually means European, then American media, politicians and public opinion).

Recently, on television, the Vice-President of the Croatian government invited all the citizens of Croatia 'to build together a positive image of Croatia in the world', which means in effect — the image of a righteous victim! The Vice-President added that even ordinary citizens could help by writing letters (surely each of us has some friends abroad!) in which they would spread 'the truth about Croatia'. The patriotic duty of every citizen — to spread the truth about Croatia — has legitimised a method which they always employed in any case with great zeal whenever invited to: denunciation of people who think differently: sceptics, 'Yugonostalgics', intellectuals who once said something critical about the present regime, denunciation of people who travel too much ('while we sit it out here bravely because our homeland is in danger'), denunciation of neighbours (he said 'fuck an independent state in which you've nothing to live on'); of an acquaintance (he said 'what kind of a state is it that has taken my two sons from me'); of colleagues at work (he said 'why are we fighting when the 'commies' are still in power') and so on and so forth. The citizens, meanwhile, as always in such cases, sincerely believe that they are carrying out a little, honourable, patriotic task.

Bit by bit, the strategy of 'spreading the truth about Croatia' has entailed several disastrous consequences: the virtually complete control of the media on the part of the ruling party, ie the state. Namely, in spite of democratic elections, all power in Croatia is in the hands of the ruling party and the president of the state (who is at the same time the leader of the ruling party), who has extensive presidential powers. These powers were approved by the parliament when they voted for the new constitution, which was not difficult because the majority of seats are held by members of that same, ruling party. Television, as the most powerful propaganda machine, followed by radio, serves the state. The main newspaper today (because of changes in the economic system, they say) is controlled by an editorial board, in which the majority consists once again of representatives of the ruling party!

Dozens and dozens of journalists have been dismissed from their jobs, their places have been taken by those who unanimously 'spread the truth about Croatia'. 'There are journalists who *think* Croatia and those who *feel* her. Croatia should not be thought, she should be felt,' said a journalist, the one we have already quoted. Her slogan typifies the state of Croatian journalism today. Sometimes Croatian journalists succeed in fighting for a more critical article in local newspapers. Of course, this can only be when the editors of the newspapers decide temporarily to improve their 'image' and so suppress 'Western rumours' that all is not well with the media in Croatia.

The 'image', which is, they say, more important than the truth at this political moment, is not only being worked on by government organisations, the Ministry of Information, Offices for the promotion of Croatia in the world; but also by newly formed non-governmental organisations such as for instance 'The Croatian Anti-defamation League'. Maintaining that 'lies about Croatia have been spread for decades', the president of the League recently announced: 'We shall endeavour to alter world public opinion in favour of Croatia, using the truth as our strongest and sole argument. It is the duty of each one of us to defend our country,

Hotel Medena, Croatia 1993: holiday houses for refugees

and that is our most important task. Slander is a more powerful weapon than a gun, a tank or an aeroplane'.

Reading local newspapers the uninformed reader might think that we were not involved in a real war but in a battle for our 'image in the world'. Newspapers abound in such titles as: 'Why the Muslims have a better image in the world than the Croats', 'How the Serbs succeeded in manipulating world public opinion and improving their image in the world', 'What Croatia has to do to improve its image in the world'. And so on and so forth.

But still, in order for the system to function, it is not enough for there to be (one-party) power, control of the media, censorship (justified by the war), ideological propaganda (justified by the exceptional situation), and constant media patriotic 'briefings' (which are in themselves 'natural'), it is not enough, in other words, to send out messages, there must also be someone to receive them.

In the autumn of 1991, the inhabitants of Zagreb (including myself, the author of these lines) went down almost daily into cellars and shelters at the sound of the air-raid warning. Fortunately this drilling of the people proved to be unnecessary, although in other towns (Zadar, Vukovar, Dubrovnik, Karlovac, Sibenik...) it was all too necessary. In the autumn of 1991, the people of Zagreb were reluctant to go out into the streets for fear of Serbian snipers (apparently disguised as chimney-sweeps, postmen and firemen!), who shot at people from the roofs. The snipers and their victims were curiously anonymous, despite the fact that they could have contributed to the process of 'spreading the truth about Croatia' (!) but also rapidly forgotten, because of new dramatic events. That is how the citizens became one, collective, threatened body, just as the enemy became one, collective, threatening body. The collective paranoia induced in this way, based on perfectly real assumptions, brought with it also a collective readiness to interpret rumours as the truth (after all many interpreted the truth as rumour). Anguished by fear, the loss of relatives and friends, poverty, uncertainty, an information blockade, the terror of war, encroaching chaos, the citizens of Croatia are today ready to grab hold of the one and only truth they are offered, like a straw. The totalitarian mentality, collectivism and conformism — which have sprung out of the perception of the nation as victim — have now become so entrenched that every objection to quite obvious, crude offences, illogicality, political amateurism, crimes, corruption, infringements of human rights — is interpreted as an attack 'against the young Croatian state', as 'anti-Croatian', and therefore 'pro-Serbian', as 'undermining the young Croatian state', as 'treason', as — 'a lie'

In order, therefore to set up a system which manifests the clear symptoms of pathological collectivism, what was required was perfect cooperation between the authorities, the state ideology, and the citizens who identify with it. The citizens will then justify their conformism with regard to obvious infringements of human rights, disregard of fundamental democratic principles, the creation of an autocratic state, etc — by priorities: our survival is at stake, this is still wartime, we're not going to worry about trifles such as the freedom of the media... . And similar arguments are used by the authorities themselves.

In the newly created collective climate all who do not speak the language of the collective are exposed to the danger of being proclaimed traitors and enemies of the people. It is a fact that the number of 'enemies of the people' (compared to the number of friends of the people) is numerically insignificant, so the same names keep turning up in the Croatian press.

The objects of public campaigns are often women (journalists, writers, artists). In a milieu that has hidden its deeply rooted patriarchalism behind socialist formulae about the equality of women and men, 'democratisation' has brought a new freedom for patriarchalism. In this sense women, intellectuals, are almost a 'natural' choice as objects of a media assassination. Along with the female 'enemies of the people' — who are guilty because they have publicly declared their anti-nationalist, anti-war and individual standpoint — some men, also intellectuals, have also undergone the media 'hot rabbit' treatment or 'blanketing'. It is interesting that few people came to their defence: occasional journalists, alternative and anti-war women's groups, the occasional friend. It is a fact that the public campaigns against 'enemies of the people' often included colleagues (members of the Croatian PEN, writers, journalists, intellectuals), politicians, but also ordinary citizens. These last in the 'Readers' letters' columns of newspapers, or, if the 'victim' agrees to a dialogue, in organised interviews on television (a kind of trial-by-television), where anonymous citizens put questions to the 'accused' and comment on her/his answers.

The collective paranoia that has been induced does not stop at individuals. In an atmosphere of quite real insecurity, and fear, with the constant sense that life is on the edge of an abyss, in an atmosphere of uncertainty and quite real helplessness — the citizens of Croatia occasionally direct their enmity at all those who *do not understand them*, or, conversely, euphorically proclaim their friendship towards all those who *do understand* them. Thus it is not uncommon to find in Croatian newspapers headlines such as the recent one: 'The French and English do not like us!' And since rumour has in any case replaced information, it is not rare for various theories of an international conspiracy against Croatia to appear in the Croatian media.

It seems that it is not only fear, aroused national (and nationalist) emotions, hatred of the enemy, vulnerability, the establishment of an autocratic system, media propaganda and war that have reinforced the culture of lies. One of the strategies with which the culture of lies is established is terror by forgetting (they force you to forget what you remember!) and terror by remembering (they force you to remember what you do not remember!). After the dismantling of Yugoslavia, after the election of the new Croatian government and the proclamation of independence, terror by forgetting was carried out in Croatia by administrative means, by means of the media and finally — by collective compulsion. 'Yugoslavia' (a country in which Croatian citizens had lived for some 50 years!) became a prohibited word, and the terms 'Yugoslav', 'Yugonostalgic' or 'Yugo-zombie' are synonymous with national traitor. The old symbols have been removed: flags, coats of arms, the names of streets, schools, squares and replaced by new ones; the language and its name have been changed (Cyrillic and Serbian have become undesirable). Almost overnight a whole system of values has been changed. So 'anti-fascists', former 'partisans', 'Communists', the 'left-wing', 'anti-nationalists' (previously positively marked terms) have suddenly become negatively marked (despite the fact that the Croatian government, including above all the Croatian president, consists largely of political converts: former communists). The formerly negatively valued nationalists, terrorist-emigrés, 'ustashas', and the Independent State of Croatia (NDH) itself, have acquired a neutral or even a positive connotation. In that sense many historical concepts and 'historical facts' have undergone an abrupt reassessment (so, for example, according to the new value judgments, the 'ustashas' did admittedly commit crimes, but on a far smaller scale than was suggested for years by the 'Yugo-Bolshevik-Greater Serb propaganda'). So, among other things, the Independent State of Croatia has been re-evaluated. The NDH is today often seen as a state that was admittedly 'Nazi', but at the same time it realised the age-old longing for Croatian statehood.

Such an abrupt transformation of values, occurring in many spheres of everyday cultural, political and ideological life has generated confusion in the heads of many citizens: bad has suddenly become good, left has suddenly become right. In this re-evaluation the blotting out of one's personal life, one's identity, a kind of amnesia, an unconscious or conscious lie have become a protective reaction which enables one quickly to adopt the new identity.

I know of a writer colleague who claimed to a foreign journalist that he was 'the victim of repression' under Yugo-Communism, that his books were banned, and that he had been in prison. That colleague was never in prison nor was he 'the victim of repression' and all his books were regularly published. I do not believe that he was lying. Exposed to media brainwashing, terror by forgetting and collective compulsion, my collegue had simply forgotten his personal history, he carried out an unconscious mental touching-up, and in the general context the spoken lie became an acceptable truth. And after all, the foreign journalist had come to hear just such a story, in his 'Westerner's' head he already carried the stereotype: the story of a repressed writer in the former Communist regime and a happy end in the new, democratic one.

I know of a Zagreb Japanologist, who terrorised the whole Yugoslav cultural scene for years with — Japan! Throughout the whole of former Yugoslavia there sprang up haiku-circles, haiku-poets, ikebana courses, anthologies of Japanese poetry, twinnings between Osaka and Varazdin, festivals of Yugoslav haiku-poets. Thanks to the activity of the afore-mentioned Japanologist, the inflation of haiku-poetry during 'totalitarianism' had given us all 'a pain in the neck'. Today the famous Japanologist claims that under the 'Tito regime' he was exposed to repression because of — haiku poetry!

Many citizens of Croatia, among them Albanians, Croats, Serbs, Muslims and others, are today experiencing difficulty in acquiring the residence document, *domovnica,* on the basis of which they can obtain essential papers, a passport, an identity card. If their father was born outside Croatia, if they were themselves born in Skopje or Sarajevo, if they moved to Zagreb from Belgrade, if they are refugees, they will come up against an unpleasant bureaucratic procedure and the possibility that they will not be granted citizenship in the country in which they were born or lived their whole life. The country in which they have lived for years is suddenly no longer theirs. And the citizens will have to forget their former life in order to liberate the space for a new one. They will adapt, conform, sign some things and write off others in order to survive, in order that their children should survive, in order that on some 'higher' state level the space should be liberated for the building of some New (this time truly new!) BRIGHT (this time truly bright) Future (this time truly a future!)

Terror by remembering is a parallel process to terror by forgetting. Both processes have the function of building a new state, a new truth. Terror by remembering is a strategy by which the continuity (apparently interrupted) of national identity is established, terror by forgetting is the strategy whereby a 'Yugoslav' identity and any remote prospect of its being re-established is wiped out. Terror by remembering has its administrative-symbolic, cultural forms as well. The names of streets, squares, institutions are replaced by the names of Croats ('of renown'); monuments are erected to Croatian historical figures, writers, politicians; the language of schools and the media is changed; textbooks are changed, figures from Croatian cultural history are honoured, and so on. Terror by remembering as a method of establishing a national identity does not shrink from national megalomania, heroization, mythization, the absurd from lies, in other words. Signs of national megalomania are visible everywhere: from proclaiming the city of Zagreb a 'metropolis', and the Croatian state a 'miracle', and 'the most democratic state in the world'. National mythomania is confirmed by 'serious' claims about the Iranian origin of the Croats and popular phrases about the Croatian state as the 'thousand-year dream of all Croats'. National mythomania tends to distort, touch up or counterfeit historical authenticity. So the latest history textbooks for primary schools are exchanging the recent heroization and fetishization of Tito and the Partisan movement for the same fetishization of the Croatian president Franjo Tudjman, that 'architect of Croatian defence', that 'great Croat' and 'man for all Croatian times'.

The terror of remembering is, of course, also a war strategy of setting up frontiers, establishing differences: *we* are different from *them* (Serbs), our history, faith, customs and language are different from theirs. In the war variant this complex (which profoundly penetrates the Croatian collective consciousness) is used like this: we are different from them (Serbs) because we are better, which is proved by our history; we always built, they always only destroyed; we are a European, Catholic culture, they are only Orthodox, illiterate barbarians. And so on and so forth.

Ordinary Croatian citizens with strong national feelings express their satisfaction that the 'dream' they have dreamed 'for a thousand years' has been realised, those with weak national feelings accept the idea that, like it or not, that dream is also their reality. Croatian Serbs in Krajina are dreaming some 'thousand-year dreams' of their own. After one set of 'truths' has been transformed into 'lies' and 'lies' transformed into 'truths', in the majority of cases the citizens will always bow to — the majority.

I heard a story about a foreign TV-reporter who happened to find himelf in some Bosnian village and paid the surviving locals DM200 to drag the scattered corpses into a tidy heap, so that he could photograph them. At the same time he did not quite grasp either where he was, or who was who, and he made a moving TV commentary about a Muslim massacre of Serbs. The corpses were Muslim.

I know of tales about foreign journalists who paid local photographers and cameramen to film dangerous scenes for a pittance (Those 'natives' need money, they're dying like flies in any case!). I know of foreign journalists who, thinking they were writing 'the truth and nothing but the truth' sold the world someone else's misery for their own well-being.

I know also about those truly courageous people who risked their lives to touch the indifferent heart of the world. No one asked them to do it, but they did. One of them is Susan Sontag.

I know also of kind foreigners, whose hearts were stirred and who sent one refugee camp a large quantity of flat irons. It had not even occurred to the kind-hearted foreigners that the 'native tribes' had had electricity for ages. Or else the irons were intended for those who really did not have any, the inhabitants of Sarajevo, so that they could go to their deaths neatly ironed.

War is like a cake, everyone wants to grab his piece: politicans (local and foreign), criminals and speculators (local and foreign), war profiteers and murderers (local and foreign), sadists and masochists, believers and benefactors (local and foreign), historians and philosophers (local and foreign), journalists (local and foreign). The war carries with it the destruction of identity but also a rapid and cheap possibility of acquiring one. For foreign philosophers the war is a new toy, a test of the elasticity of old and new concepts (the phenomenon of little nation states in Europe? Europe without frontiers or Europe with frontiers? Nationalism with positive connotations, nationalism with negative connotations? Post-totalitarianism and the New World Order?). For foreign politicians and strategists the war is a living polygon for examining a potential future; for the media an exciting adventure; for foreign readers and audiences a fix for quickening the sluggish moral and emotional metabolism; for criminals the possibility of becoming heroes, for intellectuals of becoming — criminals!

Radovan Karadzic, the leader of the Bosnian Serbs and an undoubted war criminal, is a favourite theme of many Western media. When Karadzic is being shown, the Western media for some unknown reason usually put him in the foreground. So Karadzic (a psychiatrist by training!) is able more easily to communicate with his Western 'clients'. I imagine the Western reader/viewer comfortably settled in an armchair. My imagined reader/viewer first feels secretly pleased that, thank God, he does not live in such a terrible country (after all, *they* are the Balkans, not Europe). Then he gazes at the huge, sweating head of the murderer from the wild Bosnian forests and for a moment abandons himself to romantic musings about a criminal leading the whole world by the nose. Then he mentally erases such inadmissable musings and is genuinely horrified at the 'highwayman's' barbarity. Then he turns off the television, folds up the newspaper. My imagined Western media consumer then feels an undefined sense of relief. My imagined Western reader cannot conceive that at that very moment Karadzic's dark shadow is sitting in his armchair, manipulating him, the owner of the armchair and the newspaper!

I a writer, can allow myself such a notion. Indeed, I am convinced that that outside world, that so coveted arbiter of civilization, that Europe — so called upon and so desperately depended upon by the Croats (*Danke Deutschland, danke Genscher*) and the Bosnians and the people of Sarajevo (who for months have been expecting the mythical Sixth Fleet to sail into Sarajevo) — that Europe has also played its part, bears its heavy portion of blame, has its problem of a 'Western' culture of truth and lies. And the root of that problem, whether Europe wants it or not, lies in Bosnia . . . And that is why Karadzic's dark and terrible shadow is already sitting, comfortably settled, in the armchairs of European homes.

In all the former Yugoslav territories people are now living a postmodern chaos/order. Past, present and future are all lived simultaneously. In the circular temporal mish-mash suddenly everything we ever knew and everything we shall know has sprung to life and gained its right to existence.

After exactly a round 50 years (1991-1941), by almost infernal symmetry, the second world war has sprung up again, many of the same villages have been burned down again, many families have experienced a symmetrical fate, many children and grandchildren have lived through the fate of their fathers. Even the weapons are sometimes the same: stolen out of necessity from local 'museums of the revolution', belonging to the Partisans in other words, or else taken down from attics and out of trunks, left there for fifty years by 'ustashas' or 'chetniks'.

The newly created states are also 'museum pieces': quotations, and the responses of the newly elected leaders are only references to those already uttered. Like the flash of a hologram, segments of former times appear, fragments of history; from the faces of today's leaders there often gleams the hellish reflection of some other leaders, in such a gleam the swastika is linked to the red star. The hotheads of the Balkan peoples dream thousand-year dreams, some fragments flash like reality and then sink into the darkness to yield the right to a brief life to some other fragments. In the territories of the disintegrated country, which was once shared, victims and their executioners, attackers and attacked, occupiers and occupied sometimes exchange dreams, sometimes they dream the same dream, thinking they are dreaming different ones.

In the disintegrated Yugoslav territories we are also living simultaneously the future, that post-apocalyptic one, the one that for others has yet to come. Sarajevo is a city from the future and a city of the future, existing and non-existent, a city from science fiction films and cartoons, the screenplay for a new version of *Blade Runner*, for a future version of *Mad Max*. 'I am a terminator,' said my friend soon after she had

left Sarajevo, 'I have seen so much death that I cannot be anything but —
a terminator.' My friend set off into the world. 'I must tell the world that
I come from the future, from Sarajevo,' she said.

The present in which people are dying is like the permanent running
of films from the past and from the future. 'I'm sitting in life like a
cinema,' wrote my Belgrade friend a long time ago. On a doomed ship
that is sailing nowhere, in the former Yugoslav territories, reality no
longer exists. The media perpetuation of accusations and lies has cancelled
their harsh reality. People watch their own death on the screen, they only
do not know whether the bullet that will kill them is coming from the
street or from the screen. Which comes to the same thing in any case, as
we are perhaps all dead already. 'Or else we are dead already, only our
nails are still growing just a little, as the nails of corpses do, they are
turning into claws,' wrote the Sarajevo writer Abdulah Sidran.
Perpetuating the horror destroys the horror, perpetuating the evil destroys
its weight. Ultimately, nothing has happened, if what is happening is only
a reference to what has already happened, and if what is happening is only
what is yet to come.

In this sense my story about the culture of lies also collapses like a tower
of cards, destroying itself. The truth is only (unverifiable at that!) that I
too, the writer of these lines, am covered with invisible bruises, just as my
Sarajevo aquaintance from the beginning of this story is covered with
visible ones. Soon I shall be voluntarily joining that ocean of (willing and
unwilling) refugees who are knocking at the doors of other countries of
the world. I have no illusions. In those other countries at least one thing is
undoubtedly waiting: the TV screen and newspapers. I imagine myself
opening a newspaper (and oddly I still want to) and coming across an
article written by a colleague from over there, on the other side. The
article will be about — the Serbian culture of lies. As it is my text is only
half the story, half the truth. Or half a lie, as, I imagine, my Croatian
countrymen would say.

©*Dubravka Ugresic*
Translated by Celia Hawkesworth

JAMES FENTON

The Exchange

I met the Muse of Censorship
And she had packed her bags
And all the folk of Moscow
Were hanging out the flags.

I asked her what her prospects were
And whither her thoughts did range.
She said: 'I am off to Dublin town
On a cultural exchange.

'And folk there be in Cambridge
Who like the way I think
And there be folk in Nottingham
Whom I shall drown in ink

'And when we reach America
The majorettes will sing:
Here comes the Muse of Censorship —
This is a very good thing.'

I went to the Finland Station
To wave the Muse goodbye
And on another platform
A crowd I did espy.

I saw the Muse of Freedom
Alighting from the train.
Far from that crowd I wept aloud
For to see that Muse again.

From Out of Danger, © *James Fenton, 1993.*
Reproduced by permission of Penguin Books Ltd.

EMMA **ULMANN**
NÉE A SIÈRENTZ
LE 12 AVRIL 1892
DÉCÉDÉE A NEULLY
LE 30 NOVEMBRE 1977

UMBERTO ECO

Tolerance and the intolerable

'I see no real difference between the skinheads and neo-Nazis of today and the Nazis of a generation earlier. There is the same hatred of others and the will to destruction'

In 1993, Umberto Eco, linguist, semiologist, university professor and distinguished novelist, was one of 40 intellectuals who called to all Europeans to be on their guard against the manoeuvres of the extreme right. Disturbed by the extent to which dangerous ideas are becoming commonplace and the seductive power of some of them, the signatories of the *'Appel à la vigilance'* — now several hundred — have undertaken not to take part in any publications, meetings or broadcasts which have the remotest connection with the extreme right.

In an interview with Roger-Pol Droit, Eco explains why he signed the appeal, and elaborates his theme of tolerance and the intolerable.

Critics of the appeal say that since there is no longer any right nor left — the old divisions no longer apply, new political and cultural lines are being drawn — this warning against the spread of the ideas of the extreme right has an outdated, archaic ring. In brief, your call to vigilance is out of tune with the times; is trying to re-erect artificially ideological boundaries which have already been wiped out by the tide of history. How do you reply to such criticisms?

This sort of comment is the result of a dangerous merging of the historical changes in which we are now caught up and a sort of intellectual and moral sloppiness. Let me explain.

The old European categories of 'left' and 'right' as they have existed for the past 20 years are, undeniably, no longer an adequate concept for understanding contemporary political configurations. My travels in Brazil and Argentina in the 1960s made me aware even then that the conventional differences between right and left were no longer relevant as a key to the majority of Latin America's political movements. That perception, which at the time seemed both strange and novel, now applies to the whole of Europe.

We keep on seeing parties, supposedly of the left, taking up positions traditionally associated with the right and vice versa. To cite one recent example: the PDS (Democratic Socialist Party) — the former Italian Communist Party — supported the government decision to send paratroopers into Somalia. If anyone had told me, 20 years ago, that one-time Communists would give their backing to a military expedition against a former colony, I would have said this was something out of science fiction. This development is extraordinarily fascinating, something no intellectual can remain indifferent to. New situations demand new analyses. We must not let our thinking become locked into worn-out dogmas and doctrinaire criteria. From this point of view, the upheavals of our time are a real intellectual challenge.

But it would be a great mistake to conclude that everything has changed as a result. If we think all ideas have the same value, that one must never, under any circumstances, reject anything, we end up seriously confused. The rules of the political game are in the process of change. That does not mean there are no rules, nor that we should shrink from inventing new ones. The cards have been redealt. But their face value remains the same.

For example?

I see no real difference between the skinheads and neo-Nazis of today and the Nazis of a generation earlier. They are of the same kind as their predecessors. There is the same kind of stupidity and determination to destroy; the same hatred of others and the will to destruction. The only difference is that the Nazis murdered millions whereas their descendants have so far only beaten up a few dozen.

It is our duty as intellectuals to stress that everything has changed except this: it is our responsibility to draw the line between what is tolerable and what is not. By undertaking not to contribute to journals or to take part in radio and TV broadcasts or in seminars organised by those who are associated with the extreme right, those who sign the appeal are not rejecting the changes that have taken place in our world, nor refusing to rethink things. We are simply asserting our choice not to be seen supporting trends we consider dangerous for democracy.

Doesn't this smack of intolerance? The emergence of a new form of McCarthyism even?

The accusation is absurd. Do we need to remind ourselves what McCarthyism was all about? It was an official policy of exclusion which deprived some people of their jobs and sent others to prison on the sole

Berlin 1945: Russian soldiers bring down the flags of fascism

pretext that they were Communists or fellow travellers. How on earth can one possibly compare such methods with what the signatories of the appeal did? We have taken this step from choice: a refusal to collaborate with any intellectual, publishing or media operation connected with the extreme right. Everybody has the right to say no to what they don't like.

Are you saying that you refuse, on principle, any dialogue or debate with those you consider dangerous?

Certainly not! I have no reason to turn down a proper discussion with anyone whatsoever, no matter what their views. All that is needed is that the debate should take place in circumstances that guarantee fair play. This presupposes clearly defined conditions as to the place and the encounter. Otherwise, one can find one is what I call captured by the situation, whatever one may have said.

I signed the appeal, which did not, in any case, name names or specify particular incidents, because in Italy, too, intellectuals reputed to be of the left, notably members of the Communist Party, have taken part in meetings organised by the New Right. The latter then exploited the presence of the former for its own ends: 'There you are, you see, we are no longer divided: they are with us.'

It's a well known tactic. For example, there are people who invite you to dinner only to use your presence at their table as a form of visiting card to get themselves invited to things which have nothing to do with you. Once you know what they are up to, you can politely decline their invitations. Is that a dogmatic stance? It's simply the right to avoid places where they slap a label on you. One should also warn one's friends: 'Watch out. If you go there you should be aware you're going to be 'had'. Whatever may be the substance of your remarks, simply going there is already a political act.'

You are making a distinction between dialogue and what you call 'captivity'. Could you elaborate on that?

If, tomorrow, I organised a seminar on history or philosophy in my university, I would invite specialists with very different opinions and theories from my own. And it would be our duty to confront each other's arguments as openly and vigorously as possible, even if we reached no agreement in the end. Dialogue, however robust, assumes that no-one will turn another's words or presence to his own advantage.

Capture is precisely the opposite. When the Communist Party invited intellectuals to sign a petition it had no hesitation in presenting them all as Communist intellectuals. In the same way, most Catholic organisations entice you by saying: 'You are absolutely free; you can say what you like.' But if one takes part in their discussions, there is always that sense of having been taken over: 'You are here so you must be one of us.' That has nothing to do with dialogue!

Certain organisations have traditionally been dedicated to taking over. There are places that immediately stand out as places of captivity. The business of defining, recognising these, of fathoming the pull they exert or the precise spirit of a place, is, above all, a philosophical task.

What you are saying is that the same words acquire a different meaning depending on the place or the context in which they are spoken or printed?

Quite so. It is the power of place. To take a simple example: if I praise monarchy in Stockholm, my eulogy has a quite different weight from exactly the same speech made in, say, Paris. If someone translates the interview I gave in Sweden into French, my views would appear different. The power exercised by a particular situation, by context, should never be underestimated.

Just for a laugh, imagine that you were a devout atheist and all your life your best friend had been a Jesuit. I tell you, on the last day of your life you should absolutely forbid him to come and see you. If you don't, regardless of his wishes or your own, whatever the discussions between you, a visit from a Jesuit on the eve of your death is tantamount to your signature on a deathbed conversion.

At a time when we should be working out new landmarks and new values, we must be particularly attentive to this type of thing. For some people, calling for 'vigilance' is reminiscent of the 1930s and the Popular Front. For me it is purely and simply what the work of the intellect is all about. It is by applying themselves to the business of analysis and criticism in this way that intellectuals will find new openings, new ways forward. In this sense, thought is constant vigilance, an effort to distinguish what is dangerous even when the circumstances and the discourse appear quite innocent.

Don't we run the risk of adopting a general attitude of suspicion, of living in a sort of perpetual mistrust, of looking for danger everywhere and conjuring up imaginary perils?

No, simply because the boundaries of the intolerable cross over clearly discernible thresholds. Take, for example, this business of revisionism. Every serious historian is, in the proper meaning of the word, a revisionist: the purpose of any research is to find out whether what has been said about the past is true or needs correction. Was Catiline really the swine that Cicero portrays, or was this an invention resulting from the political climate at the time? In World War I, did 600,000 Italians really die? The historian has the right to search through the archives, to be suspicious of propaganda, to reconstruct the facts and question the figures.

I see nothing shocking in a serious and incontrovertible work establishing that the figure for genocide of the Jews by the Nazis was not 6 million but 6.5 or 5.5 million. What is intolerable is when something which might have been a work of research no longer has the same meaning and worth, and becomes a message suggesting that 'if a few less Jews than we thought were killed, there was no crime'. Socrates and Christ died alone. Two thousand years and more after their deaths, humanity is still in a state of shock, still suffering remorse for the crimes that killed them.

Another threshold was crossed when revisionism turned into denial. Like everyone of my generation I saw Jews arrested, humiliated, deported. After the war I witnessed the tears of those who wept because they were the sole survivors of entire families that had been wiped out. If those who claim to be historians attempt to make me believe that the Crusades were a myth, an invention of the Red Cross, for example... well, all that was so long ago I might perhaps hesitate, be doubtful. But that anyone would want to make me believe that what I saw with my own eyes at the age of 13, like millions of others, never took place; that they would attempt to convince young people born since then, that is intolerable.

I have the right not to invite those who propagate this type of discourse and those who support them to my house; and the right to refuse an invitation to their place.

And if they say you are intolerant?

My answer is that to be tolerant, one must set the boundaries of the intolerable.

To fix such boundaries must we not be in possession of the truth?

No. That has nothing to do with it. I do not want to use the word 'true'. There are only opinions, some of which are preferable to others. But one cannot say: 'Ah. If it is just a matter of preference to hell with it!' Our life and that of others hangs on this word preferable. One can die for an opinion which is only preferable.

What difference is there between fighting for the truth and struggling for what one deems preferable without any certainty of being in the right?

If we believe we are fighting for the truth, we are sometimes tempted to kill our enemies. Fighting for what is preferable, we can be tolerant while still rejecting the intolerable.

If there are only preferences and no truths, what basis can we find for a definition of what is universally intolerable: one that the whole world can support and that is independent of cultural, educational or religious differences?

On respect for the body. One could construct a whole ethic based on respect for the body and its functions: eating, drinking, pissing, shitting, sleeping, making love, talking, listening and so on. To stop someone sleeping at night, to force them to hang upside down, is a form of intolerable torture. To forbid others to move or to speak is equally intolerable. Rape does not respect the body of someone else. All types of racism and exclusion are, in the end, ways of denying the body of another. One could reinterpret the entire history of ethics in the light of the rights of the body and the relationship of our body to the rest of the world...

Why do you think that the left — if that term still has any meaning for you — is not at one in sharing your view about the need, which you find obvious, for a new form of vigilance against the extreme right's 'areas of appropriation'?

Overall, I see three reasons. The first, in France, as in Italy or Germany, concerns the small groups that have grown out of excessive leftism. The earth is round: one cannot move too far to the left. The logical result of pursuing the most extreme, the most provocative, the most innovative idea to its conclusion, is that one comes full circle and ends up on the extreme right. Which is what has happened in certain cases.

The second reason is the worn-out dogmas of the old left. There was a time when everyone who thought differently from us was a fascist. In

HANS WINDECK/CAMERA PRESS LONDON

Solingen, Germany 1993: from the ashes of neo-Nazi attacks on Turks

reaction to past excesses of this kind, there is a tendency today to stretch out one's hand to everyone and not to identify our enemies and their areas of appropriation. It is true that one must have a finely-honed — and ultimately rare — faculty for recognising the good faith and possibly generous motives of our adversaries. But notwithstanding that, we must never justify their ideological choices.

And finally, France today has a particular historical legacy. Italy settled its accounts with fascism in the open. One knew who supported Mussolini and who opposed him. The issue has been exhaustively debated and the past holds virtually no ambiguities. On the contrary, reading the French press I have discovered that the discussion as to who was for and who against Vichy is still going on. France's cupboards are still full of forgotten skeletons whose origins are unknown. This complicates things — and perhaps explains them.

This interview was first published in Le Monde *5 October 1993*
Translated by Judith Vidal-Hall

Nationalism and
the new right

*(Left) Spain 1994: German Fascists in the uniform of Franco's Legion of the Conda
honour the Generalissimo; (Above) Poland 1994: skinheads in Warsaw demonstrate for
a 'whites only Europe': Erma/Camera Press*

(Above) Germany 1994: to shouts of 'Sieg Heil' and 'Germany for the Germans', right-wing extremists march through Halle: Erma/Camera Press; (Right) Czech Republic 1994: right-wing hoodlums rampage on the lookout for violence: Thor Swift/Camera Press; (Overleaf) Russia 1992: young blackshirts of the ultra-nationalist Pamyat take to the streets of Moscow: Tass/Camera Press

VLADIMIR ZHIRINOVSKY

A last bid for the south

Introduction by Aleksei Venediktov

There are, in the history of the world's literature, certain books which quite clearly belong to the realm of fairy tale, myth, fantasy, nightmare. Now, all too fast, one such fiction is insinuating itself into the real world: myth, fantasy, nightmare come true.

I picture Germany in 1926 as it read *Mein Kampf*, amused, bewildered, aghast. In England, France, Russia and the USA, meanwhile, the book's readership was made up of two-tenths analysts, three-tenths political commentators and five-tenths students. Yet within five years the entire world was straining to grasp the meaning of the book's every comma, realising that behind each line lay war, death and ruin.

Vladimir Zhirinovsky's *A Last Bid for the South* could be in the same league. Imperial Russia always had designs on the south: on the Caucasus, Central Asia, Afghanistan and Turkey. Zhirinovsky is merely reviving an old ideological tradition, though this time in a world with atomic weapons and other 20th century technology. Read his book before rather than after the event. It is not beyond the bounds of possibility that it could become a textbook in Russian schools — perhaps not only in Russian schools.

It is not simply fantasy, chimera, fiction when Zhirinovsky talks about resolving Russia's old dispute with England over Central Asia, India, Pakistan, Afghanistan; or about Russian soldiers washing their shoes in the Indian Ocean. It is a hymn to Russian imperialism, set to the music of Kipling and imbued with extreme cynicism and calculation.

One could, of course, argue that Zhirinovsky's book is medicine for internal use only. But were Soviet generals not inspired with such ideas when they led their troops into Afghanistan in 1979? At the time no-one explained to the Soviet people to what end, and for whom, they were forced to do this. Yet it touched every one of my fellow citizens: everyone whose father, son or brother was going out and dying there.

Zhirinovsky makes the whole country a participant in a future war. You will swim in the ocean, he says, their women will smile at you, they will crawl up to you on their knees.

And the Russian citizen senses that with every page he is tied to the significance of what is being said. The language is straightforward and easy to understand: you are better than everyone else, you are more honourable than everyone else, you are cleverer than everyone else. And that means you are more important than everyone else.

Substitute the word 'Englishman' every time you see the word 'Russian' and read it through again. What do you say? Tempting, is it not?

Vladimir Zhirinovsky believes what he says and writes. My acquaintance with him has convinced me that the man is not a writer, he is a sober and cynical politician. But he is also a romantic whose romanticism could cost not only Russia, but the whole world, very dear.

He did not write this book, he dictated it. Read it and you hear his voice, his intonation, his cry. It is, indeed, his book.

Russia's state prosecutor has begun an investigation into Zhirinovsky's activities and pronouncements, which will include several passages from *A Last Bid for the South*. Already his colleagues are saying the book is a forgery, a distortion of the truth; that everything in it has been turned on its head and taken out of context.

No, dear readers, that is not the whole of it. It is fairy tale, myth, fantasy — and nightmare come true.

We must hope that in neither Russian nor English schools will children have to study this book; that it gathers dust on library shelves. And then we can return to reading *Alice in Wonderland*.

Aleksei Venediktov is a radio broadcaster on Ekho Moskvy (*Moscow Echo*)

Translated by Mark Greaves

Russians, proud people, the 21st century will be ours! In the intervening seven years we will definitively put a stop to revolution, *perestroika* and 'Gorbastroika'. We shall have done with 'Yeltsinism'; the Poltoranins and the Gaidars will go. All this will vanish, and in the 21st century we shall be transformed, cleansed. At the moment we are 'in the bath', washing off the accumulated scabs and dirt of the 20th century. Regrettably, this sometimes means blood has to be spilled. But this is what we and our hapless land so desperately need if we are to wash away, once and for all, the satanic contagion passed on to us from the West at the beginning of this century, a contagion that has sunk deep into Russia's heart to poison the country, to undermine it from within through Communism, Nationalism, cosmopolitanism, through the influence of alien religions, alien ideas and alien ways of life. We shall have done with that. We will emerge as hard as tempered steel.

Zhirinovsky

A last bid for the south. How I long to see Russian solders wash their boots in the warm waters of the Indian Ocean and wear summer uniform all year round. Light boots, light trousers, short-sleeved shirts, no tie, an open collar, light caps. And a small Russian sub-machine-gun produced in Izhevsk... . So that any platoon of Russian soldiers might bring order to any region.

It will probably be the last partition of the world; and it must be done in the manner of shock therapy, quickly, unexpectedly, efficiently. It will instantly resolve all our problems because we shall find peace... . When we reach to the shores of the Arctic Ocean in the north, the Pacific in the east, the Atlantic via the Black Sea, the Mediterranean and the Baltic seas; and when at last we stand in a massive column on the shores of the Indian Ocean — then we shall also find peaceful neighbours.

It is not just the economy that's being destroyed. People are dying as well, all the time. Like a disease, there is a hidden civil war in the country; in certain regions it is now open war. A disease is still a disease, even though it may be hidden from view. And it undermines the living organism — just like a hidden civil war. In Tajikistan and in the Caucasus it is open war. In the Baltic and in the Ukraine it exists in hidden form. But this civil war continues, destroying us from inside, and is all the more dangerous for that. The present war in Tajikistan may be less dangerous because it will end — such wars do end — more quickly. An illness in its extreme form may be easy to heal and quicker to diagnose, and a happy outcome is more likely. But in its hidden form, it is like a fire burning in a mineshaft. Smoke rises from the ground, but the fire cannot be found. The slate and the coal may burn for years, then they explode into the open and half the town is wiped out in a flash. It is easier to douse a burning house, even when the fire is highly dangerous.

We need pluralism, openness and peace. We must stop tormenting our country, for Russia is already tired. We have exhausted her with these upheavals. The title 'USSR' is an artificial one; more artificial still is the title 'CIS'. The proper name for our state is Russia. It is an historical name and a geographical concept. But the name certainly does not signify 'a state for the Russians' — that is the 22 million square kilometres that make up the Euro-Asiatic continent. To the north, our borders are defined by the Arctic Ocean, in the Far East by the Pacific. Beyond the Black Sea and the Baltic Sea, the Atlantic defines our borders. And in the future, when we have made our final 'push south', there will be the Indian Ocean.

Of course every party is in some way like a political version of the mafia, with its leader and its own well-defined internal rules... .

Take... the history of Hitler and his party in Germany. A National Socialist Party of Germany might not have seemed such a bad idea. What was wrong with it? Work arranged along socialist lines, with a national emphasis to encourage Germany's revival. Ultimately, however, the party turned into an instrument of nationwide repression. It overturned and effectively smothered any opposition. The leader's personal qualities played their part in this. In France, by contrast, it was precisely Napoleon Bonaparte's personal qualities that made France invincible over an extended period... .

*Players in the Great Game: Colonel Grombtchevski, Russian agent (left),
and Sir Francis Younghusband, British explorer on the frontier*

Personality always plays a highly significant role in history, positive as well as negative.

Russia has been entrusted with a great historical mission. It could be her last. She must then address herself to purely national problems: the development of an infrastructure, the construction of good roads, storehouses, refrigerators, transport networks, communications centres and new residential accommodation. Russia must in part return to being a 'one-storey' country, with cottages, saunas, garages, farmsteads and gardens. These offer better living conditions than those jungles of concrete and stone. All will be well in India because its conflict with Pakistan will have ended. Russia will acquire a border with India. The conflicts between Mongolia and China, between China and South-East Asia and between China and India will cease. Japan will have determined finally what its national interests are. Peace will come to all. South Africa will receive guarantees for the existence of a white republic in southern

Africa.

But no-one will help Russia herself. And it could still happen that America will need Russia's help. Who knows whether, by the middle of the 21st century, America may not have to ask for Russia's helping hand?... . Russia must act quickly to become healthy, strong and mighty, a power whose borders look out over the sea's wide expanse.

America too will soon begin to fall apart. It too has accumulated much that is bad. It too is throwing up many problems, many multi-ethnic conflicts. America, your perestroika, your suffering, your degradation lie before you. But we Russians will not gloat when your states begin to secede, when your factories grind to a halt, when you lack sufficient food or medicine for your own needs, when people leave America for Europe, for Russia, for Japan, for South Africa, for Australia. We will not gloat when California secedes to Mexico, when a black republic is established in Miami, when Russia reclaims Alaska, when people no longer call you the United States of America but the Commonwealth of New American States.

The world should be grateful to Russia in her role as saviour. She did not win that role as reward for her ordeals: every hundred years she fulfils her historical mission. It is the nature of Russia's development. It is her awakening, her capacity to again help the people of the south to find genuine liberation so that peace comes at last to the Near and Middle East, to Asia Minor and Central Asia. Only Russia can help here. For the last time, a Russian army will prepare for a southern campaign and will come to a final halt on the shores of the Indian Ocean. Beyond, there is nothing but the warm waters of the Indian Ocean, washing the shores of our eternal friend, India, and Iraq — both Russia's strategic allies. The warm breath of the ocean will calm all those who inhabit this new geopolitical expanse, within Russia's new borders. The Russian flag will threaten no one, and the Russian fleet in the Indian Ocean will pay friendly visits to the ports of India, the Persian Gulf and East Africa. We will become friends with everyone, but with South Africa in particular. We are tied to them by special interests in the fields of economics, culture and geopolitics. That is how north-south relations will be.

We will understand one another because every family will have the home it wants — be it in a large or small town, in a village in Central Asia or the Caucasus, in the tropics, in the forest or on a mountainside... . We will live peacefully, with no dominant ideology. There will be no struggles for power, nor will one leader be able to establish a world order. Ivan and Uncle Sam will no longer frighten one another. There will be fewer diseases. Hunger should disappear because there will be enough produce; we will make sure that it reaches those in need. All this will become possible only when Russia finds a national, as distinct from an international, identity. This is not so that Russians can rise up and subjugate other peoples, but rather so that, having risen up herself, Russia can raise up other peoples living alongside her throughout this Euro-Asiatic continent, from Brest to Kabul, from Yamal to Istanbul.

Latvia will be part of Russia. Inside Russia there will be a small Lithuanian state. If people really want to live in a small Ukrainian enclave, then there will be a small Ukrainian republic.

But all this is conditional on Russia looking out over the south, coming to rest by the shores of the Indian Ocean.

There will always be those who dislike our idea. But just as in a real family there is always someone who is dissatisfied with the state of things, so in our planet's great family of nations not everyone will agree on the way things are. They should accept it for the good of the majority... .

Russia's emergence in the south would, above all, be a protective measure, a response to the fact that nowadays the threat to Russia comes from the south — from Afghanistan, which is already attacking Tajikistan, from Teheran, which plans a pan-Islamic seizure of vast areas of land, and from Ankara, which has long nurtured plans for a pan-Turkish state... .

At the very least Turkey has designs on Azerbaijan, the Caucasus and Georgia. This will make it a country of four seas: the Black Sea, the Mediterranean, the Caspian, the Sea of Marmora — even the Aegean. Russia would lose virtually everything... .

Were the entire Turkish nation to perish, the world would be unaffected. I would not, even so, wish it such a fate. But let the Turks recall their arrival in Asia

Minor, their barbaric seizure of Constantinople, where they plundered and slaughtered, subjugating all Asia Minor's peoples. Let them recall how they slaughtered 1.5 million Armenians in April 1915.

Let them recall that and let humanity's conscience shudder over an entire people slaughtered in three nights.

Meanwhile, millions of Kurds groan under the Turkish yoke and cannot live in a Kurdish state.

There is no such thing as Turkish culture. There cannot be culture when sabres are bared. And who provided the foundation for the new Turkish army? 'Janissaries' — young Slavs taken prisoner along with their parents. The parents were killed, but the young boys were educated in Turkish ways and became the mainstay of the Turkish army. It is strange that young Slavs under the Turkish flag should have wiped out Slav peoples. Who will answer for this? Who will pay for this outrage against Byzantine culture and the Slav peoples?

We must act in accordance with the will of the majority. The majority of people would be happy to see the Muslim world broken up. The Muslim threat must be removed. At present, other religions are incapable of bringing about religious wars. The Turkish-speaking world must be cleft apart.

The Russian army needs to flex its muscles. Our soldiers are tired of... spending their days in barracks in the depths of Russia not knowing who or where the enemy is, or for what they are preparing themselves both morally and physically. It would cleanse us all. And the sound of Russian Orthodox church bells on the shores of the Indian Ocean and the Mediterranean Sea would proclaim peace to the peoples of the region, brotherhood to the nations, prosperity, happiness... the end of wars and inter-ethnic strife.

Some day there will be no more passports. Residence permits are already being phased out, although they are still necessary to control the entry of southerners into Russia's European centres. They have already crawled over the Urals. Like a fungus; like cockroaches.

Moscow 1992: Pamyat's right-wing extremists at prayer

Washington and Moscow must understand that we can wait no longer, that we cannot experiment, that we cannot tear Russia apart short of destroying Europe and humanity itself. There has to be an end to meddling in the internal affairs of other peoples and countries. Spheres of influence have to be apportioned once and for all.

So let Russia make a last, successful 'push south'. I can see Russian soldiers as they prepare for this last southern campaign. I can see Russian commanders at the headquarters of Russian divisions and armies, planning the movements that will lead to the ultimate destination. I can see planes and air bases in Russia's southern regions. I can see submarines as they surface along the coast of the Indian Ocean and landing craft as they move up to the shores, where Russian army soldiers march and weapons move, while masses of tanks are shifted.

Russia is at last concluding her final military campaign. Henceforth there can be no war from the south, just as war from the north has long been impossible. In the West they will understand this. They will also understand it in the East.

In addition to civilisation, Europe also brought a corrupting influence to Russia. During Stalin's regime we were effectively a closed country. In some ways this was a positive thing — we were almost completely spared venereal disease for instance. And moral standards were, in general, high. I was at school from 1953-1964. All the girls in my class were virgins. If a girl suddenly gave people reason to think she had become sexually active, they were deeply disapproving. Until the age of 17-18 we were clean-living, well-balanced children. Nobody took drugs. We didn't sniff anything and only occasionally drank alcohol — at home with our parents on festive occasions.

I have been unable to make sense of my childhood as a whole. There were occasions when people hurt me because, as a boy, I was not physically strong. But there are happy memories — of childhood friendships at Pioneer camp, for instance. I was an outstanding student at university. I was commended for public work, as well as for assisting in preparations for a congress of peace-loving powers and an international youth festival. At times I was excluded from things. I received no state prizes, of course, nor did I produce any significant academic work or receive an academic degree... What attracted me was the living, the 'here and now'.

On the whole, I am satisfied with my life. I have achieved what I wanted to achieve; my performance has been at least, 'satisfactory'. I am leader of a political party. I was a candidate for president. Today I am known not only throughout the country, from Kaliningrad to Kamchatka, but throughout the world. In Iraq I am known as one of the Iraqi people's closest friends. In Finland, on the other hand, people are rather afraid of me. The Poles are not over-fond of me either, but I am well thought of in

Germany and by independent political forces in France; there is sympathy for my views in South Africa; and I have good relations with the Russian community abroad in Australia, Spain and Germany. I have supporters and opponents in every country in the world. I have become famous. I have personally met Saddam Hussein, who met no foreigners for two years after the war, least of all Russians. He was visited by deputies from the Russian parliament, by leaders of various parties and by journalists, but the only person he received was me, in November 1992. We conversed for four hours in his palace in Baghdad...Saddam Hussein listened and asked questions.

Translated by Mark Greaves
A Last Bid for the South *is published by Pisatel', 1993. Available only in Russian, price £6.95*

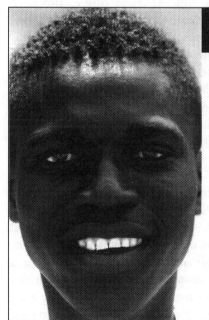

LETTER FROM LAGOS

ADEWALE MAJA-PEARCE

Living in the last days

The politics of Nigeria is either very simple or very complex; I'm still not sure which. Take the events of the last 12 months. First we had a military dictator, General Ibrahim Babangida, who promised to hand over power to an elected civilian president after eight years in office, and then promptly annulled the presidential elections, which he himself had organised, and proceeded to bribe everyone in sight to allow him to stay on indefinitely. Among those who were not slow in coming forward to receive their share of the loot were members of the two elected bodies voted in the previous year — the Senate and the House of Representatives — as part of the long-drawn-out transition to civil rule. To achieve his end, Babangida first exhausted the reserves in the Central Bank and then went directly to the national mint.

Nobody knows how much money was printed in the space of a few weeks, but Nigeria is a country where US$1.5 bn (N40 bn) of oil receipts can go missing in the space of six months (January-June 1993) and nobody is expected to ask awkward questions. Nigerian governments have never been strong on accountability, as any Nigerian journalist will tell you; but for reasons which still remain unclear, and which had little or nothing to do with the desires of ordinary Nigerians, Babangida was eventually forced to retire to his 50 bedroom mansion-cum-hotel in his home state of Minna, where he immediately attempted to unseat the local Emir in his continuing quest for power at all costs; ie, if I can't be president of the country, I can still be the religious leader of a State in the country. In his resignation speech, an emotional occasion which involved much wiping of the eyes, he explained his decision to step down as 'my personal sacrifice to the nation' (a statement which speaks volumes), and then inexplicably handed over to what he was pleased to call an Interim National Government (ING) headed by a lacklustre businessman with no political experience and even less political instinct.

Why Babangida couldn't have simply handed over to Chief Moshood Abiola, the man who had won 44% of the vote in an election deemed to be free and fair (even 'the West' said so), was not among the explanations he cared to offer a perplexed populace, unless of course it was an act of spite designed to bring the maximum confusion in its wake. If so, he might just have succeeded, but then part of the blame must also lie with the incumbent, who had already proved himself unfit for public office by fleeing abroad at the first sign of trouble and returning only after it was too late to exploit his popular mandate. Abiola's explanation at the time was his fear of assassination and his determination not to split the country 'for the sake of my personal ambition'. He had obviously missed (or misunderstood) the dramatic scene of Boris Yeltsin facing down a tank in the Russian capital when the would-be President of Russia was called upon to fulfil his patriotic duty. But Russia, unlike Nigeria, is obviously worth dying for. As for Abiola's concern about the future unity of Nigeria, the country has been splitting for more years than most people would care to count, and certainly since before independence in 1960; but perhaps the surest route to the final disintegration, should it come to that, is to stifle the collective voice even before it has had a chance properly to articulate its demands.

Back in the country at last after his extended sojourn in Europe and the USA, where he gave endless interviews to the BBC and CNN, the Chief took the illegitimate government of Nigeria to the High Court in Lagos, the commercial capital, to have it declared illegal on the grounds that the decree which brought the ING into being — Decree 61 of 1993 — was itself null and void, having been signed into law after Babangida — himself hardly legitimate — had actually quit State House for more spiritual concerns.

Surprisingly enough, Abiola won the case in what was to be one of the most sensational judgements in Nigerian legal history, but in the event the matter was settled in time-honoured fashion when General Sani Abacha, the country's second-in-command and the highest-ranking officer in the military, dissolved the government of which he was himself a member, dismissed both the Senate and the House of Representatives, and pronounced himself the new Head of State and Commander-in-Chief of the Armed Forces. And that was the end of what was to have been the third democratic experiment in the continent's most populous state, otherwise known as 'the giant of Africa'. Ten years after the military coup of December 1983, which brought to an end the Second Republic, the country is back where it started. At about the same time, the Republic of South Africa, for so long the whipping-boy of successive Nigerian dictators, is moving towards accountable government, the rule of law and respect for fundamental human rights. The world has indeed changed, but more radically than any of us had ever imagined possible. The bitter joke at the moment is that a democratic South Africa will soon be funding liberation movements in Nigeria.

In the meantime, the 'ordinary' men and women of Nigeria, that much-abused entity in whose name all manner of crimes are daily committed, are stunned at the extraordinary turn of events that delivered three heads of state between late August and early November. But to what effect? There is no credible political opposition to the boys with their toys, a fact that was demonstrated all-too clearly during the strike called by the Nigerian Labour Congress (NLC) in the very week of Abacha's ascendancy. It shouldn't have been too much, after all, to have expected the legitimate representatives of the trade union movement to be in the forefront of the agitation against military rule. Alas, not so: the executive of the NLC, which had organised the strike to protest against the six-fold increase in the price of petrol put in place by the ING in its dying days, quickly settled for a token reduction when the country's new 'strongman' warned the nation in his maiden broadcast (all seven minutes of it) against any attempt to 'test our will'. Any such attempt, he added laconically, 'will be decisively dealt with'.

More puzzling still is the long list of erstwhile democrats and would-be 'radicals' who saw fit to accept posts within the new regime on the grounds that this administration 'is friendly and sympathetic to our cause'.

They include Ambassador Baba Kingibe, the putative President's running mate in the annulled elections; Chief Alex Ibru, the proprietor of the country's leading independent daily newspaper, *The Guardian*; and Dr Olu Onagoruwa, a renowned constitutional lawyer with previously impeccable human rights credentials. Why they should imagine that any military government can possibly be 'sympathetic' to the cause of freedom is not a question that appears to trouble any of them; worse yet, all of them know very well — or should — that the experience of military rule has consistently demonstrated the exact opposite. Babangida himself assumed power on a strong pro-human rights platform, but before the year was out he had reverted to type by closing down newspaper houses, imprisoning university lecturers and generally carrying on as though the country was his personal fiefdom, which is largely what it was.

In the process, he was not above using those who were naive enough to be seduced by the trappings of power. The list of intellectuals who were co-opted to provide a veneer of legitimacy is a long one and makes for sad reading; but intellectuals usually are out of their depth when it comes to the nuts and bolts of politics. There is no reason to assume that Abacha, Babangida's erstwhile deputy and the sole survivor of that regime, will be any different from his former mentor. Every schoolchild knows that General Abacha is one of the biggest crooks in the country; every schoolchild can list the choice properties he has amassed in the course of his uninterrupted climb up the greasy pole. One might as well be living in a country where the mafia has taken control, which is the logic of military rule. The fact that the General never appears without his ubiquitous dark glasses (why are they always so predictable?) is only the most visible sign that he himself has fallen for the mythology of the gangster as politician.

To argue that Nigeria is travelling backwards at a time when the rest of the continent is democratising in accordance with the universal imperative is to assume that such wilful blindness is a viable option as we approach the next millennium. The humiliating fact of 70,000 soldiers holding to ransom a nation of almost one hundred million souls, and doing so with an impunity that beggars belief but for the fact that it continues to happen, is only exceeded by the suspicion, inescapable under the circumstances, that Nigeria is simply not ready for democratic rule, and that the country can only continue to function — insofar as it can be said to function at all — by coercion.

Consider, for instance, the shameless behaviour of the political class (so-called) in the dying days of Babangida's regime. The ease with which the retired General was able to bribe the members of the Senate and the House of Representatives was hardly surprising to most Nigerians, who expect their elected representatives to consider their own pockets first, last and always. One of the few exceptions was Dr Iyorchia Ayu, President of the Senate, whose refusal to be corrupted was instrumental in calling a halt to Babangida's megalomania, but who, inexplicably, has since joined the ranks of the new dispensation, to the disappointment of those (ie, most of us) who crave just a few examples of probity in the public domain.

As for the incorrigible optimists, those few brave souls who continue to hope against hope that the country will wake up one day and fulfil its destiny (the giant of Africa indeed!): the behaviour of the democratically-elected representatives of the people in the wake of the coup must have cured them once and for all of what, in the Nigerian context at least, is a recipe for madness. Even before the announcement that the military had taken over, but when it had become obvious that something was afoot, the torch-bearers of a free people were to be seen fleeing from their expensive hotel in Abuja, the administrative capital, for the safety of their home states. The idea that these representatives might have stood their ground and provided a focus for the nation at large was obviously not uppermost in their minds, or anywhere else for that matter. The nation, in turn, shrugged in contempt and waited to see what would happen next. Its cynicism, which has become such an integral part of the Nigerian political scene as to be perfectly unremarkable, is itself an impediment to the eventual emergence of democracy as the only acceptable form of government. It was what a friend of mine meant when he said — melodramatically, no doubt, but this is Nigeria — that we were living through the last, evil days. It is, indeed, becoming increasingly difficult to imagine where the country can possibly go from here.

22 YEARS AGO

index on censorship

STEPHEN SPENDER

With concern for those not free

There was [a] letter (published in *The Times* of 17 January 1970) from Alexander Daniel, the eighteen-year-old son of the Soviet writer Yuli Daniel, to Graham Greene, in which the young man described the trial of his father, who had been sent to a labour camp. Alexander Daniel's letter was a protest against procedures which would have seemed equally inhuman under any law. It was above all written in the name of decency and morality bound to no ideology, and it was written on the assumption that people can talk across frontiers of dictatorship and democracy — East and West — and address one another as human beings; ask one another questions to which answers can be given, in which questioner and answerer are not addressing one another as communist and non-communist but simply as human beings. 'What is it that I want of you Mr Greene? I don't know what you can do nor what you will want to do, neither do I know in general what can be done in this predicament.'

The answer to the appeal is already implicit in these uncertain questionings. That Mr Greene should listen was the answer, and although there was nothing that he could do, to publish Alexander Daniel's letter was already a form of action.

Essentially Alexander Daniel's appeal is the same as that put out in the summer of 1968 by members of the Faculty, and by students, of Charles University, after the Russian invasion of Prague, which was published in *Le Monde*. This asked that those outside Czechoslovakia should concern themselves with the fate of their Czechoslovak colleagues, keep themselves informed, follow what was happening to them. The request conveys the idea that there are or there should be international values which are those of the university. For a moment, in the summer of 1968, Czechoslovak intellectuals seem to have been buoyed up by the hope that their academic colleagues would feel that what was happening to Charles University was also happening to Oxford and Cambridge and London, Paris and Harvard and Chicago. Indeed, qualitatively and quantitatively, it was happening to every university and in every place where there is a life of the intellect. For contemporary civilisation, dependent on the minds of a few thousand people living all over the world, is a sum. And the subtraction of the numbers of those concerned with it in one country is a loss to the whole world, like the loss of some rare species, an asset to the whole world, in some particular place.

One writer — now packed away in a Russian labour camp — did have a positive idea of the ways in which colleagues in the countries of comparative freedom could help those in the lands of censorship and repression. He wrote to an English writer asking him whether it might not be possible to form an organisation in England of intellectuals who made it their business to publish information about what was happening to their censored, suppressed, and sometimes imprisoned colleagues. He insisted that such an organisation should not concern itself only with writers in Russia and Eastern Europe but throughout the world. He thought that an attempt could also be made to obtain and publish censored works, together with the news about the writers of them.

The Times also published a letter from Pavel Litvinov, appealing directly and openly for the sustained concern of colleagues abroad. A few of us decided to answer this appeal, in a direct and personal way, by telegram. The text of this message is worth recording: 'We, a group of friends representing no organisation, support your statement, admire your courage, think of you and will help in any way possible.' This was signed by Cecil Day-Lewis, Yehudi Menuhin, W H Auden, Henry Moore, Stephen Spender, A J Ayer, Bertrand Russell, Julian Huxley, Mary McCarthy, J B Priestley, Jacquetta Hawkes, Paul Scofield, Igor Stravinsky, Stuart Hampshire, Maurice Bowra and Sonia Orwell.

An organisation called Writers and Scholars International has now been formed whose aims have much in common with the sentiments expressed in this telegram... .

The main activity of WSI will be to publish a journal called *Index*, which will 'record and analyse all forms of inroads into freedom of expression and examine the censorship situation in individual countries and in relation to various constitutions and legal codes.

The role of WSI will be to study the situation of those who are silenced in their own countries and to make their circumstances known in the world community to which they spiritually belong. I think that doing this is not just an act of charity. It is a way of facilitating and extending an international consciousness traversing political boundaries... . The world is moving in two directions: one is towards the narrowing of distances through travel, increasing interchange between scientists (who take a world view of problems such as the exploration of space, ecology, population): the other is towards the shutting down of frontiers, the ever more jealous surveillance by governments and police of individual freedom. The opposites are fear and openness; and in being concerned with the situation of those who are deprived of their freedoms one is taking the side of openness.

Index on Censorship Vol 1, No 1, 1972

DIARY

RONALD HARWOOD

Sanction busting in Belgrade

December 1993

I am invited by Jovan Cirilov, the Artistic Director of the *Jugoslovensko Dramsko Pozriste* (The Yugoslav Dramatic Theatre) to attend the premiere of *The Dresser* in Belgrade in January. The British Council, which still functions energetically in the city, is to pay my fare in return for a lecture. I accept immediately since it means I can fulfil my promise to visit the Serbian, Croatian and Slovenian PEN Centres.

Friday, 14 January 1994

Because of sanctions you cannot reach Belgrade directly from London, so I fly to Budapest where the British Council has arranged for a mini-bus to meet me. I have been warned of shortages and travel armed with soap, lavatory paper and two bath plugs. We set off from Budapest at around 1pm on a journey of just over 300 kilometres. The day is dull and chill with a persistent drizzle. Time and the landscape become meaningless. Darkness falls. We reach the frontier town of Roszke and an enormously long queue of motor vehicles. I am told that the crossing can take 3 hours or more, but my driver is experienced. He dodges in and out of the queue and despite three passport checks we are cleared in no more than 20 minutes. At 8.20pm I am deposited at the magnificent Hyatt Regency hotel in Belgrade where I am met by Dr Predrag Palavestra, the President of Serbian PEN, Jovan Cirilov and a press photographer. We are later joined by Dr Robert Snell, the acting director of the British Council.

I gasp aloud when I enter my hotel room: vast, luxurious, comfortable with an opulent bathroom that boasts a towelling gown, French soap, lavatory paper and, yes, a bath plug. I turn on the television and am further surprised to see CNN, Sky, BBC World News and the usual cable junk. Dinner in the hotel dining room is also lavish.

The conversation instantly sucks me into Serbia (still officially and ridiculously called Yugoslavia) and the war. The dollar is now worth over a billion dinars; Milosovic is a suicide from a family of suicides — four, apparently, including his father — and now he wants the entire nation to commit suicide with him; petrol is the hardest commodity to come by;

Ronald Harwood

the Muslims are receiving arms from the Saudis; sanctions only bolster the regime; the poor suffer most. There isn't much food in the cities and you have to take your own anaesthetic when you go to hospital. There is much pain and a sense of despair, expressed with care and dignity.

They leave at 11pm and I sleep like the dead until 8 next morning.

Saturday, 15 January
I address a meeting of Serbian PEN. About 30 members. Some equate themselves with writers in prison and ask for International PEN to fight the cultural sanctions. I tell them I have always opposed cultural sanctions and am breaking them by attending the premiere of my play. If

governments want to censor plays and books, that's their affair but I am not going to do it for them. International PEN, I remind them, stands for freedom of expression. This is welcome but not exactly what they want to hear.

Afterwards I have a private conversation with Palavestra about International PEN's role in the region which has to remain private.

A walk around the city. I see a long line of mostly elderly people queuing for bread which, I am told, is being handed out by political parties who want votes. Another queue is for newspapers which are paid for by cheque.

In the evening, dinner at the home of Slobodan Selenic and his wife. He is a leading Serbian novelist, she a former ballerina. A handsome couple and delightful hosts. The world outside recedes. I am amongst Central European intellectuals, well-informed, cultivated, but nevertheless I have an impression of unhappiness concealed, unspoken but tangible anxiety.

Sunday, 16 January

Lunch with the critic Jovan Hristic and his new wife at their cottage which adjoins one of Tito's villas. You can see the gardens from the upstairs lavatory which gives rise to predictable jokes.

In the evening to the theatre for the premiere. Standing Room Only. Two magnificent actors: as Sir, Ljuba Tadic, who is making his return to the stage after a long absence, and Petar Kralj as Norman. The production is honest and professional.

The Dresser has now a special resonance here: to quote the press release, the play 'will, maybe, offer an answer to the question — what does art look like under exceptional circumstances and who is in need of it?' The audience applauds often and unexpectedly — the lines about rationing, barbarians bombing cities, culture being a shield etc. The reception at the end is deafening. I take a spotlit bow from the stalls but, as I do so, I know that somehow I am going to pay for this.

Afterwards, in a restaurant, the two leading actors are applauded when they enter. Twelve of us sit down to a grand meal. At another table a party of four who have seen the performance offer to pay our bill. The offer is accepted. '*Nouveau riche*,' someone says. 'War profiteers,' says another.

Monday, 17 January
Press conference. About 30 journalists and TV cameras. Predictable questions: What did I think of the performance? Do I believe writers can do any good in the present situation? To the last I answer that since certain Serbian writers are accused of being the first to let the nationalist poison out of the bottle, I presume that others may be able to find an antidote. But I am surprised that they know about my meeting four days ago with Boutros Boutros-Ghali in Geneva. Did we discuss the Balkans? It was a private meeting, I answer lamely.

Lunch with Palavestra and Cirilov. Good companions. Palavestra, a distinguished academic, has recently lost his brother who died from starvation in Sarajevo. Cirilov is thin, edgy, ironic. The cloakroom attendant, a young woman of great beauty, thanks me for coming to Belgrade. My good companions are as amazed as I am.

I give my lecture — a short history of the English theatre — for the British Council in the evening. Another full house.

Tuesday, 18 January
Up at 5.45am. In normal times you could fly from Belgrade to Zagreb in half an hour. These are not normal times. The bus journey takes 14 hours: north into Hungary, then westwards across the southern border, changing buses to enter Croatia at Barcs. No food and, worse, no smoking. We reach Zagreb around 8pm, my mind and body numb.

A board in the lobby bears a message welcoming me to the Esplanade hotel which is grand and very European. They have given me an enormous suite. Dinner with members of Croatian PEN including the President, Slobodan Prospero Novak, who was once close to Tudjman but has recently denounced him, and the Secretary, Vera Cicin-Sein. Prospero (as I insist on calling him) is large, dark and likeable. He now edits an opposition newspaper.

Wednesday, 19 January
Viktor Ivancic, the young editor of another opposition newspaper, *Feral Tribune*, has been called up into the army and the rumour is he will be sent to the front. I fax a message to President Tudjman — I am given his private fax number — protesting. I doubt if it will do any good. (A week

later I heard that Mr Ivancic had been released from army training.)

I am forcibly made aware of the pain, anger and anguish the Croatians have suffered and are suffering. They have lost a third of their country to the Serbs. They are enraged and guilt-ridden by Tudjman's adventure in Bosnia. They have a compulsion to inform: about yesterday, last week, last year, the 12th century, the thousand years before that, names, places, events, who said what, when, where. They shout at me. I say, 'Please, don't shoot the messenger!' We laugh but only momentarily. Exhausting, trying to absorb, listen, understand. They are deeply wounded and, yes, in pain.

At 5.50pm I leave for Slovenia, all energy spent. An empty train carries me to Ljubljana.

There is a noticeable change of atmosphere. Slovenia, I sense, is untroubled. My friend, Boris Novak, the President of Slovenian PEN and Milos Mikeln, the Chairman of our Peace Committee, meet me with the news that, within the last hour, Milosovic and Tudjman have signed a deal in Geneva but no-one yet knows what it means. We dine in the Writers' House where Slovenian PEN has its offices. Talk is lively and immensely enjoyable. I take a sleeping pill and am out for nine hours.

Thursday, 20 January
An hour-long interview for TV, then a press conference which lasts another hour. Lunch in a restaurant where I meet Bosnian writers who thank me for the help International PEN is giving their colleagues trapped in Sarajevo. The burden of this effort has fallen on Boris Novak who has managed to organise the transfer of enormous amounts of Deutschemarks into the besieged city. We are unexpectedly joined by a theatre director, two days out of Sarajevo and due to return shortly. Prematurely grey, thin, pale. He is highly charged and immediately attacks me for going to Belgrade — as I knew someone would. He is fierce and unrelenting. Why, he asks, have I not also visited Sarajevo? Would I have gone to Nazi Germany? (I wasn't quick enough to answer yes, if I thought I could detach German writers from the Nazi government.) 'This is genocide, we are in Auschwitz,' he cries. Milos says, 'There is one major difference between Auschwitz and Sarajevo. In Auschwitz they didn't run out of gas.' I try to explain my position: my visit could be

misused by all sides, I do not believe in the politics of gesture, I do not want the personal publicity that would inevitably result. But his eyes accuse me of cowardice and everything I say only enrages him more. Eventually the atmosphere is calmed and we part with an embrace but I am unsettled and deeply uneasy.

By coincidence, there is yet another production of *The Dresser* to see. The sizeable Slovenian minority in Trieste have their own theatre and happen to be performing the play. So, I am taken by bus to Trieste with members of Slovenian PEN. A desperately cold wind mars the sightseeing but a happy evening in every other way. The production is excellent and although it doesn't boast the fine acting of the Serbs, it catches accurately the spirit of the play.

We get back to Ljubljana at 1.30am starving. Fortunately, the restaurant in the Writers' House is still open and they agree to feed Boris Novak, Alenka Puhar, journalist and translator, and me. Within 10 minutes we are again discussing former Yugoslavia. It is obsessive. But Alenka tells me something interesting. She is writing a series of three pieces and the first, just published, is about the myth that has been created around Bosnia prior to the war. The myth makers would have us believe, she says, that Bosnia was a paradise where everyone lived in perfect harmony. Total rubbish, she says. Bosnia, she insists, was the most Stalinist, the most repressive of all the former Yugoslav republics and the reason is obvious: Stalinism was the only way to suppress the national and ethnic conflicts that have now erupted with such savagery.

Friday, 21 January
Discussions with Boris and Milos who, after lunch, drive me to the airport. I reflect on my visit. I have probably achieved nothing but at least I've demonstrated PEN's concern and learned at first hand the tortured nature of the problems. I see no glimmer of hope but know we just have to go on trying.

A last irony which, as a writer of fiction, I would not dare invent. I leave Ljubljana for Vienna where I am to have discussions about a screenplay I am writing. The subject? The assassination of the Archduke Franz Ferdinand by Gavrillo Princip on 28 June 1914 in Sarajevo. There is no escape.

ANNE NELSON

Colours of violence

America's lunatic gun laws, jealously guarded by certain sectors of the population, have traditionally given large numbers of people access to weapons of mass destruction. The idea that it is normal, desirable and socially acceptable to use them for just that is a more recent phenomenon.

Middle America's defences against the inescapable proliferation of violence in its society are crumbling fast: it's not just New York, not just the inner cities, not just the 'underclass'. The National Rifle Association defends the practice of offering semi-automatic weapons for sale with slogans like 'Guns don't kill people, people kill people.'

But the guns undoubtedly allow them to do it more efficiently.

The public is angry: Washington is caught between a vociferous gun lobby defending its frontier rights and the law of the gun in its cities. Capitol Hill is 'considering its response'.

Central to its deliberations is the connection between the excessive portrayal of violence in the mass media and violent crime on the streets. Alongside long overdue signs of movement on gun control, suggestions for controlling the quota of television violence have begun to emerge.

The debate is not about dramas or documentaries which hinge on a killing; nor on the violence of war reports. Public concern focuses on the gratuitous violence of cinema and TV that makes dialogue subordinate to the shocking visual image and saturates the audience with its morbid repetition: the kind of movie violence that propels young men to stand up in their seats, jab their fists in the air, and shout 'Aw-right!' By the age of 18, the average American child has witnessed 18,000 simulated murders on television.

As in so many US public debates, the rhetoric surrounding this one is couched in terms of 'freedom' versus censorship. There are two forms of freedom involved: freedom of expression — the right to depict violence on artistic, political or other grounds; and the freedom of the market-place — the right to make a profit from violent programmes for mass consumption, despite demonstrably harmful effects.

There is a growing body of evidence establishing the link between films and violent behaviour, particularly in the case of children watching without adult supervision.

US police files are full of copy-cat killings: the troubled teenager in Massachusetts who dressed up in a Jason hockey mask from *Friday the 13th,* and the Los Angeles thief who donned Freddy's fedora from *Nightmare on Elm Street* before murdering their victims. It is a matter of record that 35 young men committed suicide after watching the Russian roulette scene in *The Deer Hunter.* This year a child in the Midwest set his little sister's hair on fire in imitation of a comedy scene in MTV's *Beavis and Butthead.*

But the evidence is more than anecdotal. Last July, an article in *Mother Jones* cited 85 separate research studies, all of them establishing the causal relationship between television violence and actual violence. Researchers from the University of British Columbia found that two years after their area was wired for television in the 1950s, hitting and biting among first- and second-grade students increased 160%; a study of children in Chicago conducted by two doctors reached the startling conclusion that watching violent television was the best single indicator of violent behaviour as adults.

Professor Brandon Centerwall of the University of Washington found that the introduction of violent television programming corresponded precisely with a sharp rise in murder rates in the US and Canada in 1955 — and in South Africa in 1975. In both instances, the crime rate rose first in the white communities, which were the first to get television.

In the face of such overwhelming evidence, the US broadcasting industry has been forced to appeal to the First Amendment, as well as America's protection of free-market economic activity, in defence of its right to transmit violent fare, especially in daytime and primetime slots when children are likely to be watching.

But opponents of the present situation include growing numbers of law enforcement officials, medical experts and parents who believe media violence should be considered a public health issue rather than one of free expression. There is precedent for this approach to a First Amendment debate. While the US legal system provides great latitude for artistic and political expression, it can and does restrict distribution of those things it considers socially harmful. Laws against child pornography, for instance, are so severe that a current test case involves photographs of fully-clothed juveniles, in 'suggestive poses'. The First Amendment exists within a changing regulatory environment and has, in the past, responded to new evidence on public health issues. Tobacco advertising, once an enormous source of revenue, was banned from the networks as the evidence linking smoking and disease mounted. The tobacco companies cited the First Amendment and the networks fought a protracted battle for their commercial rights to no avail. The impact of tobacco commercials on children was a major plank in the arguments in favour of banning.

Violence is visually commanding, a universal language that travels well

There are voices in the movie and broadcasting industries who claim that the answer lies in pre-empting government intervention by self-regulation. But while the commercial networks have been zealous in controlling their use of explicit sexual material, the same self-regulatory mechanisms are clearly not working in the realm of violence, and current trends are set to lead to more violence, not less.

For decades, US airwaves were dominated by the big three networks, ABC, NBC and CBS, plus their worthy but underfunded cousin, PBS. The networks' audience share has plummeted over the past few years as a result of the massive inroads of cable, satellite and videotape. As commercial network audiences have dropped, so have their standards. In the attempt to recapture a bored, channel-hopping audience that they themselves have disaffected, the networks become ever more shrill, crude and action-oriented.

Nowhere is this tendency more apparent than in news programmes. Once the jewel of the networks, the nightly newscasts have had their staffs decimated, their overseas operations slashed. The flagship news programmes merely serve as lead-ins for the 'new' news format, otherwise known as 'tabloid TV'. These programmes, with names like *A Current Affair* and *Hard Copy*, borrow some of the conventions of traditional news programmes, such as the news desk, the stand-up reporter, and the investigation. Their content, however, bubbles up from the gutter: sex scandals, murder scandals and, best of all, the two in one. Lorena Bobbitt and her husband's ill-fated penis constituted a perfect tabloid TV story, as was the case of the 'Long Island Lolita', Amy Fisher, who shot the wife of her ungainly lover, Joey Buttafuoco.

It would be one thing to sing another hymn to pluralism and allow tabloid TV to occupy its niche alongside other and saner broadcasts. But if other, saner broadcasts do not get the ratings they disappear. The hour-long news documentary format, once the pride and the conscience of the networks, now clings to its single 'Frontline' slot on PBS. In the meantime, other news programmes are falling over each other to descend to the tabloids' level. Hard news, international news, investigative journalism and analytical coverage of economic and social issues are endangered species, supplanted by sensational sex and murder stories, 'disease of the week' scare stories and visually-striking but meaningless footage of disasters. The current catchphrase of the US newsroom is: 'If it bleeds, it leads.'

But a backlash has begun. In February this year, an NBC broadcast polled its audience: should violence in the news be censored? The phrasing was provocative: Americans in theory abhor the word 'censorship'. Nevertheless, of the respondents 2,468 said no but 20,300 agreed.

In Washington, a group of Congressmen and industry representatives have been exchanging harsh words on the matter; so far, suggestions for regulation have been seriously limited by cultural attitudes.

Americans are taught from the cradle to have infinite faith in technology, and no faith at all in public policy. The most popular panacea for television violence at the moment, therefore, is something called the 'V-chip', a computer chip that would be inserted in every new television set, to accompany a 'violence rating' encoded on every television programme. The V-chip would read the code in the 'vertical blanking interval' separating each video frame, so that a parent could programme it to block all programmes above a given rating.

The cable television industry has led the way in promoting this idea; it has already drafted a plan to create a new rating system with independent monitors and grading systems. Given that cable operators, unlike the broadcast networks, receive their revenues from subscriptions rather than advertising, they have the least to lose from a rating system the networks fear would scare off advertisers.

Other options include a desk-top information system on daily programming for parents, another a move to reschedule violent programming late at night, after children's viewing hours.

None of this is bad; at worst, the V-chip and its technological kin will become the newest electronic toys to be purchased to gather dust on a shelf. At best, they will be part of a rapidly-evolving electronic package that will promote greater flexibility in the use of the medium.

There is a growing body of evidence establishing the link between television violence and violence in everyday life

The problem with all these suggestions is that they lack a fundamental understanding of the modern American family, and the part television plays in them. They present one more tool to families who are already dealing with the problem. They do not address the family as it is increasingly reconfigured by divorce, two working parents, and the fracturing of extended families and communities. Across the social spectrum and regardless of race, class or income, there are fewer and fewer responsible adults present in the home to programme their V-chips, and those adults spend less time monitoring children's activities than ever before.

The answer will be more politically and logistically challenging than a V-chip. It is too much to expect the commercial broadcasters to consider what might be 'good' for the public in their programming decisions. That will be left to the international public service broadcasters — if they survive. But the commercial organisations should be held responsible for the harmful effects of their product. If, like the tobacco, alcohol and drug producers, they prove unable to regulate themselves, they must be regulated — especially where the interests of children are at stake.

The dangers of violence in the mass media may seem self-evident to Europeans, whose media environment has always been buffered by strong public service broadcasting and tight regulation of the commercial sector. They may be tempted to dismiss these problems as another manifestation of the 'American disease', so outrageous and entertaining to observe at a distance, so nerve-wracking and exhilarating to suffer first-hand.

But Europeans can no longer feel complacent. The new 'multi-channel interactive television environment' is well on its way to Europe and will alter forever the old landscape. Public service broadcasters, who have set standards of quality and suitability for the rest of the industry, will be forced to compete for audiences in new ways.

As the number of channels increases (up to 500 in the process now under way), the struggle has been economic: control of the 'information highway' itself. Programming is a secondary consideration.

It is hard to see where, in this panorama, there will be any market incentive to produce thoughtful drama or documentary work. It's easy, on the other hand, to find the incentive for violence in entertainment and news. Violence lends itself to cheap, point-and-shoot productions to fill the caverns of airtime created by the new channels. Violence is visually-commanding; as our viewer of the near future spins the 500-channel dial, violent images will register more quickly than talking heads. In the increasingly global broadcasting environment, violence travels well, a universal language with minimal lines to dub. The phenomenal box office success of the crudest Arnold Schwarzenegger films from Bangkok to Bratislava illustrate the point.

Given the withering of the state and its regulatory function, the combination of satellite and cable will present pre-teens all over the world with slasher movies in their own homes, to their heart's content.

Televised violence is only the most recent and virulent strain of programming that the lowest-common-denominator laboratory of broadcasting has come up with. There are ways to use intelligent, informed broadcasting regulation to satisfy genuine First Amendment concerns for freedom of expression. But in this transitional phase of the globalisation of broadcasting, it is the profit-driven voices of the free market who have the most to gain, that are most aggressive in staking their claim.

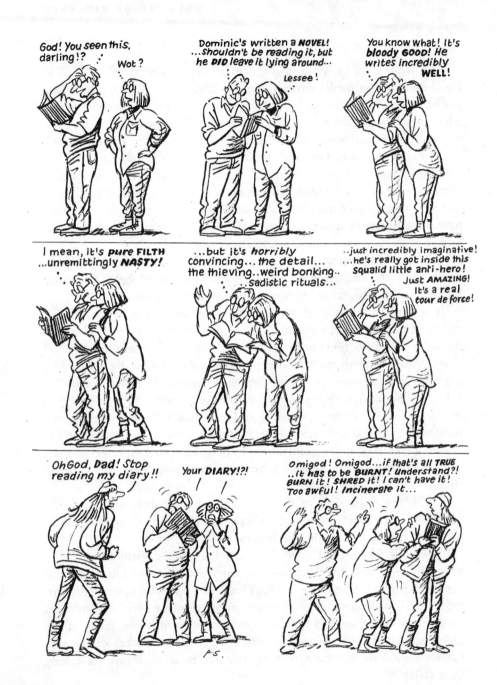

© Posy Simmonds

HUMAN RIGHTS

CAROLINE MOOREHEAD

1993: what rights?

The year 1993, in which the largest human rights gathering ever known took place, was a year of growing 'disappearances' and political assassinations, of recognition that torture is now endemic in over half the countries of the world and of the rapid spread of the most frightening violation of all — 'ethnic cleansing', the clearing away of unwanted people by terror, rape and murder.

The annual reports of the human rights organisations, published for the most part in the early months of every year, provide a rare moment of reckoning: a brief pause for thought in an otherwise unstoppable and overwhelming flood of human disaster. Those for 1993 make sorry reading. Not only has violence reached catastrophic levels in many parts of the world, but the contempt of governments for the rights of their citizens seems never to have been higher.

It was, however, also a year in which these rights were explored and debated as never before. At the Vienna world conference in June, representatives from 183 governments, as well as several thousand non-governmental organisations, met to reiterate their commitment to a more humane and tolerant world. It was the year in which Amnesty International launched a worldwide campaign against extrajudicial killings and 'disappearances', while over 50,000 of its members, in 75 countries, used their telephones and fax machines to intervene on behalf of hundreds of people threatened by torture or execution, in Urgent Action Appeals.

In recognition of the difficulties faced by minorities, 1993 was also declared by the United Nations to be the International Year for the World's Indigenous People. Even if the Vienna conference did little more than hold the line laid down in the 1948 Universal Declaration of Human Rights — that such rights are indivisible and universal and should not be tempered by national or cultural considerations — it was no small feat, given the ground swell of protest that Western human rights were not applicable where poverty reigned or religious dogma decreed otherwise.

Throughout the year, there were other marked gains, not least in the emergence of new human rights groups, particularly in Africa, born either of moves by governments toward multiparty democracy, or prodded into life by a global urge to have some say in political life. For these groups Vienna provided an extremely valuable opportunity to make contact with each other. Families of people who have 'disappeared' in the last decade, who had spent the years agitating with their own governments for justice and accountability, found common cause with other mothers and grandmothers, and have since sought ways to make their campaigns more international.

The appearance of these once isolated groups at an international forum has pushed some of the long-established Western human rights groups into rethinking their own roles, recognising their usefulness as helpers and tutors to the newcomers. Women's groups, which also emerged forcefully in Vienna, have made much of these international links, as have the many organisations dealing with censorship and the freedom to write and publish.

These last have particular reason to feel anxious. As the 1993 annual reports of the American Committee to Protect Journalists, the French *Reporters sans frontières* and the Brussels-based International Federation of Journalists make clear, journalists, editors and publishers are under great threat. While figures of those killed last year vary from organisation to organisation — CPJ counts 56 dead, and 16 others under investigation, the IFJ 75 dead and 18 under investigation — all agree that members of the press are increasingly coming to be seen as legitimate targets in their own right. Numbers of the dead and injured in 1993 were particularly high in Algeria — nine killed in the civil war between Muslim fundamentalists and the pro-Western government which has illegally kept them from power — and in Bosnia, where nine journalists died, most of them specifically targeted by snipers. Nowhere, however, has the new phrase 'censorship by the bullet' acquired more meaning than in Tajikistan, where civil war claimed at least 20,000 lives in six months in 1992, and in Turkey, where the continuing conflict between Kurds and the Turkish authorities has seen 12 journalists assassinated in 1993. *Ozgür Gündem* (see p164), a newspaper sympathetic to the Kurdish cause, started publication in May 1992. Since then, 16 of its journalists and distributors have been killed; 200 issues have been confiscated; 210 of its workers arrested and detained, and several of them tortured while in police custody.

In Bangladesh, the writer and journalist Taslima Nasreen has been threatened by religious extremists calling for her execution, after publishing material considered unbecoming to Muslim womanhood. As Ali Salem, the Egyptian writer, put it in an interview not long ago, summing up the way increasing numbers of writers throughout the world now live: 'We are not facing censorship, we are facing bullets. We are afraid not about our art but about our lives'.

Alongside the journalists under attack are the human rights monitors, gathering and publishing information on violations of human rights in their own countries. Nine of these, according to the annual reports, lost their lives in 1993, three of them in India and another three in Latin America. In Haiti, Cuba, Kuwait, Iran and Saudi Arabia many others have been silenced by imprisonment. Reporting abuses, in the early 1990s, has become an extremely dangerous business.

Violations on a far greater scale, however, are the real mark of 1993, as an 'epidemic of community violence' seems to have gripped the world. What used to be known as genocide, and now passes under the more fashionable term of 'ethnic cleansing' has taken hold in India, where 700 people, most of them Muslims, were killed in Bombay in January when police and mobs went on a rampage; in Zaire, where President Mobutu Sese Seko has unleashed a murderous ethnic conflict in Shaba — 90,000 people uprooted by mob violence — and in North Kivu — at least 7,000 people massacred; in Rwanda, Bangladesh, Sudan and, of course, Bosnia. As the Human Rights Watch report comments, violence of this kind tends 'to take on a life of its own.'

Like earthquakes, repercussions of human rights violations spread outwards in circles of shock waves, triggering more, as well as new, forms of violations. Ethnic cleansing leads by definition to expulsions, expulsions to the creation of vast populations of refugees. It is hard, today, to believe that there was a time in the late 1940s when people genuinely thought that once the refugees created by the second world war were finally settled, there would be an end to any significant refugee problem. Refugees, in 1993, grew so rapidly in number that it has become impossible to count them. Fifteen million? Twenty-five million? No one can say. A substantial part of Amnesty's annual report is devoted to an assessment of the world's response to this crisis, and to urging both international agencies and governments to take on board the causes that turn people into refugees as well as how to care for them once they have been displaced.

In the last 10 years, the annual reports of the human rights organisations have tended to concentrate on the shortcomings of governments. There has been a shift of focus in 1993. Though Human Rights Watch does devote some space to the Clinton administration's emerging human rights policy — and accuses it of being strong on theory and weak and cautious when the going gets rough — it is the international community, rather than individual states, that is under scrutiny. Governments throughout the world are proving increasingly unwilling or unable to uphold the treaties and conventions to which they are party. The tragedies of Somalia, Bosnia and Haiti have posed challenges that the peace-keeping forces of the United Nations and the deliberations of political groupings like the European Union have been unable to meet.

To counter what looks increasingly like a chaotic and ill-thought-out response to an ever more violent world, the human rights organisations are pointing to the urgent need for a 'more principled application' of tactics. Economic sanctions, and the linking of aid to improvement in human rights performance, they argue, is one weapon in the depressingly feeble armoury of human rights that has been shown to possess some bite. Selective trade sanctions, ones that target the abusers but not the abused — such as blocking export of goods made with forced labour, or restricting trade benefits to state enterprises of governments consistently guilty of abuses — and a more finely-tuned policy of sanctions, could still prove a worthwhile strategy.

The annual summaries reiterate calls, made but rejected in Vienna, for the appointment of a UN High Commissioner for Human Rights, a sufficiently senior official able to ensure that human rights issues are not ignored when the UN launches rescue operations.

In the past, annual reports dwelt most heavily on the abuses of the previous year. A stronger tone has taken over, particularly in the Amnesty International and Human Rights Watch reports, which now contain clear messages to governments and the international community. The moral and intellectual justifications of both human rights and humanitarian work are addressed in the light of 1993's prolonged debates about cultural relativism and the complicity of Western governments in continuing to fund and arm countries engaging in repression. It is no longer enough, they maintain, to impose peace on warring nations, for peace without justice remains a perpetual source of discontent. In Somalia, the UN's preoccupation with justice on behalf of its own dead, and its apparent indifference towards justice for Somali citizens, 'reduced the UN peace keepers to the level of another fighting faction'. Until the international community realises that troops and blockades cannot take the place of legal responsibility then the UN operations can only continue to founder.

The world in 1994 looks set to be no more peaceable than it was in 1993. There is an understandable note of desperation in Human Rights Watch's call for 'collective vision' to halt the slide towards ever greater mayhem.

Committee to Protect Journalists: *Journalists killed or presumed dead in 1993*
Human Rights Watch: *World Report 1994*
Amnesty International: *Report 1993*
Reporters sans frontières: *1993 Report*
International Federation of Journalists: *Danger! Journalists at work in 1993*

The following section on human rights will be a regular feature of **Index***, representing other organisations working in human rights and free expression. Contact addresses are given for those readers wishing to involve themselves further.* **Index** *welcomes information for this section from human rights organisations around the world.*

AMNESTY INTERNATIONAL

We know where the prisoners are

In the opinion piece 'Where have all the prisoners gone?' (*Index* 7/1993) Caroline Moorehead claims that thousands of people who have been gunned down by government agents could still be alive today were it not for the efficiency of the human rights movement in campaigning against political imprisonment.

Moorehead argues that the pressure put on governments by human rights organisations to release prisoners has forced states to turn to more brutal forms of repression to silence their opponents.

As is often the case, the rhetorical question posed and the answer suggested is based on an inadequate grasp of the facts. Even its initial premise is unfounded. Unfortunately, prisoners of conscience are still held in large numbers around the world, even as tens of thousands of others face death or 'disappearance'.

The question we at Amnesty International ask ourselves is not whether our success in campaigning for the release of prisoners of conscience has led to the death or 'disappearance' of people who would otherwise be alive, albeit imprisoned. The question we ask is how can we use our million strong membership and our 32 years of experience to counter governments that continue to keep thousands of people behind bars as prisoners of conscience — as well as those that murder or kidnap their citizens in the tens of thousands in a world of dramatic political changes.

Although patterns of repression do and have changed over time, the prisoner of conscience continues to be a global phenomenon — from Cuba and Peru, where we believe hundreds are held, to the thousands held in China and Indonesia, to numerous states in Africa, the Middle East and Western and Eastern Europe. Our latest annual report lists 32 countries that together hold more than 4,400 prisoners of conscience — dramatically more than the 20 Moorehead identified.

Nor can real changes be tied to the cause–and–effect relationship suggested. It is difficult to come up with a single case in which particular governments have responded to human rights campaigning for prisoners by a wholesale shift to murder. There are indeed governments in most regions of the world that have turned to mass killing or 'disappearance' over the past 30 years, but it is impossible to match such shifts to previous work for prisoners of conscience.

The real shifts that have occurred do not mean these are new phenomena. They are not. What was concealed in the past is today more apparent. Consider the wars of the decolonization period after the second world war. When tens of thousands died or 'disappeared' at the hands of the French colonial power during the Algerian war of independence, Amnesty International did not exist and independent human rights reporting was in its infancy. And even after its foundation in 1961, Amnesty International only brought political killings by governments and 'disappearances' into its mandate for action in the 1970s. Only in the 1990s has the United Nations begun to use Amnesty International's term 'extrajudicial execution' in its work to oppose what is really an age-old horror.

The most dramatic new factor in recent decades has been that the international human rights movement has enormously increased its capacity. Amnesty International and its allies have increasingly turned to exposing governments that attempt to get away with murder.

Governments' changes in tactics rarely respond to just one factor. The dramatic shift to 'disappearance' and political killings in Guatemala in the late 1960s, when political imprisonment really was largely replaced with murder, came at a time when little attention was paid to the country by the international community. Amnesty International had never had a prisoner of conscience there and had no mandate with which to confront the new tactics of terror.

Argentina, too, was virtually unknown to the international human rights community when the wave of terror burst there in 1976. The list of human rights catastrophes in Asia, in Africa, in the Middle East and, most recently, in Europe would, if space allowed, be equally eloquent rebuttal of the notion that mass murder and 'disappearance' was in some way catalysed by too effective campaigning for prisoners of conscience.

In other countries, the change in the pattern of political killings has followed in the wake of recent dramatic political changes, including shifts from military dictatorships to formal democracies and rises in levels of armed opposition violence.

Even now, the international human rights movement's development of an effective capacity to go beyond its traditional work for prisoners of conscience is still far from complete. Perhaps the organisation has been too successful in getting the message across that there is more on the human rights map that needs attention. That is one reason Amnesty International launched a campaign this year to put political killings and 'disappearance' on the international agenda once again. But the world should not forget the prisoners of conscience who are still held in their thousands across the world.

We know that Amnesty International's campaigning for prisoners of conscience has helped get them released. Since AI was founded in 1961, our members worldwide have successfully campaigned for the release of some 40,000 prisoners of conscience. And we know that we can make as much noise and have as much of an impact on armies and death squads as we have on jailers and torturers.

Anita Tiessen of *Amnesty International, 1 Easton Street, London WC1X 8DJ*

MIDDLE EAST WATCH

No one is spared

Two years after the military-backed coup that thwarted the electoral victory of the Islamic Salvation Front (FIS), human rights remain a principal casualty of the worsening confrontation in Algeria. For the present disastrous state of the country, the government and the armed Islamist opposition must share the blame, says Middle East Watch in *Human Rights Abuses in Algeria: No One is Spared*.

Released in January, the report condemns the ruling High Council of State for staging unfair trials of Islamist suspects that have resulted in nearly 400 death sentences. The New York-based organisation, a division of Human Rights Watch, is no less critical of the Islamist resistance for its targeting of civilians, including foreigners, for assassination.

The 67-page report concludes that the government, headed since January by General Lamine Zeroual, has done little to distinguish itself from the FIS-led repression and human-rights violations the coup-makers claimed to have acted to prevent. Nor has the regime taken practical steps to reopen the interrupted democratic process. The five-member High Council of State which had promised to dissolve itself by 31 December 1993 and establish a 'transitional' government, has so far failed to keep its word.

Since the cancellation of Algeria's landmark elections in January 1992,

the struggle for power has become increasingly violent; disregard for basic norms of human rights and international humanitarian law, applicable even during armed conflict, has become blatant. The state of emergency, imposed on 9 February 1992 and renewed indefinitely since then, has been used to outlaw FIS and confer arbitrary powers on the government and security forces.

Middle East Watch claims that since 1992 over 9,000 suspected FIS supporters have been dispatched to detention camps, mostly in the southern desert, for indefinite periods. Islamist suspects are allegedly subjected to mistreatment and torture while in pre-trial detention. Expedited trials in newly-created Special Courts subsequently violate their rights to due process. During the first 11 months of 1993, Algeria had the highest number of judicial executions for politically-motivated offences of any country in the Arab world after Iraq. At least 368 persons were sentenced to death (most *in absentia*), and 26 executions were carried out.

The report denounces Algeria's Special Courts for their violation of defendants' rights, highlighting in particular confessions obtained through the use of torture; incommunicado (*garde à vue*) detention of suspects beyond the legal 12-day limit before being brought before a judge; and their systematic failure to examine thoroughly and impartially allegations of abuse during interrogation.

Despite the absence of claims of responsibility for virtually all acts of violence in Algeria — other than those committed openly by the security forces — the report accuses Islamist groups of being responsible for many of the hundreds of civilian deaths that have occurred over the past year. Added to the killings of Algerians are the cold-blooded murders of foreigners, including 12 Croat and Bosnian workers at a construction site near Blida on 14 December 1993, by groups, such as the Armed Islamic Group, intent on targeting foreign nationals. Middle East Watch deplores the attempts made by exiled FIS spokesmen to justify some of these killings and calls on FIS leaders to exert their influence on their supporters within Algeria to end the cycle of violence.

No One is Spared also examines the media in Algeria which has come under pressure from the government as well as the Islamist groups. Government-imposed press restrictions far exceed what can be justified on the grounds of public safety and national security. The authorities have suspended daily newspapers; compelled state-owned television and radio stations to become government mouthpieces once more; arrested over 30 journalists, many of whom have been put on trial; threatened to withdraw public sector advertising from outspoken publications; and refused visas or work permits to many foreign correspondents.

The report highlights the cases of seven journalists assassinated since May 1993 but lists many others who have been attacked, threatened and forced into silence, self-censorship or self-imposed exile. Despite claims by government spokespersons that press freedom is constitutionally protected in Algeria, several publications — both secular and pro-Islamist, Arabic- and French-language — have been suspended, some indefinitely.

As the crisis in Algeria has worsened, Western governments have remained virtually silent on human rights abuses committed by succesive governments in Algiers and the report calls on the international community, France in particular because of its long historical ties to Algeria and its considerable economic influence, to denounce abuses by the government as well as by the Islamist resistance.
Philippa Nugent

Human Rights Abuses in Algeria: No one is spared (Middle East Watch, January 1994, 67pp). Available from Human Rights Watch, 485 Fifth Avenue, New York, NY 10017-6104

ASIA WATCH

Detained in China and Tibet

At a time when China's human rights performance is under close scrutiny in Washington, Asia Watch's February 1994 report is a timely reminder that, despite cosmetic attempts to improve its international image, political repression in the People's Republic is increasing, not decreasing. Unless international pressure is maintained and intensified, it suggests, China will receive 'a terrible signal: open season on political dissent'.

Detained in China and Tibet documents the cases of some 1,230 people detained for the peaceful expression of their political and religious beliefs. It also raises concern over torture and the need to ensure fair trials. Without doubt, 1993 was the worst year for political arrests in China since mid-1990; the report documents 250 cases. These include 216 new arrests, as well as 32 trials of dissidents that resulted in average sentences of four years' imprisonment. Almost 80% of these arrests were in Tibet where repression of peaceful pro-independence activities by monks and nuns has intensified.

Asia Watch accuses China of using prisoners as bargaining chips, hostages to be released at key moments for maximum political effect. But it is also critical of Western governments that accept these releases as evidence of progress, ignoring the tens of thousands who remain in prison and the hundreds of new arrests taking place every year.

According to Asia Watch, the true number of people detained for 'counterrevolutionary' activities is far higher than the official figure of 3,317. It claims the new publication represents the first systematic attempt by any independent organisation to compile a list of these sentenced 'counterrevolutionaries'.

The 664–page report contains two important lists of individually named prisoners. The first is a compilation of all prisoners currently known or believed to be under arrest or serving sentences in China for 'counterrevolution'. The second records the cases of nearly 100 non-violent political, ethnic or religious prisoners currently serving from 10 years to life imprisonment, most of them sentenced in the last five years, whom Asia Watch considers to be in the most urgent need of international and domestic pressure to secure their release.

In addition, the report provides information on some 460 persons detained or convicted in China for allegedly violent or other criminal acts committed during various pro-democracy, ethnic, separatist or religious movements. In view of the low standard of criminal justice prevailing in China and the general absence of safeguards for defendants' rights, Asia Watch calls on the Chinese government to make public the evidence upon which these convictions were based and, where appropriate, to reopen the cases and conduct a judicial review.

While the lists are inevitably incomplete, it is Asia Watch's intention that their publication should spur the Chinese government into a complete accounting for all its political, religious and ethnic prisoners.
Annie Knibb

Detained in China and Tibet: A directory of political and religious prisoners (Asia Watch, February 1994, 632pp). Available from Human Rights Watch, 90 Borough High Street, London SE1 1LL (£13.50 plus 15% p&p in the UK and 25% p&p elsewhere)

HELSINKI WATCH/
MEMORIAL

In the wake of civil war

In May-June 1993, members of the Moscow-based Memorial Human Rights Centre together with representatives of Helsinki Watch, travelled to Tajikistan to investigate human rights abuses in the republic since the end of the civil war. The result of their mission, *Human Rights in Tajikistan in the Wake of the Civil War*, documents how the Communist government of Emomali Rakhmanov has broken its own international human rights commitment and tolerated gross violations of human rights in the republic since it took power in late 1992. The report is a forceful documentation of human rights abuses that also provides a valuable perspective on political forces taking shape in the wider area.

In a space of only six months, from May to November 1992, Tajikistan's civil war claimed as many as 20,000 lives and displaced between 400,000 and 500,000 more. *Human Rights in Tajikistan* demonstrates that the power struggle between the old guard Communist elite and a coalition of Islamist and democratic parties, usually presented either as a battle between Communists and Islamic fundamentalists or as a gathering ethnic conflict, has more complex origins. The demographic and historical background to the conflict, as well as the nature of recent human rights abuses, indicates a tangled network of political and regional alliances compounded by the intervention of outside interests.

Human Rights in Tajikistan documents incidents of murder, robbery and violence carried out by pro-government paramilitary groups in Dushanbe since government forces returned to the capital in mid-December 1993. It exposes summary executions of opposition activists and random killings and disappearances of civilians from the Pamir and Garm regions — the eastern and north eastern opposition strongholds within the republic. Government officials do not deny the occurrence of these violations but attribute the disturbances to a general breakdown in law and order. They refuse to accept any responsibility for events and have taken no action to punish the perpetrators of the crimes. The report suggests that the government may well have collaborated in many abuses and is also likely to be aware of the existence of 'informal prisons'.

Despite its stated intention of developing political pluralism in Tajikistan, the present government has taken direct steps to eliminate the political opposition. It has banned the main parties and subjected opposition party members to constant harasssment. The opposition and independent press have been effectively silenced — although there has been no official decision to close the press — by pro-government armed groups seeking revenge for news reports published under the earlier coalition government.

Refugees and displaced persons, mainly of Garmi origin, who fled to northern Afghanistan and the eastern Gorno-Badakhshan region of Tajikistan to escape the violence of the civil war, face serious problems on attempting to return. Repatriated refugees have faced harassment and violence, have found their houses occupied or destroyed, and have been afforded little if any protection from hostile communities — mainly Uzbeks and Tajiks who supported the pro-government Popular Front and identify Garmis with the ousted political opposition.

The human rights abuses that have occurred internally in Tajikistan under the present government are put into the broader political perspective of Russian, Uzbek and Afghan interests in the area. The Uzbek government's use of the 'Islamic fundamentalist threat' in Tajikistan to justify the repression of opposition forces in its own country; the overwhelming presence of Russian troops along the Afghan-Tajik border; and Afghan involvement in arming and training sections of the Tajik opposition all fuel a complex political game that receives little attention in the international media.

Natasha Pairaudeau

Human Rights in Tajikistan in the Wake of Civil War (Human Rights Watch/Helsinki Watch and Memorial, December 1993, 64pp). Available from Human Rights Watch, 485 Fifth Avenue, New York, NY 10017-6104

INTERNATIONAL PEN

Writers in prison

'You come here to die. Forget the outside. Don't think you will get out or be judged or that anyone will care about you.'

Such were the words of a jailer to a prisoner in the Western Sahara. Yet the man had got out and was in the London office of International PEN's Writers in Prison Committee. The Committee monitors and works on behalf of over 700 writers and journalists in 95 countries who are attacked or imprisoned primarily for their use of words. For nine years the man in the Western Sahara lived in a two square metre cell with seven other men. The only light came in through two tiny holes. Prisoners were fed lentils and beans during the day and gruel at night. They were routinely tortured. Many went mad; many died. They were not allowed to write, and yet they did write. They used their half bar of soap to write plays on their trousers and memorised the plays before they washed the trousers. They found scraps of paper and wrote poetry, using thick coffee for ink. They hid their writing in their belts.

The ability of these men to imagine and to create kept them sane, the visitor said. The ability of those outside to imagine these men and to work on their behalf had at least some part in their release.

The Writers in Prison Committee of International PEN is the oldest human rights organisation working on behalf of writers, predating Amnesty. It is also the only international writers' organisation that does long-term case work for writers. International PEN has members in 120 centres all over the world — from Norway to Nepal, Chile to Congo, Turkey to Taiwan. Members write to prisoners and their families, protest to governments and work for the writers' release.

Because PEN's Writers in Prison Committee is unique in its long-term case work, one of its main focuses in the coming year will be on long-term imprisonment. Through recent submissions to the United Nations Commission on Human Rights, through repeated appeals at governmental levels, and through adoption of the writers themselves, PEN will continue pushing at the prison door. The Committee has targeted China, Vietnam, Burma (Myanmar), Syria and Cuba, among other countries.

Almost one-third of PEN's main cases are in China. At least 25 Chinese and Tibetan prisoners are serving sentences of up to 20 years. Most are held on charges of 'counter-revolutionary propaganda.' The recent releases of Wei Jingsheng and Liao Yiwu are a relief, but for each writer released another is imprisoned.

In Vietnam and Burma, long prison terms have recently been handed down against writers. Eight people involved in *Freedom Forum*, an underground magazine in Vietnam, were sentenced last April to terms ranging from eight months to 20 years. Two Burmese writers last autumn were given 20-year terms: Dr Aung Khin Sint for distributing a letter opposing an increased military role in the new Constitution, Ma Thida for 'endangering public peace, having contact with illegal organisations and distributing unlawful literature.' These convictions bring to at least 10 the number of publishers and journalists currently in prison.

In Syria at least six writers and journalists are detained solely for their peaceful political activities. Jadi Nawfal and Nizar Nayyuf are serving five- and 10-year sentences for distributing leaflets alleging government abuse of human rights. Others have been held for long periods without charge or trial — in the case of Tadrus Trad for over 13 years. One of the most blatant abuses against writers is the continued detention of Khalil Burayez, who was arrested in 1970 and sentenced to 15 years on charges related to books he wrote on the Syrian military. He remains in detention six years after his sentence expired.

Crackdowns against dissidents in Cuba in 1991 and 1992 led to sentences against numerous writers and journalists who called for improved human and democratic rights. Luis Grave de Peralta, Indamiro Restano and Pablo Reyes Martinez, serving 13-, 10- and eight-year prison terms, respectively, on charges that include the making of 'enemy propaganda', remain in detention.

Governments and non-governmental groups worldwide also try to silence the voices of their critics by harassment, short-term detention, torture, disappearances and killings. PEN's Writers in Prison Committee will continue to protest about these as well. The alarming number of writers and journalists killed recently (there were over 50 recorded killings in 1993 in countries including Turkey, Algeria, Colombia, India and Tajikistan) is also of great concern.

When a writer finally is released, even after long term imprisonment, the individual often continues to speak out. Wei Jingsheng, after over 14 years in prison in China, recently wrote in the *New York Times*: 'there is a tendency on the part of China to view the detention and release of dissidents as a hostage transaction, in which freedom for the prisoner is just a bargaining chip in an economic poker game.'

Joanne Leedom–Ackerman, Sara Whyatt and Mandy Garner of the International PEN Writers in Prison Committee, 9/10 Charterhouse Buildings, Goswell Road, London EC1M 7AT

ARTICLE 19

Campaigning and partnership

Governments that seek to restrict the right to freedom of expression — often in order to draw a cloak of secrecy over other human rights violations — are becoming ever more sophisticated in finding methods of censorship which are hard to expose and therefore to attack. In countries such as Kenya and Malawi, moves towards a multiparty state are accompanied by violent intimidation of opposition supporters; in Turkey countless legal actions against the outspoken newspaper *Ozgür Gündem* have been complemented by extra-judicial executions of its journalists and distributors, 18 of whom have been murdered in the past 18 months by unidentified assailants believed to be agents of the state security forces.

Elsewhere governments exert their influence by more subtle means such as financial control of the media through monopolies in the allocation of newsprint or the threat of withdrawal of state company advertising. Informal censorship may take the form of the strategic telephone call from senior officials to newspaper editors. Direct threats are not always necessary once a culture of fear has been created.

For human rights organisations these new threats demand professionalism. Traditional methods of protest can result in single victories — a prisoner released, for example — which are important and heart-warming but insufficient when the laws and practices remain to ensnare new victims.

As an organisation which monitors violations of the right to freedom of expression around the world, Article 19 identifies not only incidents of censorship around the world but trends in the types of censorship used by governments. Taking its name and mandate from the 19th Article of the

Universal Declaration of Human Rights, Article 19 has, over seven years, evolved a strategy which consists of challenging the laws allowing censorship, campaigning against its practice, and working in partnership with national organisations.

Protesting against bad laws, or bad interpretations of moderate laws, is an important target for campaigning because these laws allow governments to censor while proclaiming adherence to the rule of law. Article 19 identifies and exposes potentially censorial laws and calls for them to be brought into line with international standards protecting freedom of expression and information. The striking of bad laws from the statute books may signal some acceptance of democratic principles or may be a cynical move, but either way it gives greater strength to those who are fighting censorship by challenging bad practice in their own courts.

However, countries with impeccable legislation but a disgraceful human rights record are all too well known to those working in the human rights field. Good laws do not necessarily mean good practice. Informal censorship is particularly increasing in countries under pressure to show they are maintaining their international obligations as signatories to the International Covenant on Civil and Political Rights.

This puts the onus on human rights organisations to provide systematic evidence of informal and extralegal censorship, to enforce acknowledgement, action and timely information, and to insist the right to freedom of expression be protected.

The third element of Article 19's campaign philosophy is close collaboration with local partners, because only the development of a deep-rooted domestic human rights culture will protect freedom of expression in the long term. International protests are of huge value and can be literally life-savers, but the structures which encourage repression will not shift unless there is also vigilance and monitoring at the local level.

This is particularly true in countries where democracy is newly-arrived or restored. In order to support the work of local groups, Article 19 has recently published two reference books: *Press Law and Practice* surveys press freedom in 11 democratic countries; and *The Freedom of Expression Handbook* gathers over 150 court rulings protective of freedom of expression together with information on how to use national and international legal mechanisms to challenge censorship. Article 19 also facilitates links between local groups and international organisations.

Ultimately, Article 19's role is to become the generator of freedom-of-expression watchdog bodies around the world and to be a medium through which national concerns are transferred to the international level, ensuring that through coordinated campaigning action the right to freedom of expression is protected for all a country's citizens.

Frances D'Souza, Executive Director of Article 19, 90 Borough High Street, London, SE1 1LL

Insider reading.

KARIM ALRAWI

Death on the Nile

A special report prepared for *Index on Censorship* by Karim Alrawi, deputy secretary general of the Egyptian Organisation for Human Rights

KARIM ALRAWI

Goodbye to the Enlightenment

It is hard to describe what it is like to be living in a society whose culture is dying. It is not just a question of the persecution of writers and academics, nor of the tightening of restrictions on publications and the increased censorship of theatres and films. It is more than the lack of schooling that Naguib Mahfouz writes of, or the climate of censorship that Gamal el-Ghitani discusses.

It is a little like watching a large and lumbering animal slowly being sucked into the mire; it is the knowledge that what was won by past generations so painstakingly is being lost, possibly forever.

In the early part of the last century, a young man from Al-Azhar, Egypt's Islamic university, went on a journey to France. It was to have a profound effect on him and on the course of Egyptian cultural life. The young man's name was Rifaa el-Tahtawi and he had hitched his ride as a Muslim cleric whose job it was to ensure that the young scholars he was accompanying kept faith with Islam in this land of the infidel.

Instead of limiting himself to religious matters Rifaa el-Tahtawi set out to learn as much as he could about the Parisians that he encountered. He was later to write one of the most delightful accounts of a European country ever written from an Arab perspective. *Tabriez al-Abareez* must have struck many of his readers back home as strangely fanciful, as fanciful as Marco Polo's account of the lands of the Great Khan.

On his return to Egypt, Rifaa el-Tahtawi set to with great energy to translate the best of what he believed European culture had to offer. He continued despite attempts at vilification and punishment by those who feared these new ideas would threaten the social order.

The library he left after his death was to become a second home to one of the greatest figures of the Egyptian Enlightenment. Muhamad Abdu was not only a great Islamic scholar, honoured with the rare title of 'the (greatest) Imam of his age', but was also a social reformer who fought vigorously for a parliamentary system and a liberal democratic constitution.

Within 20 years of his death, the Islamic Enlightenment split into a secular progressive wing led by Saad Zaghloul and an increasingly right-wing and authoritarian fundamentalist movement led by Rasheed Rida. Both men were students of Mohamad Abdu.

During the 1930s and 1940s, the Enlightenment reached a peak that was to lay the foundations for the Nasserist period of social reforms in the 1950s and 1960s. But with the onset of the 1970s, the militant Islamic trend began to recover ground. Now, in the 1990s, it has all but swept the field.

The question 'Are you or have you ever been an atheist?' is implicit in every attack on a writer or academic. It is the charge levelled at specific artists by street corner preachers and repeated in the dozens of cassette tapes that are sold outside mosques all over Egypt. These tapes have titles such as 'The Filth of the Artistic Community', or 'Art is Filth'. Writers and artists are frequently picked on by name and damned as 'corrupters of youth', 'atheists and apostates'. Under Islamic Law both charges are theoretically punishable by death

Yet it is not only the streetside extremists who preach retribution against the artist. The official and semi-official press is no less threatening. Many people have fallen victim, without any possibility of reply, to orchestrated campaigns of vilification.

Attacks on the film maker Yousef Chahine also included references to his francophone education. This xenophobia is part of the political agenda of the Muslim Brotherhood, the inheritors of Rasheed Rida's fundamentalism. Yet many of these new middle class Islamic militants are themselves foreign-educated and run businesses or lecture at universities. Many once had socialist credentials when it paid, sometimes literally, to be a socialist. They are not interested in Islam's religious message of tolerance, but in cynically exploiting its broad appeal for political ends.

Anti-Westernism is the Brotherhood's strategy for wooing Arab

Nationalists to their ranks. It has been particularly successful since the Gulf War and the destruction of Iraq.

Not surprisingly, the Brotherhood take a dim view of Rifaa el-Tahtawi who, according to their publications, was 'a traitor and corrupter'. In one publication they call for Egypt to return to its pre-Napoleonic condition. According to the Russian Consul General in Cairo around the time, Egypt was a country with endemic disease and with less than 300 men who could read and write.

The cultural programme of the Muslim Brotherhood is a barely disguised attempt to turn the future into the past and the gains of 150 years of the Enlightenment into mass illiteracy.

In pursuit of their ideal the fundamentalist lobby have mounted virulent campaigns against individuals they think can be intimidated or whom they identify as easy targets. The latest victim is Dr Abu Zaid, who they are trying to hound out of his university post. Another ugly case was that of the novelist Ihsan Abdul Qudous who, even on his death bed, was being denounced by the Islamic press as an apostate. Leading the attack was the London-based Saudi-financed *al-Muslimoun* newspaper, which published a charge sheet they said would place Abdul Qudous in hell.

The question 'Are you or have you ever been an atheist?' is implicit in every attack on a writer or academic

The struggle being waged by the militant Islamists is a cultural one. Because Islam is the religion of the Book, the Quran is the very word of God uttered in the Arabic language. Arabic is therefore both the language of everyday discourse and the Sacred Language. When a language has this dual role using words is constantly to risk encroaching on the realm of the sacred. Yet, to be a writer is to be a creator of texts and to claim for them a truth that does not necessarily partake of the sole truth of the one sacred text. For that reason the target is writers, not merely their works.

Yet it is not just the militant Islamists who are having an open season on writers and artists. Members of parliament are also having a go. They know a good headline grabber when they see it and there is nothing that better ensures their presence on page one of the newspapers than a good attack on a writer or actor. So regular are these attacks that one could be forgiven for thinking there was not much difference between government and militant opposition.

The government's response to attacks on artists is to further increase censorship and banning orders on their works. As it is, the State Security service maintains control of the various boards of censorship through their nominee as Director of Censorship, Mr Hamdi Sorour. The 'higher interests of the state' are the latest excuse for the banning of plays and film scripts. Pop songs have to be submitted for a recording license.

Where government and Muslim Brotherhood come together is in their attempts to co-opt Al-Azhar, the most prestigious school of orthodox Islamic learning. It has long been penetrated by the Muslim Brotherhood who use it as a recruiting group for their activities world-wide.

The government needs Al-Azhar to bestow upon it a semblance of Islamic legitimacy. When the regime drew ideologically upon Arab Nationalism and Arab Socialism to justify its rule this was not a problem. A separate peace settlement with Israel put paid to Arab Nationalism and the privatisation of nationalised industries has finished off Arab Socialism.

There are two courses open to the regime to regain legitimacy. The first is genuine democratic reform. The government showed its unwillingness to follow this route when Mubarak ran as sole candidate in last October's Presidential elections.

The second alternative is an Islamic veneer of respectability. The struggle with the Muslim Brotherhood is not about ideology, but about personalities. Those in power do not want to make way for others, but unless they steal the Brotherhood's clothes they will be forced to parade naked before the Egyptian people.

In this struggle the writers and artists that the Brotherhood loathe as free-thinkers are expendable. And there are few undemocratic regimes that care much for free-thinkers anyway. The simple act of writing a short story or producing a stage play, with a plot and character development rather than a series of sketches held together with songs, has become an almost heroic act of defiance in Egypt.

Many writers are gradually surrendering to what they see as the inevitability of an Islamic regime in Egypt, hence the increased number of biographies of pious Muslims from bygone days, and the increased interest in reworking folk tales. The party organisation of the Muslim Brotherhood was modelled in the 1930s on that of the Italian Fascist party. They even went so far as to wear black shirts and parade in the streets of Cairo. Just as the rise of fascism in Europe spawned an exaggerated interest in the Volk and folk art, so now in Egypt there is a similar shift towards the folksy in art and literature. This is justified as a return to cultural roots, in the same way that Islamic fundamentalism is presented as a return to religious roots.

Egypt is turning away from the future to refabricate the past to make of it our present. Soon all we shall be left with is the sanction of a book revealed almost 1,500 years ago. Culturally it will be as though time has stopped still and has begun to run backwards.

Islam, in practice once a tolerant faith, is now the culture of the Book that bears no rivals. The veneration of the letter over the spirit has reached the point of idolatry. No other text can compare to the divinely written Quran. Its vocabulary, grammatical construction and stylistic qualities are those chosen by God. It is the ultimate text that brooks no rivals. By implication all other texts are in one way or another either commentaries on it, making its mysteries manifest, or else they are hubristic.

This view is no longer exclusive to a minority of religious militants. It is the view of even the most mainstream of preachers, such as the hugely popular Sheikh Shaarawi who appears on more television channels in the Arab world than *Star Trek*. It would also appear to be the view of the State Censorship Board.

With each new attack the province of the creative narrows. One day, the borders will be squeezed up against each other and the expurgation of the heresy of free thought will be complete. It will also be the day when time has finally rolled back: illiteracy and ignorance will again be the norm; it will be as though Rifaa el-Tahtawi and the generations of the Enlightenment had never been.

NAGUIB MAHFOUZ

Terminal sickness

Egypt's culture is declining fast. There appears to be almost unanimous agreement on this and that it is afflicting literature, the theatre, cinema, music and the arts in general. Such unanimity entitles me to wonder why we have reached such a low point. What are the reasons for such a decline?

Culture is not, and cannot be, independent of education. The state of education in our country is in crisis. It has been so for a long time now. We lack proper schools or adequately trained teachers. Classrooms are more like warehouses to cram children in for a few hours than places of education. The arts and literature are barely taught in these institutions which are run more like army barracks than places where cultural awareness and appreciation can be nurtured.

These schools lack the very rudiments necessary to generate curiosity in a child and draw out its natural gifts. There is a severe lack of libraries and reading rooms. They have no arts rooms nor space for creative activities. The environment is dull and oppressive, denying the child the possibility of developing any of its talents or learning to appreciate the creativity of others.

Having suppressed creativity and artistic appreciation in our children we now wonder why the cultural scene is so sterile, arid and devoid of any beauty or freshness. We watch our children become automatons and then wonder why our culture is so devoid of life.

The damaging influence of television is that it captures both the hearts and minds of so many people and leaves them with little time or energy to appreciate the finer works of culture. It draws writers to factory-like production of episodes in a conveyor belt of series after series. Instead of creative satisfaction they are gratified by fame and money.

Television has a role to play within the cultural environment but it should not be a means of destroying the wellspring of cultural life, replacing profundity with shallowness, and understanding and appreciation with superficiality and crassness.

Add to all this the deepening economic and social crisis we are living through and the extremist thinking it causes and stimulates, and you can begin to get a fuller picture of the dire condition of our local culture.

The picture is grim, no doubt. Nevertheless, the government assures us that it does have comprehensive development plans. We are assured that we have only to bear patiently with our present afflictions for a little while longer. We are told that there is new life on the way. Given the scale of our problems, can anyone doubt it?

Fires of Hell

Militant Islamist groups have sustained a relentless attack on Egypt's Nobel Prize winner Naguib Mahfouz. They have been successful in ensuring that the banning order on *Gablawi's Children*, first issued in 1959, is retained. Their own publications include virulent attacks on Mahfouz insisting that he will burn in Hell for the book. Their cartoons constantly depict him walking into the fires of Hell with copies of his novels.

In 1989, renewed attempts were made to un-ban *Gablawi's Children* and the monthly *Al-Yasar* started to serialise it. The Islamic press campaigned so virulently to have the serialisation stopped that Mahfouz himself asked the magazine to stop serialisation. By this stage Sheikh Omar Abdul Rahman, the spiritual leader of the militant *Gamaat Islamia*, had issued a *fatwa* excommunicating the author and calling on him to repent having written the novel and to denounce it.

EOHR

JUDGE SAID AL-ASHMAWI

What are the militants after?

Militant Islamists start from the premise that Islam is the sole valid and complete religion and abrogates all other religions. All non-Muslims, it follows, are infidels and should be converted to Islam.

An essential part of their creed is the belief that politics is an integral part of the faith, a claim they present without justification or clarification.

It is important to distinguish between Islam as history and Islam as religion. If by Islam the Islamists mean a religion, by claiming politics as a pillar of the faith they have added a sixth to the recognised five pillars of Islam — the recitation of the creed, prayer, fasting, pilgrimage to Mecca, and charity. Such a claim undermines orthodox Sunni Islamic doctrine.

But if what they mean by Islam is the history of the Muslim people then, of course, politics is part and parcel of that history. Their claim would be unremarkable and their arguments against the civil state, incorrectly referred to by them as secular, would collapse.

Militant Islamists pose the question of government in the following terms: 'Do you wish to be ruled by God or by Man?' Their question is an invitation to bestow the ruler with the divine right to oppress the ruled. It is an invitation to authoritarianism in the name of God.

The Islamists are not interested in Islam as a religion but rather as a form of nationalism. Islam as nationalism is a threat to the genuine national interests of any Muslim country: it erodes the loyalty of the citizen to his country and condemns those who oppose it as traitors and apostates. It is a certain recipe for sectarian strife and racism.

The two things that the Militants claim that they want is the application of *Sharia* and the acceptance by Muslims of *jihad* as a religious duty.

Sharia is usually translated as Islamic law. But in Arabic the word does not mean law; it means path or way and is used with precisely this sense in the Quran. *Sharia* is the way of Islam. The Islamists, however, use the term to signify the jurisprudence of medieval Muslim lawyers.

The Quran itself is not a book of legislation. Of its 6,236 verses only 80 contain unabrogated legal rulings, most of which deal with personal status and inheritance. There are only four penalties mentioned in the Quran and these are severely circumscribed by special conditions and the need for certain proof. The spirit of the Quran is compassion and mercy not punishment and vengeance.

The militants divide the world into the zone of peace and the zone of war. The zone of war is to be conquered and subjugated by Muslims by Holy War, or *jihad*. This aggressive conception of *jihad* is specifically forbidden by Quranic verses. *Jihad* in the Quranic context means 'self control' and 'self-refinement'.

For the Islamists *Sharia* is a means for authoritarian rule by divine right, *jihad* their justification for foreign aggression in the name of Islamic

Nationalism. It is an ideology that will lead to oppression and war and it is remote from both the letter and the spirit of the Quran.

RACHAD EL KOUSSY/CAMERA PRESS LONDON

The Gospel according to Al-Azhar

Two years ago, Yousef Chahine, one of Egypt's leading film makers, showed his film *Le Caire* at the Cannes Film Festival to international acclaim. In Cairo, however, the magazine *Akher Saa* accused the film of being 'obscene' and 'offending against Egypt's dignity'. The government-owned *Al-Akhbar* daily called for the director to be prosecuted.

In the eyes of its critics, this 27-minute film's major sin, it seems, was to have told the story of a young man drawn to religious fundamentalism as a consequence of social and economic deprivation, rather than for its more positive, spiritual values.

EOHR

Wisdom of the mosque

February 1994 signalled a famous victory for the fundamentalists. In a move designed to placate its critics the state handed the clerics of Al-Azhar more power over the life of Egypt than it has had in its 1,000-year history

Al-Azhar is both a mosque and a university. It was established in AD972 by the Fatimids, a Shia dynasty ruling Egypt at the time. The Fatimids set up Al-Azhar first as a mosque then as a *Dar Al-Hikma*, or House of Wisdom, from which to propagate their ideas to other parts of the Muslim World dominated in the West by the Ommayids and in the East by the Abbassids.

The political divisions of the time were extreme and Al-Azhar was expected to play its part it ensuring the victory of the Fatimids over their enemies. It was for that purpose that the mosque gradually became a school where Shia scholars could come to listen to books being read and discussed. With the fall of the Fatimid dynasty to the Ayyubids, Al-Azhar ceased to be a centre for Shia study and became an orthodox Sunni stronghold. It has remained so ever since.

The Ayyubids made no significant contribution to Al-Azhar, but their successors, the Mamelukes, did. The Mamelukes, who had been brought to Egypt as mercenaries and slaves, gradually took over the ruling of the country and eventually deposed the then monarch and installed themselves as sultans.

Much-needed repairs were undertaken and Al-Azhar's prestige increased considerably. It was also a time when Andalusia fell to the European armies and Baghdad to the Mongol hordes. Al-Azhar benefited greatly from the migration of some of the best Muslim thinkers to Egypt in search of stability and security.

With the Ottoman conquest of Egypt in 1517, Al-Azhar gradually began to lose some of its lustre. Its importance as an educational institution was downgraded. The Ottomans did, however, improve on the existing architectural structure.

But clearly the standard of education had suffered under their rule for, according to some contemporary accounts, by the time of the Napoleonic invasion of 1798 there were only 300 men in the whole country who could read and write.

The shock of the French invasion of the country and the ease with which they had been able to take Alexandria and Cairo highlighted Egypt's weaknesses. It lacked men with suitable education and expertise to handle modern warfare.

It was that need to modernise that drove Muhamad Ali Pasha, after seizing the throne, to first co-opt and then to set about controlling Al-Azhar. This he did by offering Azhari scholars government jobs and taking charge himself of the religious endowments that had allowed Al-Azhar to maintain its independence from the state.

Muhamad Ali set about creating a modern system of schooling using the endowment money to finance new building projects. He sent teams of scholars abroad to study and encouraged the translation of European texts into Arabic.

Toward the end of the 19th century a movement developed for Al-Azhar's reform. This was led by Imam Mohamad Abdu. In 1896 a new law was passed that extended the range of subjects taught to include many modern subjects and to reform the structure of the curriculum to bring it closer in line to European universities. These reforms were not held to for long as they were resisted by the more powerful resident scholars. Further reforms were introduced in 1936, but again only met with limited success. As one critic noted: 'Al-Azhar has discarded its old robes and assumed the new dress of a modern university, but nothing has really changed.'

The major changes to the structure and curriculum of the university came about with the Reform law of 1961. To maintain the careful balance between tradition and modernism the law permitted Al-Azhar a special status as a university independent of the Ministry of Higher

Education. Its president has to be a religious scholar.

During the course of this century there have been several celebrated cases of Al-Azhar interfering aggressively in the cultural life of Egypt. The first major such incident was the attack against the Egyptian writer and critic Taha Hussein for his book on *jahilia* poetry. The outrage that resulted from his claim that there is no existent pre-Islamic Arabic poetry, it all being fabricated in the post-Islamic period, forced him to revise his book, though not his theses, and republish it a year later in 1927.

Demonstrations led by Azharis culminated in scenes of book-burning reminiscent of the Middle Ages. Despite Taha Hussein's revisions the levels of resentment kept growing, until for over a two-year period from March 1932 he was deprived of state employment and the government even tried to stop him publishing or lecturing.

The first contemporary act of book-banning under the direct influence of Al-Azhar was in 1959 when Naguib Mahfouz's novel, *Awlad Haritna*, translated into English as *Gablawi's Children*, was serialised in the daily *Al-Ahram*. This novel so incensed the religious scholars of Al-Azhar that once again there were demonstrations. Naguib Mahfouz was condemned as causing offence to the prophets of Islam. Though banned in Egypt the novel was still published in Beirut and smuggled into Egypt to be sold under the counter at various bookshops.

One of the more remarkable recent interventions by Al-Azhar was the banning of a work on linguistics by the cultural critic and scholar Louis Awad. The book, *Muqadima Fi Fikh Al Lugha Al-Arabia,* was published in early 1980 and remained in the book shops for almost a year and a half during which time it sold approximately a thousand copies.

On 6 September 1981 Al-Azhar's Islamic Research Council requested that the book be banned. Dr Louis Awad challenged the decision in the courts, but the court ruled that the banning order should stand.

The objections to the book appear to be based on Dr Awad's attempts to prove that certain Arabic words were originally drawn from the language of Ancient Egypt. This may therefore affect the received meaning of certain words with a religious connotation. His argument that Arabic is an Indo-European language was also a controversial one.

During the 1980s the Islamic Research Council extended its reach over books. At the Cairo Book Fair in 1992 several books by Judge

Ashmawi were banned, as were others by less well known writers. After the threat of legal action Al-Azhar admitted to making a mistake and the books were allowed back in the bookshops.

The case that gained the greatest publicity was that of Alaa Hamid, whose novel, *A Distance in a Man's Mind* (see *Index* 2/1992), resulted in him receiving an eight-year prison sentence on Christmas Day 1991. He has not had to serve any of that time as the sentence was never ratified by the prime minister. Nevertheless it was Al-Azhar that requested that he be tried for blasphemy.

More recently Al-Azhar has preferred not to take such a prominent role in the banning of books. In a pernicious and more disturbing development they have taken to using the telephone to advise publishers and distributors directly of their displeasure, rather than issue a request for a book to be banned that State Security or the courts will then have to rule on. This has been the case with the state-owned General Book Association which has withdrawn several titles in its enlightenment series because of Al-Azhar's objections, as well a novel by Edwar Kharrat and a volume of poetry by Hassan Telib.

'Al-Azhar is a higher authority; when Al-Azhar speaks all must fall silent.'

Farouk Husni, Minister of Culture

In the present climate of intimidation Al-Azhar's displeasure is not to be countenanced by those seeking to pursue their business comfortably in present-day Egypt. Al-Azhar wields the ultimate threat of excommunication, which is as good as a death threat. The murder of the writer Dr Farag Fouda in June 1992 can leave no doubts in anybody's mind about that. Dr Fouda was gunned down outside his office two weeks after an ad hoc committee at Al-Azhar decided that 'everything he does is against Islam'. His killers have cited Al-Azhar's condemnation of Dr Fouda as their justification for killing him.

In a press release after Dr Fouda's murder the illegal *Gamaat Islamia* stated: 'Yes, we killed him... Al-Azhar issued the sentence and we carried out the execution.' The *Gamaat* are behind much of the terrorism that is taking place in Egypt now. It would be foolhardy for any writer to risk a confrontation with Al-Azhar if it is an invitation to the *Gamaat* to use them as target practice.

It is therefore this combination of official sanction and illegal terrorism that is combining to further increase Al Azhar's authority in the country.

On 10 February 1994, ruling 58/1/63 of the Council of State changed the situation dramatically. In response to Al-Azhar's request that it clarify its authority in 'confronting artistic works, audio and audio-visual artifacts that deal with Islamic issues or that conflict with Islam... preventing them from publication, recording, printing and distributing', the council both redefined the purposes of censorship and greatly enhanced Al-Azhar's hitherto advisory role in the audio-visual field.

On this date, the Council of State issued a ruling legitimising Al-Azhar's role in censoring what are termed 'artifacts of sound and sight and sound' — films, music and video cassettes — and stipulating that Al-Azhar's opinion is 'binding' on the Ministry of Culture. Though the ruling limits the application to 'Islamic issues' it also makes clear that it is up to Al-Azhar to define these limits. If the precedent of book censorship is anything to go by, Al-Azhar will set itself as wide a brief as possible.

Their master's voice

In a country where illiteracy is still over 50%, radio and television are clearly the most powerful means of influencing and controlling a population. The state operates a monopoly on both: the veneer of pluralism in the press has made no inroads on either.

The political manipulation of the media by the ruling party is most evident during news broadcasts where priority is given to the promotion of leading figures in the ruling party and state and to news items which conform with their current policy. Stage plays or films are subjected to yet another layer of censorship by a censorship committee attached to the Ministry of Information.

Al-Azhar is taking an increasingly interventionist role in deciding what can and cannot be shown on television. *Rose al-Youssef*, the state-owned cultural weekly, reported that television scripts are 'as a matter of routine sent to Al-Azhar for its approval'.

The reason most frequently given for refusal is that it is offensive to Islam to portray any of the Prophet's companions or the prophets of the Quran on television.

EOHR

FARAG FOUDA

The heart that grieves

Terrorism has developed its own culture, for there are the journalists who defend it and the philosophers who justify it, and there are those who finance it.

There are those from the clergy who meet it halfway and those senior figures in the press who hesitate before embracing it.

Which can only make the heart grieve at their duplicity.

The murders continue and the thefts continue and sectarian strife continues.

No citizen is safe.

But there is something new: the police are now being killed. Now the state itself is faced with a threat; now it sees there is no room left for compromise or dialogue. There is nothing as cruel as the words of the supporters of extremism when they write, without shame or embarrassment, that the terrorist is simply a plain honest youth whose aims are just but whose means are wrong.

It is this tune we heard when terrorists murdered the manager of an Islamic bank with his little daughter and a friend who was with them. Once again we saw the cavalcade of lawyers and opposition papers drumming out their messages of support. Compounding their own sins by supporting the sins of others.

It happened when President Sadat was murdered. His killers had already murdered and robbed Christian traders. Such lawyers and press men have made themselves partners in the sins of these criminals.

Let us take them at their word: these are innocent boys who never meant to steal and pious men who never meant to murder. These undefiled youth never meant to set off the sparks of sectarian violence.

Who then is guilty of making them believe that to steal is to be a hero and to murder is to be a crusader?

Could it be those who spilled so much ink in defence of religious extremism?

Or could it be the clergy who honours terrorists as champions of the faith?

Or the lawyers who convince the guilty of their righteousness?

It is all these who carry the beacons that lead down the path of death and theft and bigotry.

Now tell me: should the heart not grieve?

Dr Farag Fouda *was murdered on 8 June 1992 by Islamic militants after being denounced by an ad-hoc committee of clerics from Al-Azhar. These are among the last words he wrote.*

SUBSCRIPTIONS 1994

Lancaster House, 33 Islington High Street, London N1 9LH, UK

"Index has bylines that Vanity Fair would kill for. Would that bylines were the only things about Index people were willing to kill for." **BOSTON GLOBE**

1yr UK: £30 **USA:** $48 **Overseas:** £36 **Students:** £23/$35 (Worldwide)
2yr £55 $90 £66
3yr £80 $136 £99

Yes, I would like to subscribe to Index on Censorship.

❑ I enclose a cheque* or money order for £/$................
(*Sterling cheques must be drawn on a London bank)

❑ Please charge £/$ .... to my

    ❑ Visa/Mastercard   CARD NUMBER...
    ❑ American Express   ....
    ❑ Diners Club   EXP DT.................

       SIGNATURE...

❑ I have instructed my bank to send £..............
to your bank account 0635788 at Lloyds Bank,
10 Hanover Square, London W1R 0BT

NAME...

ADDRESS...

❑ I have sent £........... to your Post Office
National Giro account 574-5357 (Britain)

....

....

GIVE INDEX TO A FRIEND
EVEN ONE YOU HAVEN'T MET!

Lancaster House, 33 Islington High Street, London N1 9LH, UK

Index makes an ideal gift. Send a subscription to a friend (or several). Index will send a card announcing your gift.

1yr UK: £30 **USA:** $48 **Overseas:** £36 **Students:** £23/$35 (Worldwide)
2yr £55 $90 £66
3yr £80 $136 £99

❑ I enclose a cheque* or money order for £/$................
(*Sterling cheques must be drawn on a London bank)

❑ Please charge £/$ ....to my

    ❑ Visa/Mastercard   CARD NUMBER...
    ❑ American Express   ....
    ❑ Diners Club   EXP DT.................

       SIGNATURE...

RECIPIENT'S NAME...   YOUR NAME...

ADDRESS...   ADDRESS...

....

....

Also, you can send **Index** to a reader in the developing world—for only £18 or $27.
These sponsored subscriptions promote free speech around the world for only the cost of printing and postage.
"Bless those kind donors who have made the poor benefit from your golden magazine..." Teacher, Kenya

Index on Censorship
Lancaster House
33 Islington High Street
London N1 9LH
United Kingdom

Index on Censorship
Lancaster House
33 Islington High Street
London N1 9LH
United Kingdom

The veil is not Islamic

The sight of veiled women on Egypt's streets has become commonplace. It is a recent phenomenon and one that is growing. It is frequently attributed to the influence of the Gulf States where many Egyptian women worked as migrant labourers in the 1970s. There they were forced to don the veil by preachers and propagandists of political Islam who stressed that the veil is an Islamic dress required by the Quran and prophetic tradition.

DENIS THORPE/CAMERA PRESS LONDON

The wearing of the veil is referred to in three separate verses of the Quran and in *hadith,* sayings of the Prophet originating from a single source.

From all of these it is clear that while Islam does recommend women and girls to dress decently, it contains nothing which invites women and girls of the 20th century to don the veil. They may wear the veil, if they so choose, but should in no way be threatened or intimidated to do so; and certainly not on the pretext that it is a Quranic or Prophetic command.

The veiling of women is considered today to be a sign of faith, but in truth it is only the uniform of political Islam. The religious jurists who prevent anybody from discussing or debating this issue, by reference to the Quran and prophetic tradition, are simply serving the interests of politicians. For in truth, political Islam cares only for appearances and not for the essence.

Judge Said Al-Ashmawi

LATIFA AL-ZAYYAT

A Raid: personal papers

Any summary of the life and work of Latifa al–Zayyat without conveying what she meant for a whole generation of young writers and critics in Egypt would be an injustice to the writer and the woman. Her involvement with young people was lifelong. Her time, advice, support — and at times her praise — were given generously and without stint.

Latifa al–Zayyat was born in Egypt in 1923. After graduating in English literature in 1944, she entered the academic world. A PhD was awarded in 1957, following which she became professor of English literature at the Girls' College at Ain Shams University.

For much of her life Latifa al–Zayyat was actively involved with opposition politics and spent two terms in prison as a result. She was one of three founding members of the Higher Committee for Students and Workers whch led the 1946 uprising against the monarchy and the British occupation. In 1979 she founded, and still chairs, the Committee for the Defence of National Culture. She was among the 1,500 intellectuals rounded up by Anwar al–Sadat and imprisoned in September 1981.

She has published one novel, *The Open Door* (1960), and a collection of short stories, *Old Age and other stories* (1986). Her most recent work, the autobiographical *The Raid: personal papers* was published in 1992. It will appear in translation published by Quartet Books, UK in February 1995. She has also had a distinguished career as a critic and translator of literary texts.

Ahdaf Soueif

March 1973

In the next room my brother, Abd el-Fatah, lies dying. He does not know that he is dying; nobody in the house knows — except I. The doctors have given him three to six months. In between the nursing shifts, the manufacturing of smiles and jokes, and the forging of prescriptions so that my brother may not learn the true nature of his disease, I sit down to write. I resist death by means of an autobiography that will, however, not be completed. My brother dies in May 1973, and with his death my autobiography ends. This is what I wrote during that time:

Change has spread to the quarter where I was born in Damyetta; a city which lies in the arms of both the Nile and the Mediterranean. The district has become filled with small, ugly buildings crowded close together — so that it is difficult for me now to determine the spot where our large old house used to stand. The mosque of Shaykh Ali al-Saqqa used to provide a landmark for the house — but no longer; the mosque has been pulled down and rebuilt on an area which probably includes some of the land that used to be ours.

Although a long time has passed since our house was demolished, its image remains etched on my memory. I can even smell it still. This is not strange: I was born in the house on August 8, 1923, and in it I spent the first six years of my life. I returned to it each summer from whichever city my father was working in as a member of the City Board; from Damyetta to Mansura to Asyut, till he died when I was 12. When we moved to Cairo and until I graduated from the Faculty of Arts in 1946, I spent all my summer vacations in the old house. Time and time again after I graduated I returned to it, and what I am sure of is that it was still standing in 1949; for that is where I went when I left al-Hadra prison in Alexandria with a suspended sentence.

1967

On a day in June 1965, while my brother and the *ma'zun* sat in the next room, my husband — in a final attempt to dissuade me from completing the arrangements for our divorce, turned on his swivel chair and said:
'But I created you.'

Thirteen years of my life passed before my eyes. Three phases: first the illusion of complete union with the beloved. Then, the loss of that illusion and my mad attempts to regain it. And finally, my inaction, my paralysis. I did not want to get into an argument. I looked at him and wondered: which of those phases of my life had he created? Had he created all of them? Or had he in truth created nothing? The time had passed when I used to think of him as the source of all my joys and all my miseries; it had passed the day I was cured of my paralysis. In order to be cured, I had, among other things, to absolve my husband. And so I admitted that from first to last *I* was the one to blame for my impossible dream, my impossible madness, my impossible death. I took full responsibility and I was cured of paralysis. Here I was, getting better, *about* to get better, and I trembled in fear that my new-born being might retreat back into the womb. I wondered: had he been the project of my past life, or had my own personal happiness been my project? Had I confused the two for a while and was I now no longer confused? He had not been my project. My happiness had been my project; a project I wore myself out to actualise and went mad when it refused to take shape. I am the creator of absolutes and the prisoner of my creations. How could I distinguish between absolute happiness and absolute misery? For years I had revolved in the wrong sphere, unable to commit the act that would carry me beyond its boundaries. Years in which I was given over to paralysis by the great chasm between what I believed in and the way I lived, between the vision and the lived fact, between the dream and the reality. Years. And now I was almost getting better. I trembled with fear that my new-born being might retreat into the womb as he turned and said:

'But I created you.'

That day I would have appeared to the outsider to be a successful woman by all the agreed standards. Maybe more than just successful. At the same time I was merely the ruin of a woman although nobody knew about even one aspect of this ruin. That was my secret, and it was a secret I hid completely. I hid it from myself too, for a while. And for another while I chewed over its bitterness and I was helpless to change it. Which of those two women had he created? He had created nothing; I had created my successes and my miseries, and he had created nothing.

In the first phase, the phase of imagined union (How long did it last? One year? Two?), I achieved nothing, and I did not wish to achieve anything. It was not part of the plan that I should do anything since in his realisation lay the fullness of mine. In the shade of such imagined happiness we do not write, we do not take on a task which demands our devotion; we live the moment instead of writing it. And when I felt the ground tremble under my feet just a little, I felt a great need to write. And as soon as I finished my PhD thesis in 1957, I gave myself completely to writing my novel *The Open Door* which was published in 1960. But when I felt the ground shake and heave under my feet I wrote nothing. The most one can do in such times is to collect what remains of oneself as he turns in his swivelling chair and says:

'But I created you.'

I thought carefully before I answered. If I got into an argument I would not gain what I came here for. My decision to separate was five years old. My ability to turn the decision into an action was a month old. For a month I had been planning for the divorce meeting: through begging, through friendliness, through the mediation of friends and relatives, through threats. I did not argue, but I did not retreat. It was impossible to retreat now after I had regained at least part of my ability to act. I had retreated so often and for so long that retreat had become the pattern he and everybody expect from me.

'So what's new that you should ask for a divorce?' his older brother had asked in a family meeting to set a date for the divorce. I did not answer. Nothing was new. The new is a repetition of the old. What is new when in autumn the leaf falls from the tree? Falls — with no pain, and no regret. The leaf fell nearly five years ago. Nothing new has come to pass on my husband's side; the new is a repetition of the old. What was new had come to pass on my side; I was the active agent this time not him, I was able now to say: No — enough. I will not hide the 'no' and the 'enough' in a coma of living death. I am able to act, to struggle, to step beyond the wrong sphere until there is no longer any need to say 'no'; a sterile 'no' which takes no shape in action, a bitter 'enough' which I chew on in silence, in helplessness, and in self-hatred. I was able now to attempt to unify my mind and my heart, my vision and my life, my will and my action. The chasm between the will and the act is no longer there. I whipped myself to shift it, and my back still bears the scars.

1981

I look around me as I sit in the police car outside the gates of the Qanatir prison for women. I am impatient, impatient for the door to open, impatient to settle finally somewhere. I feel sure that whatever the material conditions, warmth awaits me here. Friends have preceded me to this prison, and friends will follow, and in residence before the latest arrests were friends who have been jailed so often that they have now become almost a feature of the Qanatir prison for women.

A sound like the clucking of chickens comes to my ears, bringing with it an odd sense of familiarity. Are they breeding chickens in the hall that separates the men's prison from the women's? I glance around me searching for the source of sound and I see two ancient trees, their massive branches crowned with thick clusters of large white flowers. And then I realise that the sound comes from the trees, and that the flowers are not flowers but masses of white egrets roosting among the leaves. The door opens and I see a warden dressed in the official grey and I almost cry out in greeting 'Sitt Aliyya!'

The warden was not Sitt Aliyya, nor was I the young woman I had been in 1949, nor was the prison the Hadra prison in Alexandria. But I entered the Qanatir prison at the age of fifty-eight with a certainty that my life was about to take on a coherent form, a form I would never have become aware of if I had not picked up those threads of my life that for a while were broken; if I had not gone back to political work, and revived the woman who had become mummified within the covers of a book, hiding from conflict.

Extracts translated by Ahdaf Soueif from The Raid: personal papers

MOHAMED MUSTAGEB

Woman

ANDRZEJ BADZIAK

A few lines on from now a terrible thing is going to occur. We shall let loose the dubious L so that he can climb up the walls of the house of Madame N, from where he will leap onto her bed and strangle her with his powerful arms, leaving her a lifeless corpse with blood pouring from her nose and soaking the whole place.

First, let it be said that N was a beautiful lady who suffered from an evident desire to be lax. A young boy related about her a shocking and mysterious story which was later confirmed by the corpse of a peddler of cloth. It had also happened that a lorry driver had stabbed her in the left shoulder with a dagger several days after her husband's demise. Of late it had been said that some swindler had helped himself to handfuls of her gold. After this so many different tales were spread abroad about Madame N that we had the feeling that every one of us must have had some sort of story with her — and that anyone who wanted to could.

The winter was a severe one and the rooms of our low-lying, narrow houses whistled and shivered with the cold. When the tea was boiling on the open fire, with its red coals giving out flames, our tales about Madame N reached full bloom, and when the smoke from the fire flooded our eyes, noses and throats, the body, the wealth and the house of Madame N were looted as material for our stories. Our cold, shivering, fumigated happiness reached its peak when each one of us would bring his skill to bear on leaving some part of his story shrouded in mystery so that we could have the joy of striving to unearth its details.

The hospital attendant was, on market day, in front of N's house. What was he doing? The narrator stops, wipes his nose and whispers: 'God knows'.

Someone else takes hold of the tail of the story and declares that he had actually seen her in the hospital seventeen days ago. What was she doing? The narrator stops and whispers 'God knows', and it becomes clear to us, then and there, that we have all met N. In the market, and on the Yusuf Canal road, and in front of the school, above the aqueducts, at the dentist's, at the office of the government land-tax collector, alongside the house of the official in charge of security in the village, inside the mill, at the railway station, at the grocer's, in the grounds of the cemetery. What was she doing? God knows.

'Hyena' specialised in helping to deliver cattle. With his sleeves rolled up, he was gradually bringing out, from deep inside the cow, the bleeding remains from the birth, when A'war leaned over my uncle's ever worrying wife and whispered: This village has got no men in it!

We all of us looked to where we had to verify the underlying reason for our village being devoid of men. There was N walking along with a swinging gait at the end of the road; she was wearing her usual black clothing that rippled in the morning breeze, giving off reflections of the sun's rays; she was wearing a headcloth that set off her beautifully fresh face.

Ten pairs of eyes encircled her as she proceeded over the canal. It was the appropriate time for 'Hyena' to extract his bloody hand from the inside of the cow and to exclaim: 'This village has got no men in it?' Quickly the conference that had convened around the cow that was giving birth became transformed into a brotherhood united in rebutting 'Hyena's' charge against the village. In a voice heavy with manliness A'war called out: 'I'll pay five pounds hard cash to rid the village of...(and he turned his face towards N with an expression of contempt). Adil answered: 'And I'll pay five,' at which Fadil called out: 'And I'll pay two pounds,' while Fagir chanted out in his ancient voice: 'And I'll pay eight.' Various offers of participation were made until the whole thing ended with 'Hyena's' voice: 'And I'll come to terms with Mr L on behalf of you all.'

My uncle's wife almost let out trilling cries of joy as she announced that she'd slaughter half the rabbits she had and give a banquet of rabbit with *mulkhiyya* in the street on the day she was brought the news that Madame N had been dealt with.

Just as every village has its own tinner, its headmaster, man in charge of its nightwatchmen, its thief, the drummer at the ceremony for exorcising spirits, the fortune-teller, the wormwood merchant, an Imam and a priest, a jobber of cattle, an official to perform marriages, a professional woman dancer, a brothel-keeper, a bone-setter, a waterwheel carpenter, a midwife, a village mayor, a water-seller, and a barber, it does in addition have its hired killer, with the village and the killer serving each other's interests.

The great L was the strongest one at that time after our village was able to boast of the five famous operations he had to his credit: he had bumped off a merchant from up north for the account of a blind woman whom the murdered man had cheated over the price of a *Kilah* of grain; he had stabbed with a spear the clerk of a neighbouring estate for the account of the previous clerk; he had cut the throat of a horseman who'd got into the habit of romping merrily around the place without so much as greeting people; he had hung up the owner of a baking oven by his feet outside the door of the oven, and as no one had had the courage to cut him loose he had stayed there till he died; the fifth operation was one in which the fisherman was killed, he and his family being put into a boat which had been untied, set alight, then sent off into the waters of the Yusuf Canal.

Of course it was 'Hyena' who came to an understanding with Mr L. When the two of them entered our street, we were all quaking with confusion, excitement and disquiet. Mr L was walking along calmly, twirling a cane stick that had been well anointed with the glory of the many necks it had busted. Once he had disappeared into the other street, we had a sense of enormous pride welling up in us. No sooner had he left the street than we were overwhelmed by the mighty answer to our question: This village is full of men. As he went quietly on his way L said to us: 'Peace be upon you.'

Also, we were waiting for the times when killing operations could take place in our village: in the early morning or at dawn, or just after the evening prayer. We were also capable of talking about the killer's fee and the method he would be employing to do away with his victim: would it be with a knife or by fire, by poison or manual strangulation, with a fibre noose or being smothered by the bedclothes. Our speculations during an exhausting week ended up with the conclusion that L would kill the accursed N by manual strangulation and at dawn directly following market day.

It was late afternoon, a time when we have no inclination to kill anyone, with the sun at the end of the day advancing, yellow, old and despondent, its rays stroking the melancholy tops of the houses.

The horizon of the village splintered and our eyes were opened in confusion as they came to rest on the scrap-heaps in the ruined buildings. The whole universe was rent by a frightful scream as Madame N's window burst open and Mr L was hurled out and fell into the street, trailing behind him his next drawn-out and terrifying scream.

The people gathered round the body of Mr L, which was all hunched up and quivering as it gave out its final gasp.

Not one of us could bring himself to raise his gaze to Madame N as she stood on the roof of her house, toweringly defiant - and stark naked - looking down at us with a smile of contempt.

Translated by Denys Johnson-Davies

MARIAM MUHAMAD

Education on the job

Censorship of the foreign press is labour-intensive and a monumental waste of time and energy. It does however, help to keep the unemployed figures down.

Egypt is a multi-layered society. At a superficial level the shop window displays democratic wares and liberal decorations; but step inside and the censorship boards and interrogation cells are hidden under the counter. In one sense at least the state is democratic: in its application of censorship to all publications..

The foreign press is as subject to regular intervention as the local press. This is usually either by the direct banning of a particular issue of a newspaper or magazine, or by removing licence of papers published in Egypt.

The *Wall Street Journal,* the *New Yorker*, the *Guardian*, and the *Economist* as well as issues of the regional *Middle East Times* are among international publications to have been banned in recent years. An analysis of confiscations and the interrogations and detentions of Egyptian journalists — as well as Egyptians who have been quoted in the foreign press — over the last year give a clear indication of the topics that are off limits for the foreign press.

Taboo subjects appear to be: the political views of the military and their attitudes to the regime; kickbacks and commissions from the purchase of military equipment; the personal wealth of key people in government; criticism of Al-Azhar and its relationship with religious extremist groups; any mention of state security and the State Censorship

Board; discussion of human rights violations.

The degree of protection enjoyed by foreign correspondents has a lot to do with their country of origin. The *Wall Street Journal* reporter who wanted to interview Sheikh Omar Abdul Rahman's son had his translator and guide threatened by state security officers to the point where he give up the idea of travelling to Fayum for the meeting. But the correspondent for Spanish Television was himself threatened by Ministry of Information officials and told that he would have his office closed and his licence revoked for broadcasting controversial material about the recent resurgence of local terrorist attacks.

It is generally accepted, though difficult to prove, that most foreign journalists' telephones and fax machines are tapped, but the most vulnerable link in their chain are the Egyptians working in their offices. Several have recently been called in for interrogation and, in some cases, been told that they should keep their eyes open for anything that would help state security. Others have been threatened and abused.

Harassment and intimidation can take many forms. Foreign correspondents who have displeased the authorities find themselves unable to obtain or renew their presidential pass. As a result they are denied access to any functions at which President Mubarak may be present.

Press departments in Egyptian embassies abroad check everything published locally on Egypt and inform state security in Cairo of anything they consider offensive to Egyptian national interests or defamatory to Islam. The correspondent of the Portuguese daily, *Publico,* in Cairo has had calls from the Egyptian ambassador in Portugal to complain about her articles; a German reporter has had complaints from the Egyptian embassy in Germany forwarded to state security.

Of all the privately owned foreign language publications published in Egypt, *Cairo Today* has been the one most willing to accommodate the authorities; the magazine's license is renewed every six months and it is vulnerable to state pressure. But even the appointment of Mursi Saad Eddin — censor of the foreign press during the 1960s and 1970s, and a state security officer for many years — as editor-in-chief, did not solve the publisher's problems.

The November 1993 issue of *Cairo Today* was withdrawn from the bookshops for publishing an article on human rights in Egypt. Eager to assist the censor in proving that there is no censorship in Egypt, *Cairo Today* replaced the banned issue overnight with another, replacing the offending article with a feature on art in Egypt. The magazine's proprietor, Bill Harrison, insists that he 'pulled the issue back voluntarily because it violated a government directive.'

Freedom's laws

The principal laws limiting free expression in Egypt are:

No 10, 1913 Public Right to Assembly Law

No 14, 1923 Public Meetings Law

No 20, 1936 Publications Law

No 58, 1937 (amended) Penal Code

No 430, 1955 Censorship of Art and Cinema Law

No 162, 1958 State of Emergency Law

No 32, 1964 Private Associations Law

No 40, 1977 Political Parties Law

No 33, 1978 Protection of Internal Order and Social Peace

No 95, 1978 Protection of Social and Moral Values Law (Law of Shame)

No 48, 1980 Press Authority Law

No 105, 1980 State Security Courts Law

Compiled by Said Essoulami, Article 19

Since April last year, three issues of *Middle East Times* have been banned for carrying articles on human rights or on the military.

Lotfi Abdel-Qader, head of the foreign press censorship board, refuses to discuss the reasons for the banning of foreign publications.

But at the offices of the Publications Authority in central Cairo, I encountered an officer furious that I had arrived unannounced. 'How do you know we exist?' he kept asking. 'Who told you about us?' He informed me that the Publications Authority's role 'is not exactly public knowledge. We do not deal with the publishers of newspapers or other publications directly. We evaluate foreign works to see if they are in line with Egyptian government policy, that is all.'

He directed us to another office of the Publications Authority in an old building in Garden City. The nameplate outside bears the name 'Press

Office'. It is here that all foreign books and magazines must be checked before gaining access to Egyptian bookshops.

The director of the Press Office was even more unforthcoming than his colleague in central Cairo. The reception area is piled high with magazines: *Time* and *Newsweek* were stacked against *Vogue* and *Esquire*. The director explained that not a single page was torn from a magazine without there being a report prepared by the censoring official. Political articles had to be checked for their possible damage to the 'higher interests of the state'.

Foreign language books are more carefully assessed. Starting with the name and telephone number of the importing agent, reports on each one include a plot summary and end with the reader's recommendations.

Refusing to answer any further questions, the director referred us to his brother who, he said, was chairman of the Department of Journalism at Cairo University. 'He teaches them and I educate them,' he said.

As I was leaving I asked him about the Press Authority Law of 1980 which stipulates that there must be no censorship of the press. 'Ah, yes,' he said, 'that is correct. But it only took the government a week to realise its mistake and set up the Press Office. That's why you are not meant to know we exist.'

JOHN TORDAI/CAMERA PRESS LONDON

Press laws and the constitution

Since 1988 there has been a marked deterioration in freedom of expression in Egypt. More frequent resort to the Special Laws, in particular, has had a marked effect on the work of journalists and writers.

The substantial battery of laws and penalties dealing specifically with the press are designed to terrorise all who work in the field. The 31 clauses dealing with 'Journalistic Crimes', include anything that causes 'hate of the ruling authorities', gives 'offence to the power structure, the army, or Parliament', or that can be construed as 'disturbing propaganda'. The degree of criminality is unaffected by the means used, whether peaceful, as in writing books, articles, or photographs, or of a more violent kind... . The law permits the presiding judge to decide on the type and level of punishment except in the case of an offence to the President, when the punishment is imprisonment.

The law also forbids the publication of lies, whether reported directly or copied from a foreign publication, and the publication of photographs that are considered to be offensive to the country's reputation or which highlight more unpleasant aspects of Egyptian life. The 1970s and early 1980s saw the introduction of the 'Special Laws'. Designed to deny freedom of opinion and expression, they are the most blatant violations of human rights in the country. The most notorious of these laws are:

1. Law of Political Parties No 40/1977
2. Law for the Protection of the Home Front and
   Social Peace No 33/1978
3. Law for the Protection of Values No 95/1980
4. Law Regulating State Security Courts No 105/1980
5. Law on the Power of the Press No 148/1980.

The Special Laws introduced new restrictions on journalists and writers, which exceeded those already applicable to the Journalists' Syndicate, and criminalised some of their activities. They empowered the Higher Council of Journalism to discipline journalists, and permitted the 'political interrogation' of journalists before the Public Prosecutor, appointed directly by the President and with the power to expropriate property and personal wealth, detain individuals without trial, deny them their democratic rights to participate or vote in syndicate elections or to pursue their employment as journalists.

The laws also permit journalists to be tried before the State Security Courts to which the President may appoint military judges, or the Courts for the Protection of Values which are set up by the Minister of Justice and to which he can appoint unqualified individuals to act as judges. These are political courts that base their judgements on hearsay and circumstantial evidence and are in violation of the constitution and the most basic principles of human rights.

Under these laws a journalist may be denied the right to work in his profession or transfer to another job. These laws can also deny him the right to join a political party or to participate in any political activity or be nominated for any professional post. Any of this may result from being accused of offending against 'the interests of the state', or inciting against 'the social order', or against the 'ruling system'. The terms are dangerously vague and elastic and can be stretched to cover any point of view not in favour with the regime.

One instance of the vagaries of these laws in application is the clause stipulating that it is an offence to insult a foreign head of state. Given the changes in Egypt's political fortunes and alliances in the Arab world since the Camp David agreement, journalists have been at sixes and sevens in knowing whom they may — or may not — abuse, and have suffered the consequences of a wrongly timed outburst.

As oppressive as the existing laws are, there have been several attempts at introducing new, more punitive ones. The law on 'Punishment of Journalists' proposed by the ruling National party in 1988, which stipulated that journalists should face mandatory prison sentences for any breaches of the provisions of the 'Special Laws', was only defeated when journalists were able to show that the real objective of introducing the law was to further restrict reporting on corruption in government circles.

A further obstacle in the way of journalists is the ownership of the press. Despite laws which authorise private ownership, Egypt's press is overwhelmingly in the hands of the state. The punishing conditions imposed upon potential owners who must raise large 'deposits' and undertake not to be politically partisan or become involved in party politics, act as a powerful deterrent to investment in the private sector. Ownership falls into three categories:

• *National papers* and magazines are published by state-owned institutions and supervised through the *Maglis Al-Shura*, a state appointed body. Their longevity and generous government subsidies give them a near monopoly of the market.

• *Party papers* are owned by the eight political parties that have emerged since 1976, plus the ruling National Democratic Party. With the exception of the daily *Al-Wafd*, all are weekly or, in the case of *Al-Shaab*, bi-weekly. They face financial hardship and problems in obtaining and publishing information from government sources which operate a virtual boycott of all except *Mayo*, the organ of the National Democratic Party.

• *Opposition party papers* need consent to publish from the state-appointed Higher Press Council which can withdraw or ban single issues of their magazines and newspapers or permanently suspend publication.

• *Society and syndicate papers* are mainly trade publications with a readership limited to members of the organisations that issue them.

Ultimate power

Martial law, first imposed in June 1967, grants the state authorities wide-ranging powers. It permits the review and censorship of all newspapers and publications before publication, as well as their expropriation and banning. It also permits the closure of print shops and publishers.

Martial law also denies the freedom to hold meetings, freedom of movement and freedom of choice of residence It permits arbitrary arrest and interrogation without charges, and house searches without a warrant. The President of the Republic can also set up special courts — State Security Courts — under what is effectively a permanent State of Emergency. He may set up Military Courts to try civilians. There is no right of appeal from these courts — except to presidential clemency.

EOHR

GAMAL EL-GHITANI

The air we breathe

Censorship by the state feeds bigotry and encourages a climate of intellectual terrorism

As an avid reader for over 40 years, there has not been a single book banned by the authorities that I have been unable to obtain and read: the best way of ensuring that a book is read is to ban it. In an age of information transfer and exchange based on technological innovations, it seems odd to be talking still of forms of censorship in minds trapped in a bygone age.

Yet despite Al-Azhar's increased banning of books, I believe the greatest threat is not from the state and its various institutions. The greatest danger comes from censorship that is part of a wider climate of bigotry that has been encouraged by the various small but vociferous extremist groups. These groups have access not just to publishing houses and to the pulpits of mosques, they also make use of the state media and television to spread their intolerant views.

Their intolerance has become so much a part of the air we breathe that workers in publishing houses have refused to allow a book they disagreed with to be published. This has happened enough times for writers to view it with concern: it points to an absorption and internalisation of extremism that leads to intellectual terrorism. State restrictions are much easier to deal with than this general climate of bigotry. At the same time, official acts of censorship feed and encourage the creeping climate of intellectual terrorism.

I have never known such a dangerous time for writers as this. Nor one in which we have been so divided and so destructive of our own creativity and the creativity of others. This time the threat is no longer directed only at our books, but at our lives as well.

MAHMOUD EL-LOZY

A theatre of censorship

The principles guiding theatre censorship in Egypt today are those formulated in Law 430 of 1955, supplemented by Decree 220 of 1976. While the former was couched in general terms and gave individual censors considerable latitude, the latter, reflecting President Sadat's turn to the right at the time, tightened restrictions on theatre and cinema to the point where any serious development of either became virtually impossible. Decree 220 gave the censor comprehensive authority over theatrical production in Egypt and reduced the entire adult population of Egypt to the status of irresponsible minors with the censor as its guardian.

And yet, despite the supreme authority wielded by him on matters theatrical, today's censor insists that there is no censorship in his Egypt. In an interview with the left-wing weekly *Al-Ahali*, the current incumbent, Hamdy Sorour, sees himself as an expurgator of corruption rather than a restrainer of creativity. He denies the common belief that the function of censorship is to protect the security of the state; he is, he insists, charged with the protection of the minds of its citizens. Censorship is the principal sponsor of the artist from whom he derives his existence.

The puritanical restrictions of Decree 220 reflect the growing influence of Gulf sheikhdoms, in particular Saudi Arabia, on Egyptian culture. In the 1950s and 1960s, Egyptian state-sponsored theatre, particularly at its home, the National Theatre, inaugurated in 1935, was a commanding presence on the theatrical scene. Deprived of outlets and with new initiatives stifled in the climate of Decree 220, it was replaced by the commercial theatre catering to Gulf Arabs and to Egypt's *nouveaux riches* who profited from the state's change in economic direction.

In conformity with their tastes, wanton behaviour, lewd allusions, and lascivious dancing are not only socially accepted but eagerly expected as long as they manifest themselves within the moralising framework of a plot, usually a tear-jerking melodrama in which retribution and expiation play an important role. In one sitting the puritan may partake of both the sinful bliss of slumming in a den of iniquity and of seeing his moral viewpoint vindicated. But puritanism has moved into bigotry; the 'veiling of actresses' threatens the very existence of theatre. No less than 21 actresses have now retired from acting to don the so-called Islamic veil and repudiate their profession in the name of religion. Since art and religion, they argue, are mutually exclusive categories, the further from art, the nearer to God. The more recent of these converts, Soheir al-Babli, once Egypt's leading actress and a star of Gulf theatre, took on the veil in June 1993 after a career spanning three decades.

Only recently, Sheikh Mitwalli al-Sha'rawi, Egypt's most celebrated television sheikh, told *Sabah El Kheir* that if he were to meet Fatin Hamama, Egypt's most accomplished film actress, he would ask her to take on the veil. The spirit of censorship has become a crucial aspect of the cultural identity of Egyptians. No one speaks out against it.

The absurdity of Sorour's claims to be the champion of high artistic and cultural standards against the growth of 'debased art' rather than a political policeman, provoked a storm of protest in the press when he banned two recent plays — both of which subsequently received accolades at home and abroad. The first of these, Nabil Badran's *Wa 'Alayna al-Salam,* a political satire on the Palestinian question, had been granted an official permit as early as 1987. Over 50 rehearsals later and on the grounds that 'new circumstances had arisen', the script was called back for re-examination and the earlier licence revoked. The minutiae of Decree 220 were invoked and stretched to their legal limit: Badran was denied the right of appeal.

The Nabil Badran case was the last resistance to censorship based on the principles of freedom of speech, artistic expression, scientific research and publication in the 1971 Egyptian Constitution. By 1990 the critics' attitude to censorship had undergone a radical shift, as their attitude to Karim Alrawi's *Crossing the Water* demonstrated.

Originally commissioned by the Royal Court Theatre in London, *Crossing the Water* was produced as a staged-reading at the American University in Cairo in Spring 1990. It was a private affair with tickets by invitation only and needed no permit. The first critical response to the play came from Ra'fat al-Khayyat in Cairo's leading evening newspaper *Al-Missa.* Al-Khayyat lambasted the play for its 'sickening' display of homosexual relationships, its distortion of history and its defeatist stance. He begged the censor to prevent a public performance — and confessed that he had not actually seen the piece.

The censor did as requested and *Crossing the Water* was removed from public gaze in Cairo. After more than a year and in response to Alrawi's attempts to produce his play in the UK, the press again moved into the attack, this time mounting a vicious campaign to discredit the playwright and his play. Ibrahim Issa of the leading cultural magazine *Rose el-Youssef* unleashed his patriotic fervour onto the unsuspecting playwright, warning his readers against foreign and domestic conspiracies aimed at subverting the nation. He was prompted to write his article, he assured his readers, out of love for Egypt and in defence of its reputation and image abroad.

NEWS ANALYSIS

MATTHEW D'ANCONA

The insolence of office

The findings of the Scott Report will be more than a comment on the misconduct and incompetence of individual ministers: at the heart of the inquiry is the public's right to know and the secrecy practised by democratic governments

When Lord Justice Scott delivers his report on the arms-for-Iraq affair later this year, he will face a Hobson's Choice of reaction. By some, he will be accused of conspiring in a government cover-up; by others, of mischievously rocking the ship of state. Yet it is to the judge's credit that he has unsettled so many people: refusing to be Establishment stooge or liberal scourge. For those who care about open government, the findings of his year-long enquiry will be essential reading.

How did the mess he has been investigating ever happen? It is now clear that the Foreign Office guidelines governing arms exports to Iraq were substantially — but secretly — relaxed in 1988. Though no goods technically considered 'lethal' were approved for sale to Saddam Hussein's vicious regime, plenty of equipment with potential military applications was getting through. As Saddam prepared the invasion of Kuwait, British firms were supplying him with munitions which could be used to make nuclear weapons and the tubing for a supergun which could fire anthrax shells on Tel Aviv.

None of this stopped the extraordinary prosecution in 1992 of three executives from Matrix Churchill, a Midlands engineering firm, for evasion of export restrictions. Had it not been for the alertness of Judge Smedley, who ordered the disclosure of crucial documents which four ministers were trying to suppress, the defendants would almost certainly have gone to jail. The government would have been saved embarrassment at the cost of a serious miscarriage of justice.

Though the political scalp-hunters hope that the Scott report will lead to sensational resignations, it will be much more than an *ad hominem* attack on the misconduct and incompetence of individuals. Throughout the inquiry, Lord Justice Scott has shown himself in command of the ethical and constitutional questions which the scandal has raised. He has pressed ministers and officials in a manner to which they are quite unaccustomed; even in parliamentary select committees. 'You have a misunderstanding of how the system works,' Sir David Miers, former head of the Foreign Office Middle East department told him. On the contrary, it seems Lord Justice Scott understands the system all too well.

In this sense, at least, the tribunal has been a victory for openness. But it has also shown how deeply ingrained the habits of secrecy are in the British administrative psyche. Unlike many journalists, I think the government's openness drive is worth taking seriously. William Waldegrave's white paper on the subject last July did not satisfy those who had hoped for a full freedom of information bill, but it left Whitehall's door ajar in a way that would have been unthinkable only a few years ago. It is a step forward.

Yet, only two months after the white paper's publication, Mr Waldegrave was reverting to a cast of mind against which his new policy is meant to rebel. Up before the Scott inquiry, he explained that 'the guidelines [covering sales to Iraq] could not be changed without the approval of the Foreign Secretary, the Prime Minister and Parliament. None of this happened. Ergo the guidelines never changed'. If this doubletalk means anything at all, it is that policies which are concealed do not exist. Who can blame Lord Justice Scott for complaining that this sort of thing was keeping him 'awake at night'?

At the heart of the inquiry's remit is the question of the Public Interest Immunity (PII) certificates which were issued before the trial by Kenneth Clarke, Tristan Garel-Jones, Malcolm Rifkind and Michael Heseltine, in order to keep vital documents out of court. Lord Justice Scott will have to decide whether they did so in the knowledge that the information withheld could save three men from prison. But he must also address the broader constitutional questions raised by this case.

PII certificates are a shockingly uncharted area of executive power which few senior officials — let alone ministers — seem to be familiar with. Their potential scope is extraordinary, covering routine interdepartmental briefings, official advice and departmental minutes as well as obviously sensitive material such as intelligence information. One treasury solicitor told the enquiry that 'administrative convenience' was enough to justify the imposition of a certificate.

But it is the sheer power of these so-called 'gagging orders' that is most alarming. Though some members of the government have claimed that the certificates are merely *advisory* documents, informing the courts of potential damage to the state, they are very rarely resisted by judges and seem, in most cases, to have the force of an executive instruction rather than a humble application.

This being so, it is amazing how slack the guidelines governing the use of PII certificates appear to be. In February, Mr Clarke argued that ministers retain the right to reject the advice of legal officers to sign certificates, while Mr Rifkind maintained that the duty to sign was binding. Somewhere in between, Mr Heseltine claimed he had been told before the trial that he was obliged to sign — and just the opposite shortly afterwards. Who is right and why has it taken a hugely expensive inquiry for the question to be posed?

Two years ago, I was involved in a special issue of *Index on Censorship* (10/1991) about defence exports and the secrecy in which they were conducted. It has been strange to watch the saga of the arms-to-Iraq affair unfold since then, putting flesh on the bones of the arguments that issue put forward. Reform of Whitehall is a slow-moving business; reform of arms export policy slower still. This summer Lord Justice Scott will go into purdah to try and make sense of it all. I do not envy him but — like scores of nervous ministers and officials — I await his report eagerly.

MICHAEL FARRELL

Farewell Section 31

Ireland gives the UK a lesson in democratic freedoms

Irish anti-censorship campaigners won their biggest victory for decades at the beginning of this year when the Irish government ended a 21-year-old Ministerial Order that banned members of Sinn Fein, the political party that supports the IRA, from the Irish airwaves (see *Index* 8&9/1993).

Suddenly, the Irish Republic, whose censorship laws had been the model for the UK's current broadcasting restrictions, was giving the UK lessons in free speech. And audiences in Northern Ireland were tuning to the Republic's radio and television stations to hear people whose voices were dubbed or subtitled under the UK broadcasting ban.

Under Section 31 of the Irish Broadcasting Act, the government could order the electronic media not to broadcast anything that, in the government's opinion, could incite to crime or undermine the authority of the state. The first Order was made in 1972 and for the next 17 years prevented Irish radio and television from interviewing the IRA, other paramilitary organisations and Sinn Fein — a legal political party with significant electoral support in Northern Ireland.

After years of campaigning by civil liberties groups and the broadcasting unions, a broader based anti-censorship campaign had been built, a new government was pledged to more openness and democracy, and the ban had been condemned by the UN Human Rights Committee. It was, in any case, becoming daily more ridiculous that at a time when the Irish and British governments were talking at — and to — Sinn Fein about a possible peace deal, the public could not see or hear Sinn Fein's response.

Unfortunately, the British government's sense of the absurd seems less developed than that of the Irish. They have resisted all calls to end their ban and it has even spread further afield recently. When Sinn Fein leader Gerry Adams visited the USA in February this year, CNN carried extracts from interviews with him on its worldwide news service. But in its broadcasts to the whole of Europe,

Adams' voice was dubbed in a US accent to conform to the British ban.

Old habits took a while to die in Ireland. The state broadcasting service, RTE, had grown so used to censorship that it seemed afraid of freedom. Extremely strict guidelines were introduced for interviews with Sinn Fein personnel. There would be no live broadcasts, no panel discussions, and all proposed interviews would have to be cleared with senior management. And the ban still applied to paramilitary groups and the Minister retained the power to ban Sinn Fein again.

RTE was so nervous that it left the first interview with Mr Adams to a small commercial radio station. All the same, the first interviews were done. The sky did not fall in. The IRA did not take over the country.

RTE gradually grew bolder and by now it all seems so normal. Sinn Fein members are quizzed about their attitude to the peace process just like anyone else, and the viewer in the sitting room may soon forget that there ever was a broadcasting ban. Future generations will wonder why on earth it was ever allowed and how it could have lasted so long.

JEFF RIGSBY

Freedom or dignity?

Old habits die hard in the new Republic of Belarus — but proposals for a new press law are not encouraging

Amid newly purchased desktop computers and piles of discarded equipment boxes, one item stands out in the spartan Minsk offices of *Svaboda* (Liberty), an eight-page biweekly covering politics and economics in the former Soviet Republic of Belarus. A framed portrait of Lenin hangs incongruously at the top of a high window, as if surveying the disorder from above. 'It's to protect the computers from sun,' one staffer told me. 'We found it on the wall when we moved in.'

Lenin's political legacy may prove to be a more intractable hazard, however. Published in Belarusian and with a circulation of just 20,000, *Svaboda* doesn't pose much of a threat to the major state-controlled dailies, which sell in their hundreds of thousands, or even to the newer sensationalist tabloids, which eschew political coverage for lurid tales of sex and crime. But the republic's unreformed media policies, together with a plummeting economy, make it a constant struggle to keep independent newspapers afloat.

Wedged between Poland, Russia, the Baltic states and Ukraine, Belarus has attracted little attention from the West since the break-up of the USSR. President Bill Clinton made a brief courtesy call to Minsk on 15 January this year, a reward for the country's willingness to give up its share of the Soviet nuclear arsenal. But the republic's Supreme Soviet, still dominated by former Communists, seems less eager to relax its grip on the press.

Belarusian law bans publication of any material which 'insults human dignity', giving aggrieved subjects leeway to take journalists to court for virtually any criticism. 'Technically, we're under the laws of the former Soviet Union,' said Roman Yakovlevsky, political editor of *Belarusian Market*, an economic weekly. Chief editor Vyacheslav Khadasovsky, says the law makes it impossible to criticise anyone with the resources to take him to court. 'Now, for example, I don't risk writing about the affairs of big companies and banks,' he said. 'Even if I have the information, I won't publish it, because I can't afford a trial.'

The editors of *Belarusian Market* describe the journal's political slant as 'liberal-conservative', supporting capitalist economic reforms that the country's hardline leaders have shied away from. But the slow pace of reform, which has led to huge inflation and a sharp drop in output, poses additional obstacles for the independent press. Shortages of printing supplies, especially paper imported from Russia, can upset printing schedules since state publications get priority. Official publications get other privileges including state subsidies.

'We have no official censorship, but all the [established] press is under government control,' said *Svaboda*'s editor Ihar Hiermancuk, a member of parliament affiliated with the opposition Belarusian Popular Front. 'The government finances it and appoints the editors of the newspapers. Every two or three months, each chief edi-

tor goes to the government and asks for more money... Every editor knows that if he gives space to opposition views, he won't be editor for much longer.'

The subsidies give mainstream papers a financial edge over their competitors, which are forced to match subsidised cover prices in order to sell. With occasional help from foreign supporters, including the US-financed National Endowment for Democracy, and from private companies in Belarus, *Svaboda* absorbs losses of roughly US$600 on each issue. 'A few businessmen are willing to pay for democracy,' says Hiermancuk. One sympathetic entrepreneur has paid for their most vital input, paper.

Svaboda has only a handful of paid staff, but has no trouble gathering the material it needs — often from journalists working for the government press. 'They give us articles which can't be published in the official newspapers,' said Hiermancuk, whose paper has been prosecuted four times for 'insulting human dignity'. 'All such articles are published under closely guarded pseudonyms which we protect even in court.'

For radio and television journalists, a controversial story can mean more trouble than for their colleagues in print. The independent television station MM4 lost its broadcasting licence on 31 December 1992, after only a year in operation. The authorities offered various pretexts for the move, charging the station with licensing irregularities and broadcasting indecent material. Dmitri Koptirin, MM4's commercial manager, has no doubts about the real motive: 'Our news programmes competed with the official news.'

MM4 stayed afloat in 1993 by producing programmes on art and fashion for Minsk's less censored cable network, as well as a popular weekly crime-news show for state television. But even this relatively innocuous work is tightly supervised. 'We work under absurd conditions,' said Koptirin. 'We air on Tuesdays, but have to submit our material for censorship the previous Friday.' The station began to broadcast again in December 1993, but subject to strict conditions, including a total ban on political commentary.

After the Popular Front's unsuccessful attempt in February this year to force early elections by calling a general strike, there is little immediate prospect of political change. But even without a change of leadership at the top, there are signs of a growing pluralism. The Front isn't the only opposition player and is scarcely a party in the Western sense; most of the country's true political parties have formed only recently, under the aegis of the Front itself. The development of a genuine democratic culture will depend on their attitudes toward press freedom, still only partly formulated — and with, as yet, no satisfactory alternative to the law of 'insult'.

Opposition models for future regulation of the press shy away from the libertarian approach of the US First Amendment towards the 'strict definitions of the abuse of dignity, defamation, and so forth' of Germany's press law, says Anatoly Sidorevich, who spent four months in prison for criticising the Soviet invasion of Czechoslovakia and now serves on the Social Democratic Union's executive committee.

The Union, he adds, would maintain subsidies for the mainstream press but reallocate them on an impartial basis in proportion to their circulation as in Finland. Like Finland, Belarus is too small a market to give newspapers an adequate financial base through the sale of advertising and, argues Sidorevich, needs subsidies to keep the press alive during the present economic crisis.

Not everyone thinks an opposition government will improve conditions for the media. In a familiar post-Communist pattern, some see evidence that militant nationalists in the Popular Front plan to substitute one brand of authoritarianism for another.

Belarusian Market's political editor Yakovlevsky, points to a draft media law prepared by the Front late in 1993, which would have given tax preferences to Belarusian-language journals. The provision was eventually dropped, in part because many urban residents in this heavily Russified republic have only a shaky command of the national language. But Yakovlevsky thinks the move was a disturbing hint of chauvinism within the opposition. 'They tend to envision a politically engaged press, and, judging by the speeches of the Popular Front and the Social Democrats, have a very strong desire to minimise the number of Russian-language publications.'

VESNA BJEKIC &
OZRENKA RADULOVIC

A right to desert

The refusal of some Western European countries to grant residence permits to young Serbs who fled their country to evade conscription, has made the question of deserters a live issue in Serbia for the first time since the early days of the war.

Failure to report for mobilisation in the Serbian army constitutes a criminal act. Belgrade lawyer Nikola Barovic, who has had considerable experience in representing Serbian deserters, claims that young Serbian men who try to return home could be arrested at the border — or any time later. In his view the issue has a political as well as a legal dimension.

The size of the problem is unknown. Estimates of the number of Serb men who went into exile to avoid the draft are often manipulated and vary widely — from 30,000 to 200,000. It is, however, known that between 20,000 and 25,000 young ethnic Hungarians from the Vojvodina region of Serbia are now in Hungary. And reports from foreign immigration organisations and the Red Cross indicate that 90,000 to 110,000 young Serbian citizens have found refuge in Europe and North America to evade conscription.

In 1991 many young Serbs obeyed the call-up of the Yugoslav People's Army (JNA) or went to war voluntarily. Some disobeyed the call-up and not a few returned home from the front. But many chose exile rather than prison. Public opinion was divided about the 'patriots' who went to fight and the 'traitors and cowards' — the deserters. One reserve member of the JNA, Miroslav Milenkovic, who was torn between the old Serb military tradition and his opposition to the war, 'solved' the problem by killing himself.

Natasa Kandic, Director of the Belgrade-based Humanitarian Law Fund, stated that in late autumn 1993 the Council of Europe adopted a resolution on the protection of deserters. This was prompted by the behaviour of certain countries, primarily Denmark, that are seeking to reduce the influx of refugees by refusing entry to deserters. Kandic said: 'The question of deserters is a major political problem facing Serbia, one which receives practically no media coverage.' She described the action of young Serbs in choosing exile rather than taking part in the war as a 'very important political stand' at a time when both the middle-aged and older generations supported the government's war policy. 'There was no political force to support the young people's anti-war attitude and protect them from the sanctions envisaged by the law. According to estimates from different sources, even the regime's own papers reckoned that in November 1991 there were about 200,000 young Serb men abroad evading the draft.' Top Serb military leaders had attributed setbacks suffered by the JNA to massive desertion.

In the view of Nikola Barovic, the legal definition of desertion is problematic: mobilisation was not preceded by any public announcement of the decision in the official gazette. Political rather than legal considerations dominated the general view of desertion.

As the fighting subsided, efforts were made to decide the fate of those who had gone abroad because of the war. In mid-March 1992, deputies of the ruling Socialist Party of Serbia, called for a ban on the return of the fugitives. Their resolution was 20 votes short of the necessary 100. À proposal by the Democratic Union of Vojvodina Hungarians (DZVM) for an amnesty of deserters, whether they had remained in the country or gone abroad, also failed.

In a sharp public debate on the issue, backers of an amnesty argued that many young men believed that the war was not being waged to protect Serbia but for other interests. Another view held that a state could not be based on law if it did not punish its deserters.

To prohibit the return of a considerable part of a generation of young men would set a dangerous precedent. A former judge of the Supreme Military Court, Jovan Buturovic, argued that amnesty would be a wise and statesmanlike gesture. Various parliamentary moves to stay proceedings against deserters came to nothing; the number of cases, if any, launched against deserters is not known.

It seemed that the problem had been taken off the agenda in Belgrade — until Denmark announced its intention to return young Serbs. Nikola Barovic said that, due to the authorities' failure to authorise an amnesty, the unsolved problem of deserters would be used for a long time as a means of pressure on the population; young men and their families would live in constant fear. He added: 'Even more tragic is the fact that this fear has the full support of Europe. West European governments are well aware of the situation here and what can happen to these young men if they are returned, but they nevertheless deny them the right to remain.'

Meanwhile, a whole new wave of young people in the cities are refusing to serve in the army — this time with the backing of their families.

VESNA ROLLER

A less than perfect right

Croatia recognises the right to conscientious objection but is liable to overlook it under pressure of the military necessity.

By early January 1994, 'more than 200 and less than 1,000' conscripts in Croatia had claimed the right of conscientious objection by asking to do unarmed military service, announced Dr Ladislav Krapac, chairman of the Commission for Army Service in Civilian Capacity, part of the Croatian Ministry of Justice. He added that only four applications had been refused.

The right to conscientious objection, which was not recognised in former Yugoslavia, was guaranteed in the Croatian constitution of 1990 and detailed in a law on the defence of the state. Members of the Croatian peace movement recognise that, unlike the other states of former Yugoslavia, Croatia has made an important step towards Western-type democracy by recognising this right, but remain critical of deficiencies in its application. Srdjan Dvornik, an activist of the Croatian Anti-War Campaign, declared: 'We still do not have a civilian alternative to military duty but rather military service without the requirement to carry weapons.'

Dvornik argued that the provisions on conscientious objection in the law were contrary to the constitution, which recognises conscientious objection against military duty rather than against bearing arms. Members of the peace movement say that conscientious objectors should be allowed to discharge their obligation in civilian services. They also demand that conscripts seeking recognition as conscientious objectors should be freed from military service until a decision is made, which usually takes three months. Peace campaigners oppose the legal provisions requiring conscientious objectors to explain the religious, moral or other beliefs on which they base their objection. In most Western countries, they claim, the right to conscientious objection is almost automatically recognised.

However, defence ministry officials argue that the state must seek to prevent abuses of the right to conscientious objection, and that only individuals who — before they were drafted — had beliefs prohibiting the use of arms can be granted the right to serve in a civilian capacity.

There is also disagreement on the question of whether those Croatian citizens who are Serbian should be recognised as conscientious objectors on the ground that they do not want to fight against other Serbs. Dr Krapac rejects such 'political and ethnic' criteria and claims they are not accepted in other European countries. But Miro Bozic, a lawyer and activist of the Civil Council for Human Rights in Karlovac, south-west of Zagreb, said many Karlovac Serbs had contacted him because they did not wish to shoot at their cousins living on the other side of the frontline near Karlovac. 'Such arguments are acceptable moral reasons,' Mr Bozic said.

Human rights campaigners reported that in a number of cases army authorities had used various forms of pressure, including imprisonment, to persuade Serbs to withdraw their applications for exemption on conscientious grounds. A special brigade, mainly of Serbs who had refused to bear arms, was ordered to wear white boots, to 'classify' it, and was sent to the front line to dig trenches and be taunted as traitors by 'real soldiers'. Similar pressure was also exerted on Croats who had refused to bear arms, the peace campaigners said.

Logically the right to conscientious objection should reduce the number of deserters, but this number has never been published. Military courts have so far dealt with very few cases. But the number of desertions may have increased following the mass mobilisations intended to fill up the brigades sent to Bosnia-Hercegovina. According to two young Zagreb students who escaped from buses which were taking them to the battlefield and are at present in hiding, conscripts were asked to sign statements saying they were going to Bosnia-Hercegovina voluntarily.

ALEXANDRINE CIVARD

A marginal press

Although Albanian is the mother-tongue of more than a quarter of its population, Macedonian broadcasting makes few concessions to its largest minority language.

MTV. The acronym, best known as the logo of a leading US TV network, signifies a very different reality in Skopje, capital of Macedonia. A Stalinesque building, looming from behind crumbling battlements, houses the state broadcasting centre, only a few cable lengths away from the university.

There is no intellectual aura surrounding these places: backwardness and a lack of organisation rule. MTV's impractical structure reflects the nature of Macedonian society at large, and the role of the Albanian

language within its news services is equally revealing: three cheers for the good old official Macedonian language.

Of the 2,300 salaried employees working for MTV's three channels, only 15 have an Albanian background. They are responsible for the news programme broadcast in Albanian on Channel 2, one of a number of programmes aimed at minority groups.

The Albanian minority numbers somewhere between 400,000 (the official figure) and 800,000 (the Albanian estimate) out of a total population of 2,000,000. Together with other minorities such as the Turks (4.8%), Hungarians (2.7%), Muslims (2.5%) and Serbs (2.2%), the Albanians have only one hour's Albanian language television each day. With less chance of promotion, lower wage rates and a greater degree of censorship than their Macedonian colleagues, Albanian journalists bear the brunt of discrimination throughout their careers. The 30 minutes of news and 30 minutes of features, received in Kosovo and Albania as well as within Macedonia, fall well short of public needs. In Kosovo the media is dominated by the language of the official government — Serbian.

The blandness of official programmes and the public's hunger for news has seen the emergence of five small local private television stations over the last two years. The genesis of these organisations is due in part to the easing of government restrictions and in part to the relative difficulty of financing an independent newspaper.

Flaka, currently the only Albanian language daily in the country, is only a 'part-time' operation, appearing only every other day. *Flaka* belongs to the *Nova Makedonija* group, still under government influence. It employs 47 people, 30 of whom are journalists. They face a number of problems peculiar to the Albanian sector of the media. Chief among these is the difficulty of news gathering caused by restricted access to sources of information. The newspaper's editor, Abdulhadi Zulfiguari, accuses the Macedonian bloc in parliament of witholding information from his news-gathering services. Torn between the Party for Democratic Prosperity of Macedonia (PDP) (one of the two Albanian parties in Macedonia), which covets *Flaka* as its political mouthpiece, and the government itself, the newspaper is the victim both of its lack of advertising resources and its poor circulation.

As well as the calamitous economic situation, there are other obstacles to the establishment of a pluralist and quality press. In the main, these involve geographical limitations, a substandard level of cultural development, the state monopoly on printing and the shortcomings of journalistic training. 'Macedonian journalists are the mirror image of our society,' states Saso Ordanoski, director of the Macedonian Information Bureau. 'Our priority is to train newspaper editors in management procedures, to improve training for journalists while making them aware of their responsibilities and to endow the profession with an ethical code of practice.'

In the long term, however, according to Saso, it is learning the ropes of freedom that will be the most perilous exercise. 'For years, journalists handed their copy to a censor who decided what they could or could not write,' he observes. 'These days it's our job to distinguish between right and wrong, propaganda and news. We have to face up to our responsibilities.'

From La Lettre *of Reporters sans frontières. Translated by Tom Nicholls*

NATHALIE NOUGAYREDE

Beware the staircases of Tbilisi

Three years after independence, the Georgian press is in a sorry state: disappearances, incarcerations and violence plague the media.

'Freedom? We still have a bit left, but I don't think it'll last,' says Tamara Chikovani, sub-editor in chief of *Droni,* one of Georgia's few independent newspapers. 'I'm worried that the authorities are going to carry on using economic difficulties as an excuse to shut us up completely,' she sighs. She has become resigned to putting up with 'pressures of all kinds'.

Last November, *Droni* published

an interview with Nodar Natadze, the leader of the Popular Front of Georgia, a nationalist movement which led the republic to independence in 1991. A few weeks earlier, on 8 October, Eduard Shevardnadze had announced Georgia's inclusion in the Commonwealth of Independent States (CIS). Scandalised by this gesture, which he regarded as 'bowing to the will of Moscow', the ageing Nodar Natadze hit back: 'Any Georgian parliamentary representative who supports this action should be strung up in public,' he declared in *Droni*. 'Some days later,' recalls Tamara Chikovani, 'the head of public prosecutions announced that our newspaper was guilty of inciting cruelty and treason. The trial continues.'

Banned newspapers, incarcerated journalists, sometimes subjected to torture, reporters who have 'vanished', acts of violence: the state of the Georgian press is a sad story. There is a certain irony in the fact that the country has been run for the last two years by Eduard Shevardnadze, erstwhile champion of *perestroika* and *glasnost*. A year of armed conflict in Abkhazia — an autonomous republic in Georgia currently seeking independence — and long months of civil war in the west of the country between Shevardnadze's partisans and those of the now dead ex-president, Zviad Gamsakhurdia, undoubtedly fostered the government's drift towards authoritarianism.

Press freedom was an early victim of the vicious crunch of military politics in a republic that became territorial prey for the 'warlords', who assumed quasi-feudal rights over entire regions. In mid-October 1993, Eduard Shevardnadze announced on television that the media had been brought to heel. The publications 'guilty of printing these provocative articles' would be subject to 'certain measures'. The result: closure of all non-government newspapers for two weeks in November, and a ban on any criticism of the authorities on television or radio. Unable to transmit because of 'technical difficulties', as the official statement explained, Ibervision, the only independent TV station, denied opposition factions access to its studios.

Throughout the autumn, journalists were questioned and detained for their political sympathies at the whim of Zviad Gamsakhurdia. Their crime was the possession of material that 'undermines the regime'. Invariably, the police claimed to have found 'pamphlets' or maybe 'a grenade'. A spokesman for Eduard Shevardnadze confirmed that five journalists were locked up in October, for periods ranging from three to 30 days. The minister of the interior categorically stated that 'nearly all of them' had been released — information unconfirmed at the end of February this year.

The most controversial case is the imprisonment of the chief sub-editor of the 'zviadist' *Iverla Spectrum*, who has been behind bars for over a month and a half. Irakli Gotsiridze, a 70-year-old, has been repeatedly beaten up by his Tbilisi gaolers. No western journalist has been let into the prison to pay him a visit. Got-siridze bears numerous scars. 'If his face has been re-arranged, the reason is that he's gone and fallen down a staircase,' explains a deadpan Djaba Ioseliani, leader of the 'Knights', the most powerful paramilitary militia in Georgia. His name heads the agenda of Eduard Shevardnadze's 'Committee for the State of Emergency.'

Several political parties have guerrillas at their disposal whose job it is to 're-establish order' in editorial drafts. Last November, a group of armed men, claiming to be members of the ultra-nationalist National Democratic Party, burst into the offices of the weekly independent *Seven Days*. The premises were ransacked and journalists were threatened for criticising the wife of the party leader.

With its record of inter-ethnic violence, the war in Abkhazia has probably demanded the highest ransom. According to a number of sources, eight journalists have been killed in Sukhumi, the Abkhazia capital, during the fighting. Following the capture of the city by Abkhazian forces, the numbers of incarcerations and cases of torture increased. Yuri Gaave, editor of *The Democratic Voice of Abkhazia*, is currently in a Moscow hospital, after being arrested in Sukhumi at the end of September. Three other journalists are still reported to be missing in Abkhazia.

Translated from La Lettre
by Tom Nicholls

HENRI FRASQUE

Chiapas: press not welcome

Not a single journalist was killed in the rebellion in Chiapas. Reporters were kept at arm's length while army helicopters shelled peasants in peace and quiet.

Who shot at Ismael Romero? On the morning of 3 January 1994, accompanied by other journalists, the reporter of the Mexican daily *La Jornada* was travelling along the road leading from San Cristóbal de las Casas to Ocosingo, in the state of Chiapas, which had been overrun for two days by guerrillas belonging to the Zapatista National Liberation Army (EZLN).

As they passed the Rancho Nuevo military base, shots were fired at the second car, despite the fact that it was clearly marked as a press vehicle, and Ismael Romero was hit three times. Fortunately none of the wounds were fatal. Although the identity of the perpetrators remains uncertain, a photographer who was with Romero in the car believes that the army was probably responsible for the attack, an accusation the government denies. In response to an enquiry by *Reporters sans frontières*, the press relations department confirmed that injuries sustained by journalists 'were not caused by weapons used by the Mexican army.' It added that 'the republican government and the Mexican army have given guarantees for, and taken measures towards, providing maximum safety for journalists in the area, particularly in places where confrontations between the armed groups and the Mexican army have occurred.'

On 5 January, to prove its good will, the government distributed white T-shirts with the legend *'Prensa'* to hundreds of journalists, photographers and cameramen present on the ground. Whether or not this was to provide the army with clearer targets is, as yet, unconfirmed. But on the morning of the same day, another group of journalists, in vehicles sporting white flags and press insignia, was attacked repeatedly by machine-gun fire from army helicopters on Santa Maria Auxiliadora, a hill near San Cristóbal de las Casas. 'There weren't any guerrillas in that area, just a house belonging to a family of peasants, and we don't know what happened to them,' recalled one reporter, a special correspondent for Agence France Presse (AFP).

In the end, a bunch of petrified journalists got away unscathed. Mistaking cameras for sub-machine guns and missing unmissable targets could have been the result of a hard night on the tequila, but was more likely a case of the army wishing to give the press a friendly reminder that it likes to quash its insurrections unobserved. The massive military counterattack which began that day came complete with a systematic blackout on media coverage, and pressmen were prevented from entering the combat zones. At the same time, directives were issued to radio and television stations 'encouraging' them to broadcast 'governmentally correct' information. 'We've not been able to carry out our work with absolute objectivity,' complain Mexican members of the Democratic Union of Journalists. In a press release they explained that the press had been forced to make do with 'what official sources tell us'. The reporters also denounced the frequent harassment and attacks to which they are subjected by elements of the Mexican army. The guerrillas, who have every interest in media attention, have not hesitated to turn to strong-arm tactics in the world of public relations. According to the weekly *Proceso,* two of its photographers were kidnapped by Zapatistas at Haixtan, before being bailed out with a 'war tax' of 700 pesos.

Translated from La Lettre
by Tom Nicholls

BORIS ADAM

Free forum

Vietnam may well be on the up and up economically, but nothing has changed in the state of its prisons nor the contempt in which it holds journalists.

Economic liberalisation has brought a rush of foreign investment: at least nine journalists are rotting in Vietnamese prisons for attempting to do their job, among them Doan Viet Hoat and six colleagues.

Between July and October 1990 they were guilty of circulating four issues of an underground paper *Dien Dan Tu Do* (Free Forum) which advocated democracy. On 9 July 1993, Doan was sentenced on appeal to 15 years' imprisonment and five years' house arrest.

While a prisoner at the Phan Dang Luu prison camp at Ho Chi Minh City, Doan drafted a letter which was smuggled out at the beginning of September and sent to international organisations who took up his case. As a result, in December 1993, the Vietnamese authorities ordered his transfer to the Xuan Phuoc prison in Phu Yen, an isolated town in North Vietnam, 650 kilometres away from his family in Ho Chi Minh City.

Translated from La Lettre
by Carmen Gibson

ROBERT MÉNARD

Shoot on sight

Since its launch on 31 May 1992, the pro-Kurd daily Ozgür Gündem *has been subjected to repression on a hitherto unknown scale. Eighteen of its employees have been killed, dozens more imprisoned and tortured.*

In his office on the second floor of the premises of *Ozgür Gündem*, a stone's throw from Istanbul's Blue Mosque, Osman Ergin, the paper's lawyer, scarcely looks up as the two police officers deliver the notice of seizure from the state prosecutor. He shrugs; since the paper was launched, all but 10 of its issues have had legal proceedings instigated against them. There are currently 190 lawsuits in progress.

Almost daily, police confiscate copies which are still on sale when the judgements are handed down. They justify their action under Article 8 of the anti-terrorist legislation that prosecutes 'propaganda' which undermines 'the national or territorial unity of the Turkish state'. Ironically, it was this same law which, when it was passed in April 1991, enabled the release of many political prisoners. The present government's onslaught on the press and all things Kurdish is a reversion to the harsher climate of an earlier regime. The Association of Contemporary Journalists, the only professional body which counts Turks as well as Kurds among its members, maintains that in the course of 1993 this law was used to imprison 150 journalists and writers. The legal system is working overtime. According to Yasar Kaya, lifelong Kurd militant and a wealthy businessman, the 190 lawsuits in progress against *Ozgür Gündem* alone amount to 9 billion Turkish lira (c. US$650,000) in fines and 500 years in prison sentences, not one of which has to date been upheld by the Supreme Court of Appeal.

After a lull in the fighting between the PKK and the Turkish army between March and May last year, fighting has broken out with renewed ferocity and violation of human rights on both sides. Ankara has been trying to establish, once and for all, links between *Ozgür Gündem* and the PKK. It is no secret that Abdullah Ocalan, alias Apo, head of the PKK, writes a weekly column for the paper under a pseudonym. In a search for more concrete evidence, the authorities mounted a raid on the paper's offices in Istanbul and South East Anatolia — official title of Turkish Kurdistan — on 10 December last year. An intensive search produced only two 7.65 pistols: purchased in self-defence, argues the paper's lawyer.

However, up to 150 of the paper's employees were arrested including Gurbetelli Erzoz, the paper's chief editor. Meanwhile, as the police spent the rest of the day combing the building, the writer Yasar Kemal held an impromptu press conference on the pavement. It was the first time Turkey's most eminent writer had come out publicly in support of the pro-Kurd daily. His outspoken, 'Enough is enough', has been taken up by many others in Turkey since.

Toward the end of 1993, the German and French governments outlawed a number of Kurdish organisations operating on their territory, claiming they were 'terrorist' operations. Ankara understood it was open season on the Kurds and the media without fear of international repercussions: a significant increase in repression coincided with the French and German announcements. According to lawyers representing the Turkish Organisation for Human Rights, the number of preliminary investigations against the press increased fivefold, at times for no more than the simple use of the word 'Kurdistan'.

To date, none of the lawsuits filed following the murders and many instances of torture against *Ozgür Gündem's* staff has led to an arrest. That Yasar Kaya's paper is in sympathy with the PKK to the extent that it never prints any criticism of Apo's party is not in doubt. But it remains the only daily in Turkey to expose the situation in Kurdistan and the daily violations of human rights suffered by its people. To silence it would deprive a whole people of a voice.

Translated from La Lettre
by Carmen Gibson

MINORITIES

PETER CALVERT

The indians of Chiapas

Remote and isolated, Chiapas remains the poorest and most deprived Mexican state. The New Year rebellion of its Mayan population had been long foretold and should have come as no surprise

When the previously unknown Zapatista National Liberation Army (EZLN) seized control of three towns in the southern Mexican state of Chiapas in the new year, it was a world sensation. Around these three — Ocosingo, Altamirano and Las Margaritas — they established a 'liberated zone'; in a fourth, the historic tourist site San Cristóbal de las Casas, they ransacked the Palace of Justice and set fire to it before retreating into the mountains to the north of the city. The former state governor, Absalón Castellanos Domínguez, was seized at his cattle ranch, bundled into a truck with two of his cows, and taken with them as a hostage. In their manifesto, *Today we say enough!*, the EZLN made their reason clear. The regional bosses (of whom Castellanos was the most hated) had stolen their lands from them. 'We possess nothing, absolutely nothing,' it said, 'no home, no land, no work, no education.'

The Mexican government, busy celebrating the success of its long negotiations for entry into the North American Free Trade Area

(NAFTA), was much embarrassed. Its first response attempted to play down the importance of the events. The second blamed them on infiltrators from neighbouring Guatemala. But, as reporters flocked to the scene from the rest of the world, it was soon clear that the official view ignored the central problem, the condition of the local people. This was not just a minor local difficulty, nor was the problem simply one of 'news management'. Within a week, the guerrillas had extended their control to the towns of San Miguel and Guadalupe Tepayac, the country was on nationwide alert, a fifth of Mexico's army had been deployed to the region, the number of dead had passed the hundred mark, and reports of summary executions and other atrocities had begun to come in. The President accepted the urgent advice of the Bishop of San Cristóbal, Monseñor Samuel Ruiz, and appointed a leading political figure to act as a mediator.

Chiapas was and is one of the most 'indian' of Mexico's states. But in a country as regionally diverse as Mexico it is not typical. Geographically the Chiapas highlands are part of Central America, rising steeply beyond the flat lands of the Isthmus of Tehuantepec. In the colonial period they formed part of Central America, then called the Captaincy-General of Guatemala. With the fall of the First Empire in Mexico in 1823 and the secession of Central America, Chiapas was left behind in Mexico. The coastal region of Soconuzco, the main route to the south, was disputed territory. This was soon annexed by Mexico and a later plebiscite confirmed that it would stay there.

However, Chiapas remained isolated from the mainstream of Mexican life. The immediate benefit of this was that the region was largely untouched by Mexico's civil wars. There were two major revolts in the 19th century against what the Indian majority saw as continued Spanish-style domination by the big landowners. Otherwise they continued to maintain a structure of village life and family relationships that had endured for more than a thousand years. Even the Revolution of 1910 aroused only distant echoes, since its contesting parties were largely excluded from Chiapas by the decision of the then Bishop of San Cristóbal to arm the peasants. When, in the last military revolt of 1929, General Cándido Aguilar took refuge there, his men deserted and his colleague General Salvador Alvarado was murdered by his own troops.

JULIO ETCHART/REPORTAGE

But the long-term consequences of isolation were serious. Even in the reforming 1930s the local inhabitants found many of their petitions for land reform ignored by the government in Mexico City. Land reform was both late and incomplete. On the other hand, in 1950, with the extension of the Pan-American Highway to San Cristóbal de las Casas, their traditional ways of life, for almost the first time since the Conquest, were abruptly broken. Within a decade the buses sweeping through the state capital, Tuxtla Gutiérrez, on their way to and from the frontier, were accompanied by an influx of new ideas, new products and new government initiatives.

Ethnically the inhabitants of Chiapas are Maya. Their languages are part of the Maya family of languages, the dominant one of which is Tzotzil, the language of the 'people of the bat'. Other indians taking part in the revolt come from the Tzeltal and Chol.

The Conquest brought Christianity. Churches replaced pyramids. Towns replaced the old ceremonial centres. The use of Spanish for trading purposes slowly spread. But the villagers maintained their traditional way of life, though today Tzotzil is not taught in schools. 'Encapsulated' in their hamlets, the villagers' structure of public offices was slowly adapted to the new order and they transferred their ceremonial observances to shrines in nearby mountains.

As the Harvard Chiapas Project's study of Zinacantán demonstrated as recently as the 1960s, even their economic system proved resistant to change. Important, even essential, new products — chickens, pigs, donkeys, machetes — were accepted. But the trading patterns remained the same as those that can be reconstructed for the ancient Maya. Many still wear traditional brightly-coloured woollen garments, live in thatched wattle-and-daub houses and practice 'slash and burn' agriculture. But as their numbers have increased, they have outgrown the diminishing amount of land left to them. Some have, with government encouragement, set out to claim new landholdings from the lowland Lacandón jungle, home to the tiny band of nomadic Lacandón indians.

But, despite ineffective attempts to preserve what remains, two-thirds of that has now vanished. On most indicators, Chiapas today ranks as the poorest and most deprived Mexican state. A third of the households have no electricity, 40% have no running water. The state ranks last on major

Mexico City 1993: 'Give us back our land'

indicators of literacy (which means, of course, literacy in Spanish). It is also the state with the most persistent accusations of human rights violations, especially the use by landowners of *pistoleros,* in conjunction with the army and the police, to drive the Indians off their lands.

Three things have acted to precipitate the crisis which had long been foretold: the discovery of oil, making one of the poorest states overnight potentially the most energy-rich in the nation; the dismantling by the Salinas government of the trade barriers that protected Mexican farmers from an influx of cheap grain from the USA, and threatened them with instant bankruptcy; and, paradoxically, the efforts of the government to avoid this. Chiapas was targeted for special assistance under the government's anti-poverty Solidarity Programme. But its traditional patrimonial structures were left untouched. And with a former governor, Patrocinio González, serving as interior minister in President Salinas' cabinet, any hope of appeal to the central government seemed to have been cut off. Revolutions tend to break out in a changing situation: when things that have got better suddenly get worse, or when, having got worse, they start to get better.

BABEL

SABINE GOODWIN

Unrecognised in Israel

The first in a series focusing on the voices of those seldom heard, rarely listened to: voices silenced by poverty, prejudice and exclusion

Palestinians living as Israeli citizens within the recognised borders of Israel today constitute 18% of the population. Since the creation of the state in 1948, the Arab Palestinians (totalling 800,000, excluding the population of East Jerusalem) have suffered discrimination and become second-class citizens of a democratic state which continues to deny them fundamental human rights.

Around 50,000 live in 'unrecognised' villages, many of which predate the creation of the state; others were established near their original sites following evacuation and demolition during and after the 1948 war. Since then, the villages have not been 'recognised' — recorded — on official maps. This, say government authorities, is because they have been built on designated agricultural land. This has not prevented the later construction of Jewish settlements on or near the site of an evacuated Palestinian village.

Since their villages are unrecognised, the homes of the 'Arab Israelis' — the official designation — who live there are illegal; despite repeated applications for building permits, villagers are prohibited from constructing new buildings or adding to existing ones. The majority of the 120 villages are not linked to any water network nor connected to any electricity grid. None have access to government health services or sewerage systems. They rarely have an official school, and are usually several kilometres away from main roads with public transport. Children are forced to walk long distances to get an education; most, particularly girls, do not continue beyond elementary schools.

Control of the land is used by the Israeli government to maintain the Jewishness of the state: 93% of the country's territory is in government hands. The casualties of this land policy are the land and property rights of the indigenous Palestinians. Dina Rachewsky, director of the Division of National and Regional Plans at the Ministry of the Interior, claims that official aerial photographs taken before 1948 support the Israeli claim that there were no villages on the sites of the unrecognised villages. These include villages I visited which have graves going back more than a century. She also disputes the figures provided by Palestinian organisations of Arabs living in these villages. The Association of Forty, an organisation which groups all the unrecognised villages in the north, has a census of the north and Haifa regions amounting to 10,000 people. There has been no official census of the Bedouin in the Negev desert in the south since 1983, but associations working in the region estimate that of the 80,000 Bedouin, around 40,000 live in the unrecognised villages.

Between 1976 and 1986, three committees were set up by the government to examine the problems of the unrecognised villages. The Markovitch report, published by the last of these in 1986, exacerbated their situation. Arguing that Arabs who had already built houses were law breakers and should not be granted retroactive permits, the report recommended an iron fist policy. It urged the demolition of thousands of houses against which demolition orders had already been issued, and proposed the institution of a special category of 'grey houses' denied any access to services: those living in the so-called 'grey areas' could continue to do so for a period determined by the relevant district planning committee. It insisted that once a house was deemed unsuitable for habitation it would be destroyed. The report also proposed to empower district commissioners with the ability to issue administrative detention orders without resorting to the courts.

The government is determined to force people off their land. The villagers are equally determined to remain where their families have always lived and where their forefathers are buried: to stay on their land and continue their agricultural tradition; to live, legitimately, in the houses they have built.

If life in the villages of the north is harsh, in the south conditions seem even more hopeless. The majority of the Bedouin are no longer nomadic; approximately half have moved to seven officially designated settlements located in 20% of the pre-1948 Negev desert area (the rest has been taken over for military operations), while the remaining 40,000 live in unrecognised settlements under constant surveillance and threat of demolition. Electricity is provided by generators which are only switched on for a few hours in the evening. Water is installed at the expense of the villagers, often from a neighbouring kibbutz which may turn it on and off at will. There are elementary schools in the south but they are overcrowded, ill-equipped and standards are low. No health facilities are provided by the government and medical help can be miles away. Every month an aeroplane flies over the villages checking for illegal building; demolition orders follow with one month in which to comply. The Bedouin are denied access to planning permission and legal redress is lengthy, expensive and usually fruitless.

Domeida 1993: children of the villages

The Bedouin live with constant pressure from the 'Green Patrol' of the Ministry of Agriculture and the Israeli Land Authority to move to one of the seven designated settlements — 'concentration settlements' to their inhabitants. Although there is electricity and water, there is no sewerage, housing is cramped and there is no land for any kind of husbandry. The settlements lack any economic base or employment. According to

ASSOCIATION OF FORTY

AbuCaf, Israel: soon to be taken over

Rachewsky, the new regional plan for the Southern District proposes to enlarge the seven Bedouin towns and give them agricultural land.

Unlike the villages in the north, which since 1988 have united to fight the state in the Association of Forty, the Bedouin tribal culture militates against any concerted action — the only possible means of change. Above all, they are unwilling to believe that a legitimate government can and will take away their land. Many of the Bedouin hold the title deeds to their land conferred during registration under the British Mandate. Though apparently worthless today, their owners retain their faith in the pieces of paper that evidence their ownership of land they have occupied often for more than 200 years.

Esther Levinson, a town planner working with the Association for the Support and Defence of Bedouin Rights, explained the difficulties she met in working with the Bedouin. The town of Omer, for instance, is expanding and, according to existing plans, will soon take over the land of AbuCaf. A naive disbelief in the unthinkable has inhibited any action by the Association on behalf of the Bedouin of AbuCaf to fight the takeover.

In the north, the unity of the Association of Forty has begun to have an effect. In May 1992, six of the 40 unrecognised villages were recognised by the government. In Domeida in the Galilee, the situation has already improved dramatically despite bureacratic delays and the enormity of practical problems. The villagers are still waiting for a proper map of the village and planning permission for the installation of services; but a road to the village has been built and a telephone for the 380 inhabitants has finally arrived.

But despite Rachewsky's assurances that her department has recently made arrangements for the villages to have water, telephone and other services, for most of them nothing has changed. The 300 inhabitants of Arab El-Naim still live in the tin shanties they built on the remains of their old stone houses destroyed by the Israeli army in 1964; demolition orders are a daily fact of life; on the fragment of land unappropriated in 1964 there is no water supply and agriculture is impossible.

Children from Arab El-Naim go to school in Sackhnin some 10km away, but it is rare for a child to complete high school. In Ein Hud, which has the only official elementary school in the region, children who wish to go to school beyond eighth grade must travel 15-20kms.

In Israel discrimination adds a further dimension to the usual divisions of rich and poor, those with rights and those without. And the two communities are always in each other's sites across the divide. The village of Ein Hud is built some 2km away from its original site, now inhabited by Israeli Jews and known as the 'artists' village'. From their illegal homes and makeshift dwellings, Arab families, who were moved by the military for six months and were never able to return, overlook their former homes. Driving over the hill towards Arab El-Naim, a warren of tin shanties, you can see the tower blocks and villas of Jewish Karmiel. The other lifestyle is always in view.

Alone among the members of the Association of Forty, the villagers of Kumeirat finally bowed to government pressure and left.

Today and every day an old man returns to Kumeirat to sit beneath a tree staring at the land that once belonged to him and his family. Other families come when they can. They speak of their trips like wedding parties; they take a picnic and sit beneath a fig tree near to their soil. They still grow vegetables and fruits on this land there is nothing, they say, that tastes so special.

Life under threat

The Palestinians of the unrecognised villages talk of a life characterised by government oppression, disappointed hopes and fear of the future. Worst of all, they say, is the constant threat of demolition

In El-Sayyed, Ayesh tells his story. 'I built a large house for my growing family on my land. After serving the demolition order the authorities came to knock it down. I dared to build another in its place. Again a demolition order was deposited at the door, only this time I had to pay a fine of 5,000 NIS (around US$3,000) and was ordered to demolish the house myself or to pay the authorities to do it for me. It was February and it was snowing really hard. I pleaded with the authorities to let me and the family stay at least until the weather improved: my wife had given birth just a few days previously. They wouldn't listen; I got my friends and we demolished the house ourselves.

'I bought an old bus for the family to live in. Every day for six months the Israeli Land Authority came and told us we had to leave the bus, that it was illegal.'

The family now lives in an open tent — technically also illegal — where we sat to talk. What was more important to Ayesh was that he had stayed. As he showed me his old bus, still there in the village although the family are forbidden to live in it, he asked, 'Am I mad? Do you think I am mad to have stayed with all these problems? Sometimes I wonder if it is me who is wrong to feel the way I do'

In AbuCaf, Abrahim speaks about his house which was demolished in 1988. 'I was sentenced to five months' imprisonment for building the house illegally. I was a schoolteacher for 17 years. I spent two months in Ramle top security jail and completed three months of organised labour after taking the case to the High Court.' Convinced he was used as an example to frighten others, he told me: 'In the real Israel, we are the slaves.'

In Rumeihat, Nazma was issued with a demolition order for her house in early November 1993. 'A few months earlier I had built a two by two metre extension. I am nearly 75 and I broke my leg and I couldn't go to the toilet in the bushes behind the houses any longer. I've lived in this house for more than 20 years, in conditions hardly fit for a donkey.

'If an illegal extension is built onto an already illegal construction, the whole building will be issued with a demolition order. When the man from the Ministry of the Interior came in his jeep to take pictures, I knew what would happen. Within weeks I was issued with the demolition order. The same thing is happening to my brother. Thirty years ago he built a shed for his animals. Now they are going to demolish it just because he renewed the corrugated iron roof.'

In Arab El-Naim, there are no water supplies. Residents complained: 'We have to transport our water supplies by tractor from neighbouring villages. It is expensive and the quality of the drinking water is perhaps not what it should be. Two years ago there

SABINE GOODWIN

Nazma of Rumeihat

was an epidemic of jaundice in the area as a result of contamination, and one child died. The use of water has to be carefully calculated; we can't grow any kind of fruit or vegetables on the land that remains accessible to us because there simply is not enough for everything. A water pipe was installed by the Association of Forty eight months ago, but the Misgav Council still refuse to connect the pipe to water supplies at a Jewish settlement only one kilometre away.'

In Al-Azazmeh, a village of 10,000 people, things are even worse. 'The village is situated opposite Ramat Trovat, an industrial chemical site responsible for the disposal of national toxic waste. We live in a permanent cloud of industrial dust. We are permanently exposed to the odours of a nearby power station. Women have miscarriages and children feel ill and dizzy. The plants and olives we grow just die.'

ASSOCIATION OF FORTY

Domeida: the water has arrived!

'I wanted to go to school, but because of the costs and the danger my parents wouldn't let me,' explained a girl in Ein Hod. 'If we want to continue after the eighth grade we have to travel 15-20kms. Transport costs 600 NIS a month. It is 3.5km by dirt track road to the main road, and it is dangerous to walk it: it's not just that it's isolated, there are wild animals roaming the area. We girls don't usually go on with our education.'

While I was still in Ein Hod, the only girl from the village who does go to school in Haifa, 20km away, arrived back exhausted after walking the 3km short cut, steep and uphill all the way. She was too tired to talk to me.

'If someone is sick in Ein Hod, we have to make the 3.5km journey down the dirt track to the neighbouring kibbutz where there is a health centre,' the women of the village told me.

'It is impossible for most of us in the unrecognised villages to continue our farming tradition. Even if there are water supplies, it doesn't seem worth growing crops when our ownership of the land is so uncertain and transitory. Like the rest of the Palestinians, we have become a class of low-paid migrant labourers. We Palestinians have always been land owners and farmers, but as immigrant Jews are taught how to till the land, the Palestinians are excluded from continuing a tradition they are more than qualified to pursue. There is no economically viable work in the villages, nor any provisions for employment in the seven designated settlements in the south. Men have to go off to work all day, leaving the women and children alone and isolated without vehicles.'

'I do not hate the Jews, I hate the government and what they are doing to us.'

'We despise the system that does such things to us and the people who run it.'

In Arab El-Naim, Mohammed, then 4, still remembers what happened the day the army came to destroy his village in 1964. 'One morning the men left for work, but an hour later they returned because they had seen so many soldiers surrounding the village. Then the soldiers came and told everyone to take what was theirs and leave their houses. People who refused to move were dragged out. Everybody was herded to the top of the hill behind and had to watch as the army took four hours to demolish and destroy their homes. The people came back and built tin shanties, all they could afford at the time, on the remains of their old stone houses. Today demolition orders are issued every time we attempt to improve these same tin houses.'

From Rumeihat, a group of 10 houses within yards of the recognised village of Ipnin, the lights and buildings of modern Haifa are directly in view. Nazma is confronted with the contrast every day as she washes her own clothes and dishes by hand, with water from a bucket. I ask her what she feels about the distance that separates her life from that in the city. Her answer is fatalistic: too many years have passed and she has ceased to hope for change.

Mohamed, Nazma's brother, speaks of Israeli democracy. 'There is only one democratic day in Israel and that is the day of the Knesset elections. Even then they don't leave us to enjoy that day but come bothering us with their empty promises to improve our situation. Do you feel that this is a democratic state when you go from an Arab village to a Jewish settlement?'

'The identity of the Palestinians who are forced to live in this way depends on the land, on our land. The soil is part of our culture and our existence. The land is our heritage, our roots. It is where we belong and we can never rightly leave it.'

In Kumeirat, a woman describes the unique taste of a single green pepper, as if the whole meaning of life was in that flavour.

'The El-Okbi were made to leave their old tribal village of Hura in 1951. We were told it was because of Israeli military operations, and were assured that we could return within six months. From 1952 until his death in January last year, my grandfather Sliman El-Okbi, the sheikh of the tribe, tried to get the land back,' Sliman's granddaughter Sanaa tells me. 'The El-Okbi tribe remained and still remain in the now illegal settlement of Hora. The government moved us here legally in 1951, but later they declared the site illegal. He never felt it was right to develop our place here; he always believed we were going back to our land.'

Their own land remains empty, nothing there, just a closed area for military operations. The original village was flattened and everything destroyed. Sanaa showed me the remains of her great-grandfather's gravestone strewn on the ground as the bulldozers left it. 'We stay here where they moved us because at least we can keep animals and grow what we need in a way that reminds us of our heritage and our land. We refuse to be treated like dogs: to move to the new legal settlement of Hora would be like giving away all our dignity and freedom.'

Most villagers speak positively about the Palestinian-Israeli peace process, but felt excluded and uncertain what the future held for them. 'What peace?' they asked. 'They have sold us for the peace,' Mohammed says. 'For there to be peace in the Middle East, there must be peace inside Israel first. There is no such peace.'

'They must admit that we are citizens too. Until they do, we will live here and die. We will never leave,' says 64-year-old Hujirat of Sarkis.

Sabine Goodwin spent time in the unrecognised villages in 1993 and again in 1994. She wishes to thank the Association of Forty and the Association for the Support and Defence of Bedouin Rights.

SABINE GOODWIN

Arab El-Naim 1993: home from school in Sackhnin

REVIEWS

ALBERTO MANGUEL

One thousand and one years of censorship

The Arabian Nights: a companion
by *Robert Irwin*
Allen Lane/Penguin, 1994, £20 pb

Several years ago, in Madrid, a taxi-driver pointed out to me the capital's uninspired monument to Cervantes. 'He wrote *Don Quixote*,' the driver informed me. 'It's a book so mammoth, it runs to hundreds of volumes and no-one has ever read it in its entirety.'

Vastness is one of the attributes of fame; generations of enthusiastic worshippers have multiplied the volumes lost in the Library of Alexandria, the beds in which George Washington slept, the number of Casanova's mistresses, the weight of Orson Welles, the splinters of wood rescued from the True Cross. Much the same can be said of the seemingly infinite collection known as *The Thousand and One Nights* which began life sometime in the Middle Ages as a hundred or so linked tales and now occupies, in Sir Richard Burton's translation for instance, sixteen pompous volumes. A thousand nights must have appeared to the earliest audience as an immensely vast time for Sheherazade to tell her stories; adding one final night was a stroke of genius that lent this vastness a terrifying precision. To speak of *The Thousand and One Nights* rings incommensurable and also true.

It is perhaps this far-ranging fame ('Fame is footnotes,' someone once said) that has led historian and novelist Robert Irwin to conceive of his informative and entertaining book as a 'companion' to the *Nights*. Less a companion than an introduction and less an introduction than an illuminating postscript, Irwin's book is not one to have at hand while browsing through the *Nights* — an activity I recommend as haphazard and solitary. Mia Gerhardt's *The Art of Story-Telling* (which Irwin generously praises) and the copious and scholarly notes of Edward Lane that accompany that other celebrated translation (Lane's notes were also published independently as *Arabian Society in the Middle Ages*) are 'companions' in a practical sense — but not Irwin's. Instead, his book is a romp of related essays on Oriental storytelling, low life in medieval Cairo, Arab erotica, sexual customs of the East, the history of the *Nights* as the history of its translations, and what Irwin calls 'Children of the *Nights*' — the inheritors of its literary tradition.

The first question anyone reading the *Nights* must ask is, what *Nights* are we reading? For centuries, Europeans have read variously censored versions (many of which Irwin analyses in a chapter aptly called 'Beautiful Infidels'). The first translator, Antoine Galland, who published part of the *Nights* in French in 1704, coyly excised from the stories all material he considered pornographic; Sir Richard Burton, in 1885, went the other way and highlighted the erotic aspects of the *Nights* with violently misogynistic and racist footnotes. Joseph Charles Mardrus, whose French version was published between 1899 and 1904, added to the *Nights* many ludicrously apocryphal passages and what Irwin calls 'revolting little anti-Semitic embellishments'.

For the European translator, the *Nights* had to fit either the notion of an Orient too crude to be apprehended — except implicitly — by an educated European audience, or so earthy that it had to be rubbed into the faces of that same audience too delicate for their own good. Translation became not the rendering into one language the text of another, but the tailoring of the foreign text to suit the translator's sensitivity. For the English reader who wants a fairly accurate version, Irwin recommends two, unfortunately incomplete. Husain Haddawy's (1990) and N J Dawood's (1973).

The *Nights'* sense of vastness is increased by the knowledge that, properly speaking, the collection has no beginning. Irwin devotes many pages to track the theories regarding the *Nights'* inception. According to Irwin, 'one of the oldest surviving manuscripts from the Arab world', dating from the 9th century, includes a fragment bearing the title *Kitab Hadith Alf Layla,* or *Book of the Tale of the Thousand Nights,* and 15 opening lines in which Sheherazade (spelled Shirazad) makes her earliest appearance. It is probable that this version was, in turn, a translation from the Persian; other orientalists have traced its origins to Mongol, Chinese or Indian sources, to the narratives of Homer and to the *Epic of Gilgamesh.* Such diverse genealogy adds nothing to our reading of the *Nights* but reinforces the stories' universality; it explains less the book's coming into being than the sense of communality all readers experience when sharing the exotic adventures. The *Nights* are remote and mysterious, but in an oddly reassuring way.

The most obvious aspect of the *Nights* is that its stories are both astounding and familiar: they take place in a realm where the impossible is probable and where lives are well plotted and death serves a purpose. Appalling misogyny, sadistic violence, political and religious dogmatism surface in the *Nights* (as Irwin points out), but this is not what the reader remembers. No quiet desperation here: *Weltschmerz* is cast out to the sound of thunderclaps, *ennui* vanishes in puffs of genie smoke and under the glare of hidden treasures. We are all chosen, like Aladdin, for some mysterious design which we will accomplish after many tribulations and which will no doubt redeem us, we are all at the mercy of that night-blind camel, fate (the metaphor belongs to the poet Zuhar Ibn Abi Salama), nudging our knife-wielding hand, like Sinbad's, into the heart of our dearest friend. We are all betrayed like the King of the Black Isles or rewarded like the man who found his treasure in a dream. It may be helpful to remember that these magical and faraway plots precisely reflect our immediate and humdrum realities.

The *Nights* never had an audience that demanded from it documentary reality. Its Arab listeners followed in the stories the accurate labyrinth of a contemporary Cairo [where a new edition was removed from sale only last year. Ed] distorted by fantastic adventures, or else lost itself in the hazy labyrinth of an imaginary Baghdad made present through meticulous plotting. In either case, realism didn't matter: what mattered was that somewhere in the world extraordinary things happened to ordinary men and women, as well as to vizirs and princesses. Under other skies, the *Nights'* European audience peopled the stories with dread of what lay abroad and desire for what was foreign, and made real in their readings an imaginary place which was all dreams and shadows, and which nevertheless carried with it a sober seal of authenticity: had not the Arab storytellers themselves told these tales about their own people, tales which Galland first of all, and then Burton, Mardrus, Littmann and other reputable scholars so painstakingly translated for a Christian audience?

As Irwin points out, 'the *Nights* has received short and rather patronising shrift in general histories of Arabic literature' and in the present-day Middle East it 'is not regarded by Arab intellectuals as literature at all.' But little goes to waste in art: what one society will not use, another will treasure, what one sees as trite, another will recognise as rich and exotic. Edward Bulwer-Lytton is remembered for the first line of a notorious novel — 'It was a dark and stormy night' — which has become a catch phrase of the uninspired imagination. In Japan, the translation of Bulwer-Lytton's books in the late 19th century broke the Celestial Empire's literary isolation and provided Japanese literature with a fiction model that would eventually produce the masterpieces of Tamzaki, Kawabata, Kobo Abe, Shusaku Endo. The *Arabian Nights*, the soap-opera of the majestic Arab literature, nourished among the infidels such luminaries as Diderot, Montesquieu, Voltaire, Samuel Johnson, William Beckford, Horace Walpole, 'Monk' Lewis, Goethe, Dumas, Tolstoy, Byron, De Quincey, Coleridge, Wordsworth, Tennyson, Dickens, Oscar Wilde, Robert Louis Stevenson, Washington Irving, Edgar Allan Poe, Melville, Joyce, Chesterton, Proust, Jorge Luis Borges, Salman Rushdie, and the 'almost 700 hundred romances in oriental mode published in France in the eighteenth century'. 'It might have been an easier, shorter chapter', says Irwin, 'if I had discussed those writers who were not influenced by the *Nights.'* Among the incorruptibles: William Blake, Evelyn Waugh and Vladimir Nabokov.

Irwin's enthusiasm in his subject has most probably led him to meander, to repeat a number of facts with irritating frequency, and to make a few mistakes: a slip of the key attributes to Ulysses's encounter with the Cyclops in the *Iliad;* a curious use of the adjective 'naïve' qualifies the ways in which the *Nights* are supposed to have influenced the fictions of Borges — but these are quibbles. When Irwin strays from his point, the reader is rewarded with all kinds of arcane wonders. During these excursions, we are informed that Cairo thieves sent tortoises with lit candles on their backs into the houses they wished to burgle; if the house was occupied, the owner would cry out something like 'Oh, look! there's a tortoise with a candle on its back, I wonder what it's doing in my house,' and the thief would be thus warned off. We are reminded of the innumerable hells promised by Allah, in the least of which are one thousand mountains of fire, on each mountain seventy thousand cities of fire, in each city seventy thousand castles of fire, in each castle seventy thousand couches of fire and on each couch seventy thousand manners of torment. We are told of the curious Cairo archive known as the Geniza, assembled by medieval Jews who, in awe of the name of God, refused to throw away any scrap of paper that might bear His name and thereby preserved all manner of writings, from laundry lists and prayers to marriage contracts and poems. We are initiated into the delights of bums (both male and female) which the medieval Arabs quite rightly held in high esteem. We are warned against the *udar,* a monstrous creature that rapes men and leaves them to die of a worm-infested anus. We are taught to interpret old-fashioned gestures such as striking the left hand against the right (to signify regret), putting one's finger in one's mouth (to indicate that someone is like one's own soul) or biting one's hand (to show repentance). We are retold some of Sheherazade's choicest tales (such as the marvellous ordeal of 'Judar and His Brethren', which I, for one, had certainly forgotten, in which the hero must confront a demon in the shape of his mother and, *pace* Freud, force her to undress), whetting once again our appetite for those endless nocturnal adventures. And this alone would suffice to recommend Irwin's book: as a bait to revisit or (blessed innocence!) to enter for the first time the convoluted and magical *Nights*. 'This *Companion*,' says Irwin in his Introduction, 'may serve as a guide into the labyrinth, but it offers no route out. But then, having entered the maze, why should one ever want to leave?' As most readers have found out for their joys, one does not.

SUZANNE GIBSON

The right to a language

Ours by Right — Womens Rights as Human Rights. Edited by Joanna Kerr, Zed Books, London/North-South Institute 1993, £12.95 pb, £32.95 hb

In the name of human culture, tradition and religion, women are genitally mutilated, bought and sold as commodities, forced into marriage, tortured and imprisoned in the home, executed without trial by menfolk who think them unchaste, compelled to reproduce, denied rights to their children, debarred from economic independence, excluded from political participation. In some of these activities the political state and its agents are directly implicated. In others, men act of their own volition, in their own cause, but with the state's support or connivance. But these acts are not violations of human rights.

Apparently, no human right is violated when the wrong is in accordance with the traditions of a culture. Nor, it seems, is a human right a right when holy writ decrees an evil deed be done. And a human right abused is not a human wronged when the harm is done away from the public gaze and by an unpaid agent of the state.

But no: this cannot be. If it were, then what role would there be for the international human rights movement? *Of course* respect for human rights must transcend the particularities of culture, religion, state agencies. Except, that is, where the victims of human rights violations are women. Then it is different.

The contributors to *Ours By Right* wish to redefine violations of women's lives as violations of human rights. They have enlisted the unapologetic absolutism, and the unimpeachable moral authority, of the language of human rights on behalf of the women they represent. This language is impartial and unashamedly universalistic. It makes no apology for its repudiation of self-serving claims to sovereignty by governments; it determinedly refuses to countenance the evasions and excuses of those who violate its terms; and it continues dogmatically to assert what it knows is right. For all these reasons, the language of human rights is powerful. Women's rights activists in the developing countries, women at the bottom of the bottom, need just such a language.

And so do women in the developed world, but not for the same reasons. Contemporary Anglo-American feminism is bereft of the moral clarity of human rights discourse. It will never be perceived as impartial, committed as it is to challenging privilege long believed to be legitimate. Allied to a politics of identity and of respect for cultural diversity, Western feminism has become unable to declare itself a universal movement for all women. Stumbling over all the differences of race and class within the developed world, it is tripped up by the assertion, for instance, that genital mutilation is practised by women of certain cultures by their own choice.

And Anglo-American feminism has become less certain, decreasingly dogmatic, perhaps, in the face of the counter-arguments and complexities of sexual politics. So for women in the West, invoking the language of human rights signals both a desire to describe the real harsh pain of women's lives and an attempt to recast feminist ideals into a more resilient, a less yielding, form.

Read this book, though I doubt if you will enjoy it. Being based on the proceedings of a conference, it is not so much a collection of essays as a gathering up of talks. In consequence, all the pieces are short, frustratingly so in some cases, a mercy in others. Some contributions are frustratingly vague in their reportage of women's human rights violations. Others are frustratingly narrow in scope. But there are interesting and insightful papers here too. There is an informative essay on the telling diversity of misogynistic Islamic laws, by Marie-Aimée Hélie-Lucas, international coordinator of the 'Women Living under Muslim Laws Network'. There are concise strategic papers by Charlotte Bunch and Dorothy Thomas and a particularly interesting essay by Elizabeth McAllister on the hazards of attempting to use development aid as a means of procuring change in developing countries.

But in Joanna Kerr's concluding summary we sense emergent differences between conferees over priorities for change, cultural diversity, the role of first world women. The

JP CHARBONNIER/ CAMERA PRESS LONDON

unease echoes past disagreements and perhaps prefigures future rifts.

The language of human rights is powerful because it expresses a single, simple principle: no state can justify using coercive powers against its citizens as a means to political ends. (Human rights instruments do include the so-called 'second generation' rights to socio-economic security but not even in the developed world are these treated with any seriousness.) The language of women's rights has, on the contrary, become more complex and thus less compelling not because we talk too much, but because the matters we must talk about *are,* quite simply, more complex. Is the seductively powerful language of human rights so powerful that it may testify to such complexity and yet still retain its strength? I doubt it.

DORIS LESSING

Mad dogs and Chinamen

The Lost Boat. Avant-garde fiction from China. Edited by Henry Y H Zhao & John Cayley, Wellsweep Press, London, 1994, £7.95/$14.95 pb; £14.95/$23.95 hb

This collection of 'five short and three long short stories' is described as 'avant-garde' and the preface warns that it is meant to be read as literature, not, as fiction so recently has been in Communist countries, only from a social point of view. In this usage 'avant-garde' means writing that has had the brakes taken off, is no longer expected to whitewash reality: 'avant-garde' does not mean the writing is experimental, only that it speaks its mind.

We are told Chinese writing has been influenced by García Márquez, Borges, Salinger, but there is nothing of that here. This is realist writing. All these stories are brutal, violent. That has been China's experience this century. So it is not easy to read the tales solely with an eye to the literary quality, though even in places where the translation seems to be rough it is clear they are as good as anything written anywhere now.

For people in the West — that is, people interested at all in China — now is a time of revelation about that country. The biographical novel *Wild Swans*, by Jung Chang, which has been a best-seller in Britain, described, through the lives of three women and their men, three-quarters of a century of tumultuous experience. The latest films from China, *Blue Kite* and *Farewell My Concubine*, as well as the earlier *Red Sorghum*, tell the same story. All testify on the one hand to atrocious cruelties and suffering and, on the other, to the extraordinary robustness of the Chinese, who seem to survive everything fate can throw at them with morale and optimism intact. When a British publisher — Jonathan Cape — recently held a competition for novels written by people under the age of 30, twenty or so novels from Communist China were entered. They were in English, sometimes very good English, causing one inevitably to think how unlikely it is that any Britisher could write a novel in Chinese. The other surprising fact was that the subject of every one of these novels was the Cultural Revolution and its ravages. And when I was in China last year, sooner or later every conversation turned to that, after all, so recent upheaval. And with a balanced and reasoned assessment of it, although the people discussing it were all victims. There is a saying in China that from time to time there must come a century of upheaval, and then things go back to normal. Perhaps the apparent equanimity — certainly stoicism — is because, after this so terrible century, people expect things to settle down again.

Reading this collection it is necessary to remember that even if nothing of the kind is included here, stories (and novels) light in tone, humorous, even roaringly funny, are being written and published in China.

There is another surprising thing. Chinese writing is accessible to the Westerner, not at all — as I find with Japanese writing — exotic.

We are reading about people like ourselves, people who react as we do, whose hopes and expectations are the same, who think and judge as we do, even if their capacity for endurance seems well beyond our own. Incest, murder, war, executions, tortures, floods, earthquakes — so what's new? That is the note. Sometimes, though, a familiar chord: the war stories come from the same level of knowledge as Isaac Babel's.

The title story by Ge Fei is set in 1928 and civil war. 'The war had made him weary of these minor nuisances. He knew it was quite common for the relatives of soldiers killed in action to turn up unexpectedly at HQ and these strangers clutching notes with the names of their sons and husbands written on them would make ridiculous demands — asking for the belongings of the dead men or trying to find out all sorts of details about the solders' last hours.'

And now a surreal tale, 'The Mad City' by Wen Yuhong, that moves from the butchery of dogs to cannibalism, but is really a metaphor for political savagery. 'The following day in different markets across the city, sixteen real attacks on customers actually happened, one after the other — all of them just like the brothers'. Customers were seized, strung upside down from the branch of a tree —

and butchered. Within the next few weeks the whole town was infected with this madness.'

And there are many more in this volume, as startling and as different from each other as those above.

With China taking its place as a major power in the world, and with so much being written there, it is inevitable that more and more of its literature will be translated. Already we can see that this is a rich and varied feast. Meanwhile here is a sample — a nibble, as it were. The many titles of unknown novels and short stories, the many writers of whom we have never heard mentioned in the preface to this collection give us an inkling of what we may hope for.

Picture overleaf:
Wuxuan County: John Gittings

WEN YUHONG

The mad city

A dog was hanging upside down in a tree, a great gash torn in its belly. Two young men were in the process of tearing out the hot, seething innards — one grasping a dagger dripping with blood, the other's hands caked in blood. They were working with intense concentration. The spectacle was so horrible that passers-by could not bear to watch.

These last few years they must have slaughtered some four hundred dogs. Their techniques became more and more sophisticated. Every time they butchered a dog their spirits were soothed and they felt a special kind of pleasure. Whenever they saw a living dog leaping about or jumping up and down, they stared as if they couldn't believe their eyes. How could any dog be as happy as that, how dare it have the nerve to shake its head and wag its tail like that — right under their very noses. Their fingers would start to twitch as if they could already see the animal dismembered and subjugated, struggling powerlessly — its fresh blood dripping down. It was as if they could already see the steaming, palpitating organs and intestines — as well as plate upon plate of over-stewed, dog-meat chop suey.

They were blood brothers, totally inseparable and united by a bond of total dedication to one another. I don't know when, but there certainly must have been a time when they started this business of slaughtering dogs. They would hunt through the lanes and alleys of the town, and at each Korean noodle-house they'd be asked to go off and butcher a couple of dogs. The expenses they received were meagre, just a dish of casseroled dog-meat and something to drink. Drinking was something the brothers really did well; they could put away oceans of booze. They didn't eat much, but could easily get through several pints. They would drink till their faces were flushed, their heads swollen, and their foreheads covered in beads of sweat which dripped down onto the dining table.

Their lips were a dark purple, the corners of their mouths were fat, and they each had a mouthful of great, healthy, yellow teeth. It didn't matter if the beef stew wasn't tender, their sharp teeth would twist and grind away at it, gnashing backwards and forwards this way and that, and in no time they'd manage to gulp it down. When they were on the booze they could drink half the night away, and there wasn't a single Korean noodle-house that dared to kick them out. There was nobody who had seen the brothers drunk. They didn't talk to other people but once in a while would yell at the landlord to get them some food — 'Hey landlord, more food!' — in their rude voices, snapping their thick, yellow fingers. Afterwards they would talk to each other saying things nobody understood and laughing uproariously in their vulgar way.

When dogs saw the brothers coming it was as if they could smell the stench of butchery coming out of them. They would tear off, as fast and as far as possible, leaving not a trace of their existence behind. In the evenings, if the brothers went past houses where dogs were raised, the dogs inside would let out the most frantic howls — as if they never expected to live to see another day.

The brothers would invariably look at one another and burst out laughing, proud of their reputations.

They always kept gleaming daggers tucked into their belts, so the police didn't dare to meddle with them. The brothers both had official licences for this profession of specialist dog-butchers.

They rode huge motorbikes, wearing helmets and dressed from top to toe in leather. They would zip past your head tossing out great peals of laughter.

AS soon as the tradesmen saw the brothers coming into the market they would start to get agitated. They would rush forward to welcome them and exchange a few words of greeting, then give them a few samples of their goods.

When their hearts were set on the prospect of blood the brothers could not sleep. Their minds were focused on one thing and one thing only — butchery and more butchery. If there were no more dogs, they would make do with cats or even hunt rats. These creatures they would pin out on wooden planks, cruelly ripping open their bellies, and with their bare hands pull out the moist, slimy, sticky and still pulsing insides. At such moments they felt profoundly satisfied and totally forgetful of worldly things. They would hold the innards in their hands for a long time, gently squeezing them and delicately savouring the feel of the slippery organs, and only when they were cold, their vitality quite sapped, would they throw them away and rip out some more. Their greedy mouths would split wide-open, erupting with great belly-laughs. That was what they were like — a pair of hands still dripping blood onto the ground, and nearby, little corpses, still stretched out on the board, bellies completely voided. Hearts, livers, intestines were scattered any-old-where, on walls, floors, ceilings — here a string of intestines, there a large pool of bile — and a rising stench of rottenness which filled the whole room. Then they would sit down at the table, staring at their hands and watching intensely as little by little the blood there darkened and hardened, while the corpses slowly stiffened on the boards.

Then they were dead tired, their strength as exhausted as if they had fought some heroic battle or subjugated some band of marauding invaders. After a while, when their fatigue had abated and they were fed up with admiring their spoil, they would gather up all the bodies and innards, scrape the blood and bile off the walls, and toss the whole lot into a large cauldron of boiling water, sprinkle it with a pinch of salt and pour black soy sauce over the top.

THIS was the strangest city I had ever seen in the entire course of my life. I've been to all sorts of places, and passed the time of day with every kind of character — I've been genuinely shocked, frightened and disgusted by abnormal psychology, paranoia and barbaric cannibalism. But I have never before seen such a place, one with such a multitudinous population, yet all enveloped in such a suffocatingly negative pall.

A winding river coiled around the outside of the town, always threatening to flood. Inside, there was only a shallow, all but dry stream. I went to look at it, and even in summer, on days of torrential rain, it barely came up to a person's waist and was only something like a metre deep. The brackish water glinted in the sunshine. Wide banks of anaemic yellow sand were piled up along the shores on both sides. A reinforced steel bridge rose out of the sand. It was suspended high above the water, extending end to end fully a thousand metres. In summer the local kids played naked in the water. On both sides, the steep banks were overgrown with tall artemesia.

Other parts of the town had no stream at all. Of course the public park had a lake where rubbish floated — scraps of bread, ice-lolly papers, clumps of grass and other things people chuck away. The lake was the size of a mere pond but was crammed with innumerable pleasure boats, all bashing into each other, crashing and banging, sometimes producing a peculiar shrieking sound. A moat was in the process of being constructed around the outside of the city. I wondered if it was fated to become like the lake — filthy, stinking water and annoying scraps of waste paper.

You can imagine how dry the town was, mad winds and dust making everyone irritable. Huge numbers of chimneys gushed thick smoke out over the town, and the stench of sulphuric acid from the chemical factories spread everywhere. The city was so big, with such an enormous population and such strange varieties of madness. Truly I've never seen anything like it.

THE day came when the brothers' behaviour suddenly became the established norm in the city. Every young person copied them, studying their good example. Dog-slaughtering hadn't existed as a mania till then, but in the twinkling of an eye it permeated every corner of the city. Every day the doors of the Trade and Industry offices were crowded with people trying to wangle licences to set themselves up as professional dog-butchers. They queued up in long lines, all packed together. And hosts of young people streamed out of factories, institutions and schools, rejecting their previous work or study, and swaggering onto the streets to join the flood of frenzied dog-butchers. Each of them rode a great motorbike and zipped past your head. They had daggers tucked into their belts and they crowded into bars to drink themselves silly. They muttered streams of weird nonsense and let off peals of obscene laughter. And they began to hunt rats and cats, tossing intestines and internal organs about all over the place, afterwards throwing them into great pots of boiling water, stewing them till all the goodness was boiled out of them, and then gulping down the soup.

What the brothers did one day became all the rage in the city the next.

ONE day at a street market in the western part of the city, a young man arrived who wasn't acquainted with the place. He was a beef trader, tall and strong, clever and capable. When the two brothers entered the market at noon, the other tradesmen dropped their business and rushed forward to greet them. One after another they let the brothers pick out whatever goods they fancied. The young beef trader, however, just stood in front of his carving board, wondering what all the fuss was about. Why on earth should anyone want to lick the boots of rat- or cat-catchers. He and the two brothers stared at each other. The brothers' huge, gamblers' mouths and flat butchers' cheeks made the young man shudder.

That afternoon a mad wind started up, lifting the sand and even turning stones. Bits of cabbage, shreds of paper, rotting vegetable leaves, everything was whirled up suddenly into the sky. In front of the crowd, the two brothers tied the young butcher up, stuffed his mouth with pig offal, and hung him upside down from the branch of a tree in the market — in the same way they had done with the dogs. At that time of year the tree was almost bare. At the base of its trunk there was a huge, pitch-black hole full of creepy-crawlies. The brothers stripped the young man naked, tossing his clothes into the hole, then with a single slash of their knife, slit him from stomach to gizzard. His pale green intestines burst, slip-slopping, out. The mass of people crowded together in the market watched with the greatest relish. A gang of young men who were the brothers' particular fans didn't miss the least nuance of expression or movement of hand, keeping tabs on even the least discernible details. Some of them even acted out the scene at the same time.

That evening the exciting news of the brothers' deeds reverberated round the town. The business was discussed with glee in every household.

Like the eyes of wild animals glaring out from the jungle, lights blazed from every building, every house, penetrating the murky haze of the dimly-lit streets. Out of every window poured great gusts of laughter, as well as sounds of cursing. This went on till well past midnight when the lights were finally extinguished. On the streets outside it was pitch dark and a cold wind was blowing. Laughter just like the brothers' laughter, continued to spew out from the lips of the sleepers, bursting out of windows, ricocheting around and echoing wildly. Sleep-walkers rose from their beds, grabbed their food-choppers and began to whet them against the sides of big pickled-cabbage pots.

All night long the dreamers' ravings kept pouring into the dark sky above the town. They mumbled unspeakable horrors. There was the ceaseless rasping sound of sharpening knives. And on top of it all there was a continuous cackling of blood-curdling laughter.

THE following day in different markets across the city, sixteen real attacks on customers actually happened, one after another — all of them just like the brothers'. Customers were seized, strung upside down from the branch of a tree — and butchered.

Within the next few weeks the whole town was infected with this madness. Not only young people but even those of more advanced years were butchering right, left and centre. All night long terrifying sounds poured out from the city. The dreamers' sleep-talk became more and more horrifying, making your flesh creep. All night long, the awful sounds of knife-sharpening became more and more oppressive and nerve-racking. It was as if the whole town had been filled with a crazy singing and dancing—the slashing of hundreds of icy, gleaming knives.

THE municipal government sent in the local police to capture the brothers. But some people noticed that even in the ranks of the police there were many who had been responsible for butchering their 'clients'. The police stormed the brothers' residence, kicking in the front door, assault weapons at the ready. But the place was empty — just a cauldron of rat meat and innards stewed to a pulp. The police put down their weapons and shouted to the inn-keeper next door to bring them a pot of something alcoholic, then wrenching off rat thighs and scooping up portions of their innards, they sat down to feast, gorging themselves with great mouthfuls.

WITHIN a few days the brothers had reappeared in the city. They were still just the same, daggers tucked into their belts, riding great motorbikes, and rampaging about with a murderous look in their eye.

THE city was constantly enveloped in dense yellow smog. In the doorways of every shop there were fortune-tellers and palmists, young and old, men and women. Each of them clutched a great wad of gaudy cards and was dressed in a black padded coat covered with grease, stains and dust. They yelled loudly, bustling about this way and that through the crowd. The rain dripped slowly down from a grey sky, and yellow leaves covered the city, flying about or sticking soggily all over the black tarmac on the roads. The roads were pot-holed and loose stones rolled about on them. Every day the people flowed back and forth to work in great winding serpents; gathering, then disappearing into fathomless nooks and crannies

In front of the cinema and the theatre, people were bored stupid. Particularly since the theatre's doors had remained tightly closed for years. At the cinema they showed the same film, day in day out, three hundred and sixty days a year. The soundtrack coughed and spluttered out of a broken-toothed old projector. The ushers, both young and old, who were supposed to look after things, just fumbled about in the dark playing poker.

There were two occasions every year when there would be a remarkable hubbub on the playing field. This was when there was a national or international football match. Several hundred spectators would be crushed to death or trampled flat as they tried to catch a glimpse of the exciting battle. The young men who came out onto the field over successive months were like wild, unbridled horses. They would dash about hither and thither, bumping and bashing, twisting and turning, frothing at the mouth, hair all dishevelled.

THE first time I came to this town it happened to be right in the middle of the season of mad winds, during the time of year they called 'the fall that just *kills* you'. Gust upon gust of buffeting wind had demolished all the houses. Even hotels and large buildings which had been built to withstand earthquakes — all had collapsed. Spirals of dust swirled around on the road lifting a frenzy of waste paper, rotting wood and bits of old roof-tile. Enormous trees had come crashing down and lay silently on the sides of all the roads. Slender willow twigs grew up and danced proud in the angry wind. And on top of everything there was the black smoke rising silently from the rubble, the mad wind fanning it out everywhere.

I saw crowds of people, huddled group after huddled group of them, all sitting in the broken shells of the razed buildings. They threw poker cards down on the table with exaggerated force. On the corner of the tables a dark, carelessly stacked pile of banknotes was already heaped up. These people were dressed in long woollen coats and sucked hard at their cigarettes. Their brows were lowered and their foreheads furrowed as they clutched their cards in a death-like grip. The dark smoke painted their faces black and yellow, and the north-east wind, hooting and whistling from the rafters, came in bursts of hot waves. I saw small children huddled at random amongst the crowds. They too were smoking like old troopers, their penetrating, childish screams grating on the ears. All around were pieces of rotting wood, crumbling bricks — and right under their very noses, a tide of cockroaches and other insects scuttling back and forth in unbroken currents.

ON an empty part of the square, the two brothers had set up a boxing ring. Anyone who came to see the fight had to pay ten dollars. A great beast of a dog was brought out into the ring. Wearing only the scantiest of trunks and grasping their daggers, the two men did battle with the dog. The brothers had specially trained these dogs, and every day fed them wildcat, hare or rat — alive. This had turned the dogs into savage beasts. When they were hungry their eyes blazed, they bared their fangs and their ears pricked up. Their cavernous red mouths hung wide open, long tongues lolling out, and they let out blood curdling howls. They would leap at the brothers immediately, their sharp claws stripping bloody scales from the brothers' bodies and reducing their skimpy trunks to tatters. The men too became like wild animals, mouths hanging open and revealing their strong yellow teeth. Ducking and diving this way and that way, they would await the moment to seize their chance — to plunge a dagger down into the dog's throat. With the dog's claws still deeply embedded in their skin, there would be a little glugging noise, and gradually the dog's grip would be relaxed. It would stretch out and its body stiffened.

The audience watched goggle-eyed. Holding their breath, bodies utterly still, they would stare unblinking as the dogs leapt at the brothers.

Whatever the weather, whether it was blowing a gale or pouring cats and dogs, every day at mid-day the brothers would bring a dog into the ring for a performance. In order to experience the exquisite spectacle of this fierce battle, people would come from all over — some even by train from several hundred miles away. It didn't matter whether gales had destroyed their homes, or if they were soaked to the skin, their whole attention would be riveted, just waiting for the destruction of the howling dog.

EVERY day a battalion of girls trailed after the brothers. Their lips were painted bright red, their faces plastered white as paper, and dressed in the most fashionable clothes. Facing the crowd, they and the brothers would egg each other on with the most vulgar obscenities — and raising a storm of laughter from the audience.

There was one girl who had been with the brothers for a long time. Whatever the time of the year, she always wore the same black dress. She was one of the town's best-educated girls. People said her parents had agreed to her marrying a young man who had money as well as education. The townsfolk were green with envy.

But in this town, things are always twisted. The young man had graduated from university not long before. People used to say, look at him, he'll go far. He began to frequent bars and dance-halls, cleaning-up with his talk and his dancing. People still said that he was intelligent and capable, and sooner or later he'd be a high-ranking official. But the next morning he was discovered having committed suicide on his bed.

On the evening of her wedding the girl came running out. The following day, wearing a black dress, she appeared on the square with the brothers.

Like the brothers, she chain-smoked, which turned her nails yellow and made a green light shine in her eyes. She drank one glass after another too. She drank until steam came out of her mouth and she couldn't drink any more.

But she remained both lovely and exquisitely elegant. Her eyes became darker and colder, like the light in the winter sky. People often discussed her, and said that these eyes were strange. Her gaze seemed out of focus as if she wasn't looking at anything, and yet at the same time as if she could see everyone. Even when she looked at the brothers she appeared at a loss, as if looking at them without seeing them. She didn't laugh or cry, and didn't get angry; her voice and expression revealed nothing about her, but made it seem as if she was endlessly dredging the bottom of the ocean for a lost needle.

She got on extremely well with the brothers, thinking up ideas for them, as well as giving them her body. On New Year's Eve she got them to buy five hundred dollars' worth of fireworks, and then in the evening let them off in one fell swoop. The sky was lit up for all of three hours. She got the brothers to wrap up a dog's heart — bloody, dripping and still warm from the little bit of life left in it — and send it off to an old boyfriend. When he received it the young man nearly died of fright, and screaming for an ambulance, was rushed away to hospital. And she got the brothers to put on masks and rob a bank. Then, taking the bills they had snatched out onto the square, she threw them up in the air, watching with immense gratification as people leapt as high as twin-storeyed houses, a forest of arms reaching up to grab the beautiful notes. She and the brothers all wore daggers, and whenever they saw a parked car, they slashed deep holes in its tyres, then faded away into the night.

She also got on very well with the gang of girls who trailed after the brothers. She never interfered with them, just stood quietly to one side, watching as they and the brothers teased and flirted with one another. She never wore make-up and seldom dressed up, but was, nonetheless, wonderfully turned-out, with her glossy hair swept back off her face naturally.

She liked to drink till she was tipsy, and would run out completely naked and roll in the snow. She liked to go out in summer storms, without any protection — the rain-drops all whipped up in the streets by the wind — running through the heaviest rain and get soaked through.

The other females in the gang were jealous of her status with the brothers, and practically the whole town detested her, but each time they thought of murdering her, she was saved by the brothers, who discovered the plot in the nick of time and put a stop to it.

THE police started a hunt for the brothers and for her. They put an end to the fighting in the square, which set everyone complaining. The brothers' dog-butchering licence was revoked. And at every Korean noodle-house a platoon of policemen was stationed to keep watch over the landlords so that they wouldn't hire the brothers to go dog-butchering.

IT seemed to be the most peaceful day of my stay in the city. Every street, large or small, was flooded with yellow uniformed policemen. They grasped electric batons, had rifles slung from their belts, and their shouts thundered out everywhere. The landlords were forever putting glasses of beer into their hands. 'My dear officer. Sir, please do have one on me. Have one on me.'

It appeared that the young people with daggers slung at their waists were no longer to be seen. Nothing was to be heard except the policemen's motorbikes hooting eerily. At the doorway of the cinema, people were still bored stupid. The theatre was closed fast.

NOW it is winter, and the murky yellow waste gases are still spreading out over the city. The choking smell of sulphuric acid, of dust and of coal smoke is denser than ever, permeating every corner of this place. The trees on either side of the main roads have become pitch-black and heaped up by the side of the road, even the spoilt snow is pitch coloured, ulcerated with a thousand holes. The biting north wind blows right through people. And at night-time the city is still filled with stories of horrors recalled by the dreamers, and the sound of sharpening knifes.

I thought the city really would quieten down for good. On the day I left, I asked a policeman standing beside me — the same kind of young man as the brothers — 'Have you really killed them as people say?' He gave me a sly look and told me in a low voice that the brothers had secretly joined the police long ago. Seeing my surprise, he went on with even greater pride. 'The brothers are going to start up again in the spring, this is just a period of rest and consolidation. The cat is hibernating now. It's like this every year.' He spoke without the least trace of caution. 'And the girl?' I asked. 'What about her?' 'What girl?' His brow furrowed with distaste. 'They killed her ages ago.' 'Killed her? — the brothers?' 'Ah, no—it was the gang. When the brothers were off their guard, they took their chance and killed her.' He put his hands round his own throat to show me. 'She was a real pain in the arse you know,' he added.

From The Lost Boat: Avant-Garde Fiction from China, *selected & edited with an introduction by Henry Y H Zhao (Wellsweep, 1993)*
Illustrations by Vladimir Sieladcou

JOHN GITTINGS

The truth behind the fiction

The Chinese government says it is a vicious slander. Some anthropologists say it is a myth which never actually occurs. Wen Yuhong's story *The Mad City* is clearly an allegory for the suppressed violence of a sick society, whether it is that of China or the modern world. But there is an authenticated instance of cannibalism in recent Chinese history which vividly illustrates the social pathology described by Wen. Friends of China — among whom I include myself — have difficulty in coming to terms with this episode but it has to be honestly faced.

For a very short period of time, in conditions of immense political turmoil and social disorder during the 'Cultural Revolution', in a few districts in one region of China, victims of factional fighting were not only slaughtered but carved up so that portions of their bodies — livers, hearts and flesh — could be eaten. The worst outbreak of this 'revenge cannibalism' took place in Wuxuan County, Guangxi Autonomous Region, in May-July 1968, where some 70 victims were recorded. The evidence consists of the following: (1) interviews carried out in 1986 and 1988 by the dissident Chinese writer Zheng Yi, published abroad last year after he went into exile; (2) official reports of the Chinese authorities which Zheng obtained. These date from the early 1980s when the 'crimes' of the Cultural Revolution were being secretly investigated. I am satisfied that they were authentic; (3) my own conversations in the area, which were brief but confirmatory.

Chinese history has recorded many instances of 'revenge cannibalism' — though some no doubt are literary inventions — over more than two thousand years. Combatants in other societies vent their victorious rage against the defeated in other ways, by rearrangement of the body in obscene postures, mutilation or dismemberment — witness the pictures of US Marines with severed heads in Vietnam. In China the victor may demonstrate extreme contempt for the defeated foe by consuming parts of his body. Treading on dangerous ground, we may speculate that China is a more 'oral' culture than ours.

The practice also has a presumed therapeutic value. There was a tradition of 'eating (another's) heart to nourish (one's own) heart'. Bread soaked in the blood of an executed criminal was supposed to have medicinal value — the theme of a famous short story by the 20th-century writer Lu Xun. But why did it only happen during the Cultural Revolution, and as far as we know only in parts of Guangxi?

Guangxi was still, in Chinese terms, a very 'backward' region in the 1960s. The people of Wuxuan, tucked in a fold of the Great Yao mountains, were particularly deprived. They had a reputation for violence: the great but savage Taiping Rebellion of the mid-19th century had emerged from this very area. In 1966-68 the Communist Party's orderly system of control was torn apart by Mao Zedong's Red Guards. The 'masses' were told to wage 'total war' against the 'class enemy' but were easily manipulated by rival leaders. Desperately poor and starting from a very low political base, they were easily won over by demagogues, opportunists and psychopaths. The ideal of a new revolution to mend a flawed socialist society soon faded.

After two years of confused struggle, there was a sudden escalation of violence in Wuxuan in mid-1968, first to mass killings and then to cannibalism. At first only a few ate human flesh in secret, or mixed it with pork to lessen the shock. Later it was even served at drinking parties. The sequence of events had the same surreal character as that described in *The Mad City*. Finally the Beijing government, alerted by a brave local Communist, ordered the army to move in.

This short story invites us to contemplate the depths of human nature under extreme conditions: who is to say that in different ways and in different places, it could not happen again?

MICHAEL GRADE

The state of the nation

Secrecy has always been a problem in Britain. Today, more than ever, it threatens the public's right to know, says the chief executive of Channel 4 Television UK

It remains an unhappy fact of British life that all journalistic enterprises continually come up against the barriers of secrecy erected by the powerful in their attempts to prevent the public being told. To take a small, topical example, the Scott inquiry. Why are cameras prohibited from the proceedings? Who decided? On what basis? And why didn't we kick up a fuss?

But my general interest in the issue has been sharpened by the position in which we in the electronic and print media now find ourselves. The public's right to know is under an even greater threat.

It is easy for some to dismiss campaigns for freedom of information as journalistic special pleading. They claim that journalists only want to promote their careers through sensational scoops, that newspapers only care about circulation and television about ratings: the usual stuff about competition and market forces and all that.

But what lies at the heart of any campaign for freedom of information is not simply the journalists' right to publish but, of course, the public's right to know. It is that fundamental right which is under growing threat. A combination of circumstances has brought us to this unhappy position. The most important of these is undoubtedly a perceived rise in concern about the activities of some of the tabloid press.

Normally one wouldn't take this ritual media-baiting too seriously. There is an almost inevitable cycle in these things and, every few years or so, bashing the press becomes a popular national pastime only to disappear as soon as more substantial issues arise.

I say 'national' pastime but the truth is that the pressure we have seen over the last 12 months for measures to control the press is of a very different order from the past. First, it has come more from politicians — by coincidence the very subjects of much of the reporting which is complained of — rather than from the public at large. And second, there is the real threat that it will result in legislation.

The argument so far has centred largely on alleged invasions of individual privacy by the press. Yet there is little indication or evidence that the ordinary public are bothered about the issue at all. You know that when politicians use the well-worn cliché 'widespread public concern'! Television is subject to the jurisdiction of a curious quango called the Broadcasting Complaints Commission which can investigate allegations of unfair treatment of individuals including, for example, that their privacy has been invaded by programme makers. In the light of the recent furore about invasions of privacy, it is interesting to note that the issue of television invading privacy has not greatly concerned people who complain to the Broadcasting Complaints Commission. In 1992 only four of the 50 complaints entertained by the Commission concerned privacy and that was not a particularly unusual year: figures for previous years reflect similar proportions.

Privacy may not be a concern at the forefront of the public's mind but it is exercising policy makers and I am afraid that until recently, at least, the press has been losing the arguments. Sir David Calcutt recommended in his report that there should be statutory controls to protect privacy; Peter Brooke is examining the introduction of legislation which would make certain physical invasions of privacy criminal offences; the Lord Chancellor's Department has produced a consultation paper suggesting the introduction of a new tort providing a general right of privacy. The only consolation — and it may be a sign that the tide is now turning — is that the attempts by some politicians to blame the government's predicament on the activities of the press have failed to convince.

The Secretary of State for National Heritage, in his public utterances on the issue, has always recognised that the question of legislation on privacy is a very delicate one. The balance between an individual's right to privacy and the public's right to know is delicate and you upset it at your peril. There will always be different views on the cases at the margin and no-one would condone every activity of the tabloid press. Yet one of the strange aspects of the current situation is that people do not seem to recognise that the existing law actually provides a good deal of protection for individuals' privacy.

Freedom of information is the journalists' right to publish and the public's right to know

Take the case of the publication of the photographs of the Princess of Wales in a gym. The truth is, as the Princess' lawyers have shown, that the existing law may already provide protection for someone in her position. She obtained an injunction preventing further publication of the pictures and has issued a writ for the seizure of the negatives and payment of profits. The interesting fact about privacy is not, as so many commentators seem to suggest, the absence of regulation — the most common characteristic of the British system — but rather the presence of a whole plethora of regulations with real teeth.

There are laws of trespass and breach of confidence as well as quite draconian libel laws and highly restrictive official secrets legislation. The fact that these are balanced by no written constitution, no specific guarantees of freedom of speech and no freedom of information act, mean that far from having a press that can run rampant over individual rights, journalists operate in a highly restrictive regime. The powerful have a range of existing weapons at their disposal to prevent publication of stories and programmes which go against their interests and to keep secret information which ought to be in the public domain. One only has to look at the way the late Robert Maxwell and others played the system to realise just how effective these can be in the hands of a shrewd and ruthless manipulator.

A new privacy law would tilt the existing balance even further against the public right to know and strengthen the protection of those who are legitimate subjects of journalistic inquiry.

But the problems do not stop there. Take Northern Ireland — an area in which the commitment to free speech is bound to be most rigorously tested. Perhaps the most ludicrous of all the restrictions under which the media is forced to operate is the Home Office ban on reporting Northern Ireland: the legislation which prevents British television showing members of Sinn Fein (and others) from speaking in their own voices on our screens outside election time. It has to be one of the most pointless restrictions on free speech ever imposed on a democracy. The idea that representatives of legal political parties elected by proper democratic processes in part of the United Kingdom cannot be heard in their own voices on British television is, frankly, an international embarrassment. An embarrassment heightened by the welcome decision last week by the Dublin government to lift their own version of the ban *(see p152)*. The position is that now residents of Northern Ireland will be able to see members of Sinn Fein speaking in their own voices on a whole range of issues on Irish television — which most in Northern Ireland can receive — but not on British television. It is bizarre.

It is all too easy to use television as a scapegoat for the failures of modern society

The prime minister instigated a review of the ban which was carried out by Peter Brooke. A high level delegation of all UK broadcasters visited Mr Brooke to express their united opposition to the ban. [In vain. Following the UK government's outrage at Gerrry Adams' visit to the USA, the government announced in January 1994 that the ban would remain. Ed].

Some politicians offer a rather facile view of journalists' objections to the ban. If you're against the ban, they say, you're aiding the terrorists. We say if you're against the ban you're in favour of democracy. We all abhor terrorism and would do nothing to offer the perpetrators of violence any succour. To our mind, however, a healthy, confident democracy ought to be able to cope with hearing these people in their own voices — if only because it would let us subject them to the same rigorous cross-questioning we apply to mainstream politicians and their ilk. The government's argument in favour of the 'Sinn Fein ban' are convincing arguments for proscribing Sinn Fein. It is time that politicians stopped using the media as the scapegoats for society's more intractable ills.

Reporting Northern Ireland is the area in which attempts to control the press are, not surprisingly, the most prevalent. Channel 4 had dramatic experience of this with our *Dispatches* programme two years ago. It investigated alleged collusion between the security forces and Loyalist assassination squads and was subjected to a concerted campaign of denigration by the Northern Ireland authorities and the most intense scrutiny by the Royal Ulster Constabulary itself. Eighteen months of investigation by the RUC produced no charges and nothing which has shaken Channel 4's belief that the programme raised genuine issues of public importance. In one of the most distasteful episodes of the investigation, the authorities attempted to charge the programme researcher with perjury, arresting him in a dawn raid at his house in London. Six weeks later, the charges had to be dropped for lack of evidence.

This sort of harassment of legitimate and honest programme makers going about their proper and lawful function can only be designed to dissuade people from asking difficult questions about policy and activity in the most sensitive part of the United Kingdom. We all appreciate that the security forces in Northern Ireland have a desperately difficult and dangerous task to perform, but their activities must be open to journalistic scrutiny if the fundamentals of our democracy are to survive.

Probably the most worrying legacy of that programme, however, is that journalists are left in the position where they have no right to protect the anonymity of their sources if courts order otherwise. This is particularly true under the Prevention of Terrorism Act where the combination of the police powers of seizure and the unusual requirement on individuals to provide the security forces with information, place journalists in the position of having to disclose confidential sources or face the full force of the criminal law. The ability to protect sources is an essential tenet of a free and independent press. Journalists must be able to operate as a source of information independent from the state. These provisions are a significant restriction and should be removed.

Attempts to restrict freedom of speech, however, are not confined to political and security issues. There is increasing pressure on areas of general artistic freedoms — those normally covered by the term 'taste and decency'. As I have said, it is all too easy to use television as a scapegoat for the failures of modern society whether it be terrorism in Northern Ireland or violent crime or the growth of the so-called permissive society. Politicians can easily pick selectively from the schedules to blame us, to take a topical example, for encouraging cynicism and lack of respect for national institutions. If what they mean is that television encourages people to question — that it stops them simply accepting what they are spoon-fed by those in authority — then I plead guilty without hesitation. What value is television if it doesn't inform in this way?

However, if they mean to imply that we only criticise and never celebrate, they couldn't be more wrong. British television is questioning, it does reflect and stimulate the national debates. But that is only a small part of our prodigious output. There are acres of schools and further education programmes, there are many programmes celebrating the arts, telling the success stories of British industries, British sporting heroes — many of them brilliant ethnic minority role models. There are programmes celebrating the joys of religion, soap operas where the survival instincts of the family unit form the core of the series, programmes raising money for worthy causes.

I do not believe for one moment that facile attempts by politicians of all parties to blame the media for society's more intractable problems are likely to convince the public. It was suggested last week that we are systematically undermining the established structures of our society. Not from where I stand. If the public questions, say, the forces of law and order, isn't that more likely to be the result of the many miscarriages of justice exposed by television and newspapers over the last few years — not least the Birmingham Six and the Guildford Four? If the monarchy is under scrutiny, is it the media's fault that the heir to the throne's marriage has broken down? Is it really television's fault that the Church of England is split over the issue of women priests? I could go on, but I hope the point is made.

I need to cover one last area of restriction: namely an attempt to strangle our culture. Television has to reflect changes in taste and behaviour and terrestrial television today is undoubtedly more sexually explicit than it was 15 years ago. But it is demonstrably less violent — at least on terrestrial television. However, pressure from one interest group means we now have the sort of television equivalent of watch committees reviewing every scene, questioning every word. There are three of them: our licensing body, the Independent Television Commission, the Broadcasting Standards Council and the Broadcasting Complaints Commission. Their mandates overlap and it now appears that they try to outdo each other to demonstrate their toughness with broadcasters.

Nor is it always clear that they reflect public concern. Early in January, Channel 4 had to publish a Broadcasting Standards Council adjudication against a fine drama series we had transmitted called *The Camomile Lawn*, based on the best selling novel by Mary Wesley. The BSC objected to the use of one four-letter word soon after the 9 o'clock watershed. It was one word, it was after the watershed and it was a direct quote from the novelist's text. They received only one complaint. Yet such are the obsessions of these new puritans that dramatic context is irrelevant. We all have to conform to some norm of what is thought by our 'betters' — the great and the good — to be right and proper; everything must be counted, measured and controlled. Nobody I know in television wants an unregulated free-for-all. But judgements like *The Camomile Lawn* case give regulation a bad name. The BSC only exists to repress freedom of expression, to curb the artist, the writer, the director. If it is seen to repress, it loses its raison d'être. It belongs on the scrap heap with the watch committees and the Lord Chamberlain's blue pencil. Content regulation is best left to the ITC: they are experienced and they have other things to regulate as well.

I fear I have presented a gloomy prognosis — an uphill struggle to reverse the trend. Freedom of expression, the public's right to know and journalistic freedoms in general are threatened with greater restrictions in Britain today. We await with interest the specific proposals arising out of William Waldegrave's White Paper on Open Government to see whether they will go any way towards improving the situation. But I wouldn't hold your breath.

This speech was given at the Campaign for Freedom of Information Awards, 1994

ROBERT McCRUM

Indifferent death

Indifference, public apathy and arms sales have enabled Indonesia to get away with murder and genocide in East Timor

East Timor is back in the news, and not before time. The crimes of genocide committed on this small, remote half-island at the eastern extremity of the Indonesian archipelago have been documented often enough by *Index on Censorship*, but they have gone largely ignored by the world community for nearly a generation. Ever since Indonesian paratroopers drifted out of the dawn on the morning of 7 December 1975, East Timor has suffered not only the agony of a bloody occupation but also the torment of international indifference. From time to time the fate of the islanders becomes news. Then silence descends once more.

But now, in 1994, change is in the air. There is pressure in print and on British television. The Clinton administration has acknowledged — as yet, not more — the gravity of the issue. The UN is examining violations of human rights. The British Foreign Office is reportedly nervous about the increased attention focused on East Timor, as well it might be. The British government is the number one seller of arms to Jakarta. The question remains: how have the East Timorese survived nearly a generation of neglect and indifference?

They have lost, in the course of the last 20–odd years, at least 200,000 people (out of an estimated population of 700,000). They live from day to day under constant surveillance and the threat of intimidation, imprisonment and torture. Yet they have not given up.

Journalists cannot visit East Timor, so I and photographer Julio Etchart went as tourists. We found an extraordinary and moving determination by the people of East Timor to resist the Indonesian invader.

In particular, the East Timorese are sustained by the Roman Catholic church, led by Bishop Carlos Ximines Belo. The Bishop has to walk a diplomatic ecclesiastical tightrope. His priests are less constrained. They are, almost without exception, more or less actively in the East Timor liberation struggle. Among several Roman Catholic missions we visited in the course of our stay, there was one — at a location it would be dangerous to disclose — that seemed to epitomise the courage and tenacity of the church and its faithful congregation, and their determination to pursue a path of stubborn opposition to Indonesian oppression, often in the face of great hostility.

The mission is far from the capital, Dili, and takes nearly a day to reach by bus or motorbike. It is situated on the edge of an extensive forest region occupied by members of the small, fragmented and ill-equipped resistance movement. It is in these remote parts that the real battle for East Timor's independence is being fought out.

When we arrived, we were obliged to register with the local police garrison, after which we made our way across a stretch of waste ground, into the mission compound and, as we had been advised in the capital, asked to speak to the priest, whom I shall call Father Rodolpho da Costa.

Father Rodolpho is 40 years old. He was born in the north of the island and came here about seven years ago. He has an air of quiet certainty, a strong sense of humour, and a shyness that

Bishop Carlos Ximines Belo

vanishes when he stands before his congregation. In this parish, over 90% of the population is registered as Roman Catholic, and Father Rodolpho takes pride in the increasing attendances at Mass.

The mission and its church are at once a school, a surgery, a place of recreation, a refuge, a social centre, and a source of inspiration. Throughout the island there is a sense that the church is the administration. Beyond the walls of the mission there are spies, policemen, informers — the army of occupation. Inside, there is teaching, prayer and song. Father Rodolpho said he would try to arrange for us to make contact with members of the armed struggle. He said it might take some time. So we settled down to wait.

It's a simple life at the mission. There's no running water, fitful electricity and a basic diet of rice and stewed lamb. Father Rodolpho rises at five. At six, school starts, and will go on, in different parts of the mission compound, all day. Portuguese is spoken freely here. '*Buonas dias*', said Father Rodolpho, coming in for breakfast at eight. By midday it's swelteringly hot.

At about four in the afternoon, Father Rodolpho celebrates Mass. The church is always crowded. There is nothing routine about these prayers. I saw many people kneeling in tears. Some will also make their confession.

On that first day, in the lull before supper, Father Rodolpho talked about his life and work here. We also spoke of politics. He is not afraid to address political questions in his church. 'When I speak of corruption and injustice,' he says, 'the military don't like it.' Then we talked about the struggle for independence. Father Rodolpho made the comparison with Yugoslavia. He remarked that President Suharto could be seen as a kind of South-East Asian Tito, holding together a loose confederation with a combination of military muscle and massive economic expansion (GDP has expanded by a staggering annual 7% for the past several years). Indonesia is made up of about 13,500 separate islands, many with aspirations to independence, and there's no doubt that the violence meted out to East Timor is intended as a deterrent to others in Aceh and Irian Jaya. After Suharto, what next? 'This is a society threatening to fly apart at the seams,' said Father Rodolpho.

Another day passed. There were many comings and goings. An officer from the local Indonesian battalion paid a visit. He asked, 'Who is staying at the mission?' Although we had already registered with the police, this inquiry was more pointed. Father Rodolpho replied: 'I have two tourists from London.' Later, he told us that a new, crack battalion had just arrived from Java to strengthen the campaign against the guerrillas. Indonesian propaganda claims a reduction in troop levels. We saw no evidence of this.

After our siesta on the second day, Julio and I paid a visit to a local notable, Antonio Anastasio da Costa Soares. As his name suggests, this fine old gentleman has a family pedigree that can be traced back to the days of Portuguese rule. He is a great survivor. He has lived through the Japanese invasion, has seen the return of Portuguese rule, then the brief declaration of Timorese independence in 1975 and then, finally, the Indonesian invasion. Unlike many of his age, he had survived the occupation unharmed. He insisted that, despite everything, his country was still, as he put it 'the same Timor.'

Late on Saturday we were joined by a man who agreed to be identified only by his first name, Jose. He is the local organist and he had come to practise for Sunday Mass, but he's no ordinary musician. Jose is 25 and is under permanent detention at the local barracks. When the Pope visited Dili in 1989, Jose organised the student protest and was arrested. He is still in detention, but at least he has survived. His plight is known to Bishop Belo and to the International Red Cross. He has no idea when he will be released. He has no books, no newspapers, no radio nor TV — his weekly visit to the mission is his only contact with the outside world.

This is a society whose language has been doubly terrorised. First there is the fear of torture or death. Then there is the language terrorism, more subtle, but just as brutal.

After Mass on Sunday, we drove out with Father Rodolpho to a remote village in the forest. It was a sobering journey, full of first-hand evidence of the attempted extermination of the East Timorese. In this cul-de-sac 50 people were machine-gunned. Under that palm tree is a mass grave. Over there, on that hillside, is a well-known killing field. Finally we reached our destination, a 'new' village of about 1,100 people. Before the massacres of the 1970s and 1980s and before relocation it numbered some 4,900. Here, as everywhere in East Timor, you see children, teenagers and young adults — but no 30- or 40-year-olds. They have all been killed. There was also a platoon of Indonesian troops and the usual complement of informers in residence. We found a group of young people watching a boxing match on the village television. I wanted to ask questions, but no one would talk. Father Rodolpho spoke to the village leader who became edgy and nervous. His eyes darted this way and that. He was evidently afraid. He knew he was being watched. He would not speak.

This is a society whose language has been doubly terrorised. First there is the fear of torture or death. Everyone has lost a sibling or a parent or a grandparent, often in circumstances of the most appalling cruelty. As in Cambodia after the Khmer Rouge, the people are in a state of shock. Then there is the language terrorism, more subtle, but just as brutal. The older generation grew up speaking Portuguese. After the invasion, this became associated with the resistance movement, and now it is only used in murmurs behind closed doors. The official state language is Bahasa Indonesia. For the rest, the local language, Tetum, is the speech of everyday life, but deprived of the freedom to express the basic desire for independence and justice.

'The world refuses to pay attention to what we sacrifice, families, homes, lives... We have been given many fine words, but we are still dying, every day we are still dying.'

On the afternoon of the third day, still waiting to make contact with the guerrillas, we walked a little way out of the town, and found ourselves being directed by the local people to the scene of a cock-fight. A large crowd of young men and boys had collected around a small, wire-fenced arena. Almost everyone was chewing 'mascar', a kind of betel, and their reddened lips and teeth contributed to the blood-thirsty atmosphere. As we arrived, the excitement was mounting. Razor-blades were being strapped onto the claws of two fighting-cocks. In another corner there was furious betting. The cocks are held, beak to beak, to arouse hostility. Suddenly, they are released and there's a flurry of feathers and squawking. Then a shout goes up. One of the birds has been slashed. Bright red blood drips onto the earth. The winning bird is snatched up by its owner and held proudly aloft. The other bird is gasping in a corner, a dirty heap of plumage. In a few minutes it will be dead. In the area around the cockpit,

Dili Harbour 1994: Indonesian landing-craft from the 1975 invasion

several other cocks are tethered waiting to fight. Some owners parade their birds for the inspection of the punters. Another round of betting. Another fight. Another death. For a people who have endured what the Timorese have endured, a few dead birds must seem insignificant.

Night fell. We had been told to be ready for a meeting with a member of 'the armed struggle'. The hours ticked by. Finally we met a young man from the resistance movement, and learned of the desperate situation now facing the freedom fighters of East Timor.

The guerrilla I spoke to, Joaquim Guterres (not his real name), had been close to the guerrilla leader, 'Xanana' Gusmao, who is currently in prison serving a 20-year sentence. In his opinion Gusmao had allowed himself to be arrested and made a political prisoner to dramatise the plight of the East Timor resistance movement to the world: Gusmao could (and did) attract the attention of the world's press. There was no question of Gusmao's continuing psychological presence among the guerrillas, however. 'He is our Nelson Mandela,' said Joaquim Guterres.

Gusmao has been replaced, in the field, by a young leader named Konis Santana, but the armed struggle remains in dire straits, short of arms, supplies and new recruits. There are, perhaps, no more than 1,000 men sustaining the clandestine movement, of whom less than half carry weapons. I asked how, in these circumstances, the resistance could ever hope to succeed? The young man opposite shook his head fiercely. He had no real answers, only a desperate faith in his cause. 'Indonesian troops are killing our people every day, but I am 100% certain we shall succeed. We shall always have the support of the people and we love our freedom. We shall never give up.'

We talked on. Joaquim Guterres described the activities of his fellow guerrillas, their Maubere code-names (Lan-Wai, Fuluk, Loro-Talin, Ular Rihyk) and their day-to-day living conditions. He admitted a frustration at the isolation of the Timorese people. 'The world refuses to pay attention, no matter what we sacrifice, families, homes, lives... We have been given many fine words, but we are still dying, every day we are still dying.'

As in Cambodia after the Khmer Rouge, the people are in a state of shock

Sometime after midnight Guterres said he had to return to the forest, and handed over messages for fellow resistance workers who have somehow managed to flee abroad. Then he disappeared silently into the dark.

Next morning, we bade farewell to Father Rodolpho and walked with our rucksacks out of the mission, back into the town. The bell was tolling for Mass. People were hurrying towards the church as usual. Across the street, local informers watched our progress from their mopeds. Now, writing this in the security of the West, I worry, as any journalist must worry, about the safety of those I have described. I had discussed this point with Father Rodolpho who remained impressively calm. 'You are welcome here,' he had said. 'You must write about what you have seen. What is important is that you tell the world.'

LEGAL

ANTHONY BURTON

Bernard Simons

'Swift sailed into his rest;
Savage indignation there
Cannot lacerate his breast
Imitate him if you dare,
World-besotted traveller;
He served human liberty'

WB Yeats

Bernard Simons aged 52 died in Madrid on 29 May 1993 shortly after delivering a powerful lecture on the practical aspects of the use of Human Rights Conventions in criminal cases. He was attending a conference of the International Bar Association of which he was a vice-chairman. In his lecture he asserted that as a lawyer practising in the criminal courts in England and Wales 'one risks a negligence action if one does not constantly have at the forefront of one's mind the possibility that once a client has exhausted the local remedies there may be grounds to apply to the European Commission for a remedy.' This perception encapsulated Bernard's breadth of vision as a brilliant tactician and lateral-thinking lawyer. He was a pioneer among radical lawyers, never afraid to take on even the most unpopular causes of the time. He detested injustice. His proactive, innovative, persistent but always measured style guaranteed his clients the certainty that the judicial system would be tested to its limits.

Lawyers have to listen but few are good listeners. Bernard possessed that rare ability.

His unwavering commitment to human rights cannot be better demonstrated than by his concern for the plight of men incarcerated on death row in Jamaica and Trinidad. Following his representation of Michael X over 20 years ago, he discovered an esoteric 'in forma pauperis' procedure whereby at his own expense he was able to take on the cases of poor men on death row for final appeal before the Privy Council in London. It was his belief that such work had to be done, if lawyers were to justify the basis of their vocation that the poor and oppressed were to be represented without fear or favour. Probably his greatest achievement, which, ironically, only became known after his death — the case having been prepared and argued with his friend and colleague, Geoffrey Robertson QC, before he died — is the landmark decision of the Privy Council in the case of Pratt and Morgan *v* The Attorney General for Jamaica, where the Privy Council ruled that to execute someone after holding that person in suspense for more than five years will amount to inhuman and degrading punishment. The decision has worldwide ramifications and may influence the US Supreme Court where a test case is expected to be launched shortly.

> **'The case brought home to me how a few well chosen words impeccably uttered in a well modulated voice could bring about a man's death.'**
>
> *Bernard Simons on the case of Michael X*

Bernard balanced the stress of his work with an infectious sense of humour which included the ability not to take himself too seriously. In the 1960s and early 1970s, Bernard along with a crop of Release-spawned radical lawyers travelled the national circuit of magistrates courts defending individuals charged with possession of cannabis. At the time the offence still attracted a real risk of imprisonment. In 1992, as president of the London Criminal Courts Solicitors Association in a rapturously greeted speech to its members at their annual dinner, he told an anecdote about his early days as an advocate on the circuit. Having explained that he generally made the same plea in mitigation for every possession offence, he was at risk, like an actor in a long run, of allowing his mind to wander onto more interesting topics such as what he was going to cook for dinner that night. In his own words, 'I had started my plea and lapsed into the usual reverie. I came to, some 10 minutes later, and noticed the Bench, the Clerks and indeed my client were looking at me in total amazement as if my trousers had just fallen down. I staggered on to the end and sat down. When I came out of Court I asked my client what had gone wrong. He said, "Well you started out alright, but you suddenly started dictating your speech to the Magistrate. At the end of each phrase, you put in a comma, at the end of each sentence a full stop. You told them when you had reached a new paragraph, you spelt all the hard words such as marijuana, and at the end you told them you wanted double spacing and two copies by lunch time". I fled from the back of the Court to London'.

Numerous writers, artists and performers were the beneficiaries of Bernard's special blend of skills as a lawyer. His love of literature and his own ability as a writer and broadcaster made him a libel lawyer par excellence. It led to frequent and successful skirmishes with the media, amongst whom he had so many friends. His firm belief in the freedom of information led him into conflict with government, notably during his defence of Howard Marks and the journalist Duncan Campbell who was prosecuted for exposing the truth about GCHQ.

Bernard did not pay lip service to human rights but through his work attempted to educate others as well as protect the interests of the individuals he served. I can think of no better way to preserve his memory than to dedicate a regular column to him in this magazine, the aims of which are at one with his own.

ANDREW KELLY

Silent witness

Britain's new Criminal Justice and Public Order Bill threatens to abolish one of the most ancient and important legal privileges protecting the rights of British citizens.

The right to silence is an ancient privilege fundamental to the criminal justice system in the United Kingdom. In contemporary law the right provides for the appropriate balance of power between state and individual, protecting the latter's presumption of innocence and right not to incriminate him/herself, and imposing on the state the necessity to bring — and prove — its case.

The principle that no accused person or witness could be forced into self-incrimination developed at the end of the Middle Ages in response to the practices of the Court of Star Chamber, which exacted confessions by imprisonment, pillory, mutilation and torture.

Arguments for its abolition also have a history: Jeremy Bentham contended that 'innocence claims the right of speaking, as guilt invokes the privilege of silence'. But the right has never been so seriously threatened as by the proposals in the Government's new Criminal Justice and Public Order Bill.

In England and Wales the 300 year old right operates with few exceptions and is encapsulated during police questioning in the standard caution: 'You do not have to say anything unless you wish' (Code of Practice for the Detention, treatment and questioning of Persons by Police Officers). It is also a statutory right during trial: 'The failure to give evidence shall not be made the subject of any comment by the prosecution' (Section 1, Criminal Evidence Act 1898). Under various statutes there is a duty to disclose information to the Inland Revenue, Customs and Excise, a Serious Fraud Office inquiry and a variety of other inspectors, who can compel answers on pain of contempt of court.

It is this right that the new Bill promises to abolish altogether in England and Wales. Under its provisions, a court or jury, in determining whether there is a case to answer or whether an accused person is guilty of the offence charged, may 'draw such inferences as appear proper' if the accused fails to mention relevant facts when questioned or charged; refuses to be sworn at trial or, having been sworn, refuses to give evidence; or fails to account for objects, substances, marks on an object, or his presence at a particular place (Sections 27-29). The Bill means that the judge must call a silent witness to give evidence and that inferences from his silence may be treated as corroboration of any evidence against him.

Certain safeguards are contained in the Bill, namely: an accused cannot be convicted solely on the inference from silence; the facts must be ones which he could be reasonably expected to reveal; and the court may exercise a general discretion to excuse an accused person from answering. However, these provisions permit a wide discretion in their interpretation, for which no statutory guidance has been given.

The right to silence has already been removed in Northern Ireland. Douglas Hurd, then at the Home Office, set up a Standing Advisory Commission in 1988 to examine how to make changes in the law. Before the commission had even received evidence, the law was changed by the Criminal Evidence (Northern Ireland) Order 1988, a statutory instrument issued by the Secretary of State. The first the commission heard about the change of law was in a newspaper report. The provisions of the 'Order' mirror those in the new Criminal Justice and Public Order Bill.

After an initial reluctance, judges in Northern Ireland have come to use the order more and more, and its implementation has given rise to real concern for the operation of two fundamental legal principles enshrined in international law. First, since the enactment of the Order, the courts have ruled that once a *prima facie* case has been established, a judge may draw inferences of guilt from an accused person's silence during police questioning or at trial. This has the effect of lowering the standard of proof necessary to establish guilt. Experts agree that its application has eroded the principle that an accused person shall be considered innocent until proven guilty, as set out in the International Covenant on Civil and Political Rights (ICCPR) Article

14(2) and the European Convention on Human Rights (ECHR) Article 6(2). The UN Human Rights Commission, the European Court of Human Rights and two UK Royal Commissions have all held that the right to silence is fundamental on those grounds.

Second, an accused person is left with no reasonable choice between remaining silent and making a statement. In the case of R *v* K S Murray, the House of Lords, in a Northern Irish Appeal case, expressed the dilemma faced by an accused: 'he cannot be compelled to give evidence, but must risk the consequences if he does not.' Such a provision could contravene the international standard on the right not to testify against oneself or confess guilt, as set out in ICCPR Article 14(3).

On 18 January, the European Commission on Human Rights ruled that a convicted man, John Murray, could pursue a claim that the abolition of the right to silence in Northern Ireland breaches Article 6(1) of ECHR. Should the European Court on Human Rights decide in his favour, the UK Government will be under strong pressure to retain the right of silence in England and Wales and to revoke the Northern Irish Order. The European Court of Human Rights has held previously that an accused person, in France, had a right to silence, under Article 6(1).

Senior legal figures have criticised the Criminal Justice Bill. On 19 January, Lord Taylor, the Lord chief Justice, said he and other judges were seriously concerned by Clause 28 of the Bill, that requires judges to call the 'silent' witness before the jury. He stated that 'the jury may well regard a decision not to testify as showing the defendant is defying the judge'. He argued, however, that there should be some limitations to a defendant's right to silence during police questioning.

Government claims that new safeguards will protect the innocent are challenged by recent research. Helen Fenwick, Lecturer in Law at the University of Durham, claims that whilst the videotaping of police interviews is probably worthwhile, it would not provide adequate protection in the absence of the right to silence. If anything, videotaping, she adds, could lend a spurious credibility to confessions and would increase pressure on the accused to testify against themselves.

Her argument is supported by Irving and Hilgendorf's study showing that the removal of the right to silence would increase psychological pressure on suspects and could lead to false confessions and miscarriages of justice.

Ministers have suggested that removal of the right will lead to a reduction in crime. This claim too is contested by recent findings. Research by the Royal Commission on Criminal Justice showed that only about 2% of all suspects who relied on the right to silence were acquitted. This suggests that abolishing the right would have no significant impact on the rate of crime or convictions.

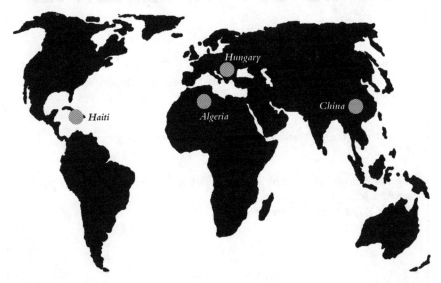

Flashpoints

New lords, new laws

'Roll up that map', the British prime minister William Pitt said as Napoleon's armies swept through Europe, 'it will not be wanted these 10 years'. Now, nearly five years since the rationale for the Cold War collapsed, we too have become accustomed to new maps, new leaders, to the armies of change that have swept through our world.

The changes wrought in the meltdown of the Soviet empire, however, have not met the promise of the trumpeted New World Order. Economic liberalisation has generally occurred without a concomitant liberalisation in the political sphere and the ideals of democracy have been sold out to the interests of a narrowly construed economic necessity.

In **Hungary**, the state tightens its grip on senior appointments in the media, and 'reasons of economy' are used to justify mass sackings in state radio. This is just the latest wave in a steady erosion of the independence of Hungarian public broadcasting over the last two years. That each erosion can be traced back to the extreme nationalist leader Istvan Csurka (who has openly advocated political manipulation of the media); and that Csurka's Hungarian Justice and Life Party is preparing to fight the general election starting on 8 May, is not coincidence. Such premises lead to the inexorable conclusion that the economy served by these sackings has less to do with saving money than with economy of discussion and debate.

The domino effect that toppled governments from the Elbe to the Bering Sea was brutally halted in Tiananmen Square. But in **China**, too, an economic restructuring has taken place, without an accompanying political restructuring: *perestroika* without *glasnost*. The US has attempted to make the renewal of China's Most Favoured Nation trade status contingent on greater respect for human rights. But since the US evidently has more to lose — financially — than China from any alteration to the status quo, the vague threats emanating from Washington sound distinctly hollow. Indeed, the visit to China in March by US secretary of state Warren Christopher coincided with a marked crackdown on dissident activity. The hollowness, in turn, of Beijing's vague promises of greater openness is further underlined by the recent restatement of the laws against proselytism, reapplied to counter the threat posed by the spread of Islam to China's ideological purity.

Which all goes to show that one person's heresy is another's orthodoxy to be enforced, if necessary, at the point of a gun. In **Algeria**, militant Islamists are fighting to impose religious purity in the face of a discredited military-backed regime. Writers, artists, intellectuals are inevitably caught in the crossfire: with at least five journalists killed since October 1993, Algeria is probably the most dangerous country in the world for the practice of journalism.

For harassment of the press to occur, however, there must be a press to harass. In **Haiti**, where another military regime holds sway, in defiance of increasingly impotent international opposition, the media are suffocating under the stranglehold of UN-imposed economic sanctions. Independent radio stations and newspapers, the only peaceful opposition to General Cedras and his thuggish *attachés*, are facing closure due to fuel and newsprint shortages.

The world, undoubtedly, has changed. At least, the map *looks* different now; new insignia adorn the lapels of the new strongmen, who find ever more ingenious methods of stifling dissent; and a rigorous economic orthodoxy has supplanted the old political certainties. But for those who seek to restrict access to information; for those who would impose silence through economic pressure, manipulation of the law, or through the threat or use of the gun; for these, it's business as usual.

Adam Newey

A censorship chronicle incorporating information from Agence France Presse (AFP), Amnesty International (AI), the World Association of Community Radio Broadcasters (AMARC), the Central American Centre for the Protection of Freedom of Expression (CEPEX), the Committee to Protect Journalists (CPJ), the Canadian Committee to Protect Journalists (CCPJ), the Inter-American Press Association (IAPA), the International Federation of Journalists (IFJ), the Media Institute of Southern Africa (MISA), International PEN (PEN), Radio Free Europe/Radio Liberty (RFE/RL), Reporters sans frontières (RSF), the BBC Monitoring Service Summary of World Broadcasts (SWB) and other sources.

AFGHANISTAN

Two foreign correspondents, Terence White of AFP and John Jennings of AP, were captured while covering fighting between the two main rival Mojahedin factions, the forces of former defence minister Ahmed Shah Massoud, and Hezbi Islami, the party led by prime minister Hekmatyar. The journalists, accused of being military advisers to Massoud, were held at a Hezbi Islami military camp and beaten. They were eventually released on 15 November 1993. (RSF)

ALBANIA

In November 1993 the student newspaper *Reporteri* was banned, reportedly for its condemnation of the proposed press law which would restrict freedom of information and

permit confiscation of newspapers. The law would also specify who can publish or edit newspapers and provide for the punishment of journalists who criticise the president, parliament or visiting foreign dignitaries. (RSF)

A Tirana court banned local journalists from reporting the trial of 10 former politburo members on 13 December 1993. Foreign journalists had already been banned from reporting the case. The defendants, charged with 'violating the equality of citizens' by abusing state funds, were found guilty on 27 December and sentenced to between six and eight years in jail. It is feared that the precedents set by the ban could undermine the right to a fair and open trial. (SWB)

It was reported in January that Shygyri Meka, deputy editor of *Zeri i Popullit*, was arrested after the newspaper published an article attacking President Sali Berisha; and that Nazmi Sina, a Tirana news vendor, was arrested for publicising an article in *Populli Po* which criticised the president. (*East European Newsletter*)

Martin Leka of the daily paper *Koha Jone* was found guilty of slander and sentenced to 18 months' imprisonment on 25 February. However, both he and the paper's editor, Aleksander Frangaj, were found not guilty of disclosing state secrets. The charges arose from publication in January of a defence ministry order on the use of firearms by members of the Albanian armed forces. (SWB, RSF)

'We burn unsold copies.'

ALGERIA

Photo-journalist Djamel Bouhidel, who worked for the weekly *Nouveau Tell*, was shot dead on 5 October 1993 in Blida. And on 14 October Mustapha Abada, a former head of Algeria's state television ENTV, was shot dead in Algiers. (RSF)

Editor-in-chief of the daily news programme on ENTV, Smaïl Yefsah, was murdered on 18 October 1993 near his home in Bab-Ezzouar, Algiers. Several independent and state-owned newspapers withheld publication on 20 October and issued a joint statement condemning 'the genocide organized and executed by the forces of fundamentalism against the intellectuals and all the defenders of freedom and democracy in Algeria'. (Article 19)

The body of Youssef Sebti, lecturer at the National Institute of Agronomy and an Arabic-language poet, was found in his home in El Harrach on 28 December

1993. His throat had been cut. (PEN)

Olivier Quémeneur, a French cameraman working for the Australian Broadcasting Corporation, was attacked and killed in the casbah area of Algiers on 1 February. An ABC colleague, Scott Allan White, was seriously injured in the attack. (RSF)

Abdelaziz Smati, a producer working for ENTV, was seriously wounded after being shot by two gunmen outside his Algiers home on 14 February. (CCPJ)

Abdelkader Hireche, a journalist in the news department of ENTV, was shot dead by two men near his home in Algiers on 1 March. (RSF)

Recent publications: *Algeria: Assassination in the Name of Religion* (Article 19, December 1993, 14pp); *Human Rights Abuses in Algeria: No One Is Spared* (Human Rights Watch/Middle East, January 1994, 67pp) (see p100)

ANGOLA

Gustavo Costa and Aguiar dos Santos, stringers for the Portuguese publications *O Publico* and *Expresso*, were both reported to be receiving anonymous death threats in late December 1993 because of their investigations into alleged government corruption. (Angolan Journalists' Union, PEN)

On 13 January the state-run station Radio Nacional de Angola called on journalists to

be 'patriotic', and not cover stories which could constitute a threat to national security. A similar broadcast on 14 January referred to 'a certain correspondent of South African radio', believed to be a reference to Mario Paiva, an Angolan journalist who works for South Africa's Channel Africa. Paiva believes he was singled out because of his recent reports criticising a government investigation into the persecution of the Bakongo people. (MISA)

ARGENTINA

Several unknown people attacked the headquarters of the Press Workers' Union (UTP) in Buenos Aires on 14 November 1993 and badly beat union official Miguel Galivan. The office later received threats warning them to halt investigations into recent attacks on journalists. (IAPA)

The body of sports journalist Miguel Bonino, who had been missing for four days, was found floating in a river near Buenos Aires on 15 November. Suicide has been ruled out as a cause of death. (IAPA)

Government files released in December (*Index* 4/1992, 4/1993) reveal that up to 1,000 suspected war criminals and Nazi collaborators were allowed into the country after 1945, and that successive administrations were active in blocking attempts to bring them to justice. (*Sunday Times*)

Soccer star Diego Maradona fired several shots from an air gun on 2 February, injuring

several journalists gathered outside his house. (CCPJ)

Julio Torres Cabanilla of the paper *La Razón* was badly beaten in Buenos Aires on 3 February, apparently in retaliation for his coverage of popular protests in President Menem's home province of La Rioja. (IAPA)

AUSTRIA

On 24 November 1993 the European Court of Human Rights ruled that the Austrian government's monopoly on broadcasting was a clear violation of Article 10 of the European Convention, which guarantees the right to freedom of expression. The Court praised the government's stated aim of achieving objectivity, impartiality and diversity but argued that a monopoly is the most restrictive means of achieving pluralism. (Article 19)

AZERBAIJAN

On 11 September 1993, the entire print run of the opposition newspaper *Azadlig* was seized and destroyed, apparently because of articles and cartoons critical of President Guiedar Aliyev's policy of rapprochement with the Russian Federation. (RSF)

Three Canadian journalists, Dick Gordon and Douglas Alteen of the Canadian Broadcasting Corporation and Mike Trickey of Southam News press agency, were expelled from the country on 11 February. Despite having authorisation to visit camps of

refugees displaced by the conflict with Armenia, authorities claimed the journalists lacked the correct documents. (CCPJ)

BANGLADESH

Abdul Mannan, a press machine operator, was shot dead during a gunfight in the newsroom of the paper *Ittefaq* on 14 January. The shooting reportedly broke out between two groups backing the rival claims of two brothers to the editorship of the paper, the country's largest daily. (United Press International)

BELARUS

On 30 November an open letter to the government from editors of several major newspapers, including *Zviazva*, *Sovetskaya Belorussiy*, *Vechernyi Minsk* and the state-owned *Narodnaja Hazieta*, warned that the economic situation, and the fact that energy has to be bought in Russian roubles, had brought the Belarus printing house and its papers 'to the verge of closing'. (SWB)

The oppostion newspaper *Svaboda* failed to appear on 15

February after the printing works received a telegram purporting to be a government ban. The official whose signature appeared on the telegram later denied all knowledge of it. (SWB) (see p153)

BENIN

Jean-Luc Akplogan, a Radio France International reporter, had his accreditation withdrawn on 27 January for interviewing a union leader following an illegal anti-government demonstration. (RSF)

BOSNIA-HERCEGOVINA

John Hasek, a Canadian freelance journalist who was severely injured while covering the Balkan conflict in June 1993, died in hospital in Prague on 1 January. (CCPJ)

On 28 January all three members of a crew from the Italian television station RAI, Marco Lucchetta, Dario D'Angelo and Alessandro Ota, were killed by mortar fire while leaving a hospital in Mostar. (AFP)

Jadran Svetska, a Dutch journalist, was detained by Croatian militia near Prozor in mid-January while travelling with a German aid convoy. (PEN)

Recent publication: *Former Yugoslavia: The War Crimes Tribunal One Year Later* (Human Rights Watch/ Helsinki, February 1994, 26pp)

BOTSWANA

University students in Gabarone were denied official permission for a demonstration

against alleged ministerial abuse of development funds on 4 February, on the grounds that not enough police were available to escort the demonstrators. One thousand students assembled at the university on the day of the march but some 200 riot police stopped them from leaving the campus. (MISA)

BRAZIL

João Alberto Ferreira Souto, owner of the daily *Jornal Do Estado*, was ambushed and shot dead near his home in Vitoria da Conquista on 19 February. It is believed that he was killed because of his critical investigations of local politicians. (IAPA)

BRITAIN

Four senior ministers were recently accused of routinely suppressing information which showed the government had broken its own guidelines on arms sales to Iraq. Two of the four, president of the board of trade Michael Heseltine and Kenneth Clarke, chancellor of the exchequer, have said they will resign if the ongoing Scott inquiry into the arms sales finds that they acted improperly. William Waldegrave, the minister for open government, admitted on 8 March that ministers sometimes lie to Parliament. (national press) (see above p150)

A scene of two women kissing in Channel 4's *Brookside*, the first British soap opera to feature a lesbian relationship, was cut from an edition shown on 15 January, reportedly to avoid embarrassment to viewers and possible criticism from the Independent Television Commission. The volume of complaints at the self-censorship has since encouraged the station to screen another kiss. (Channel 4)

The government admitted in late February that Britain's largest-ever overseas aid grant, worth £234 million, to build the Pergau dam in Malaysia, was given in return for a contract for the sale of British arms worth £1 billion. The admission contradicts persistent previous denials on the linkage between arms sales and aid. (national press)

Plans by the police, revealed in early March, to keep computer records on some 8,000 New Age travellers, with details of their vehicles, nicknames and associates, are to be challenged under the right to privacy in the European Convention on Human Rights. (*Guardian*)

The British government's proposals to abolish a defendant's right to silence, currently at the committee stage in the House of Commons, have provoked unprecedented opposition from the senior judge, Lord Chief Justice Taylor, the Police Federation, lawyers and civil liberties groups. The European Court of Human Rights is expected to rule soon on the removal of the right to silence in 1988 for terrorist suspects in Northern Ireland courts. (national press) (see p150)

In September 1993 Bulgarian

journalists' unions called on parliament to remove a section of the 1992 Labour Law which allows national radio and television stations to dismiss journalists without prior union consultation and without right of defence. It is reported that 45 Bulgarian Radio journalists have been sacked under the law and two more threatened with dismissal. (IFJ)

On 29 December 1993 the Union of Bulgarian Journalists reportedly dismissed the director of its newspaper *Podkrepa*, Boyan Daskalov, for publishing articles in the paper that contradicted union policy. (SWB)

On 27 December 1993 Fidele Nduwayo, a journalist with the independent bi-monthly *Citizen*, narrowly escaped being kidnapped by three men who, according to witnesses, fled the scene in a government-owned vehicle. (RSF)

At the end of 1993 circulation of the opposition newspaper *Crossroads of Ideas* was prohibited by the Ministry of Communications, apparently in connection with an article published on 15 December entitled 'National Heroes or Head of Tribe of Decapitators'. The article dealt with the attempted coup of 21 October, in which President Melchior Ndadaye and other senior members of the country's first democratically elected government were executed. (RSF)

Recent publication: *Burundi: Le Choix de la Censure* (Reporters sans frontières, January 1994,

52pp plus appendices)

The information minister announced on 23 November that any journalist who criticised King Norodom Sihanouk would be arrested. A week later, however, the King said that press criticism, short of 'unfounded, unjust and defamatory' statements, was allowable. (RSF)

The 7 March edition of *Le Messager* was seized by the authorities because it contained articles on the conflict with Nigeria which had not been cleared prior to publication. The editor, Pius Njawe, has been accused of 'not respecting censorship'. Another weekly, *Challenge Hebdo*, was suspended in February for publishing an interview with a former associate of the president. *Le Nouvel Independent* has been publishing in defiance of a banning order since the end of 1993, when it ran an article alleging the president's involvement in a counterfeiting operation. (RSF)

Toronto-based painter Eli Langer was committed for trial under the country's new Child Pornography and Corrupting Morals law on 17 January, after police raided an exhibition of his work in December 1993. The exhibition included five paintings and 35 drawings depicting sexual acts between children and adults. The new law, which has been widely criticised, makes it an offence to own, make, exhibit or sell anything that depicts a sexual act by anyone under 18. (*New York Times*)

CHILE

In November 1993 the Navy prosecutor recommended that former intelligence officer Captain Humberto Antonio Palamara Iribarne (*Index* 5&6/1993, 8&9/1993) be sentenced to 540 days' restricted liberty in connection with his book *Ethics and the Intelligence Services*. (PEN)

The 22 November 1993 edition of the daily *La Epoca* was seized after the paper defied a court order prohibiting the publication of information concerning a murder case before the court. (IAPA)

Francisco Herreros Mardones, editor of the magazine *Pluma y Pincel*, and Juan Andrés Lagos Espinoza, editor of the weekly *El Siglo*, were sentenced to 300 days in prison by a military court on 13 January for publishing an article by Herreros which criticised the Supreme Court's decision to transfer the investigation of a 1974 disappearance to a military tribunal. (AI)

CHINA

Author Jia Pingao's novel *Fei Du* (Abandoned Capital) was banned in October 1993, owing to its 'gratuitous' sex scenes. The book, China's unofficial best-seller, is a tale of corruption and vice in a Chinese city. (CCPJ)

On 10 November 1993 it was

'A dissident? Where? Where's there a dissident?

reported that China was ready to discuss allowing the International Red Cross access to some 3,600 political prisoners detained for counter-revolutionary offences. (*International Herald Tribune*)

The case of Fu Shenqi (*Index* 8 &9/1993) was heard on 12 November 1993 at the Dafeng re-education through labour camp in Jiangsu province. He and his wife were both allowed to attend the trial and he was also permitted to speak. However, his solicitors were not permitted to present their whole testimonies nor to call witnesses. (PEN, AI)

It was reported on 17 November 1993 that Qin Yongmin and Yang Zhou, members of a new pluralist movement, were arrested only hours after a 'peace charter' had been signed in support of a multi-party political system. They were arrested for 'violating laws and regulations'. Yang

Zhou was released after six weeks, but on 25 January it was reported that Qin Yongmin had been sentenced to two years in a camp for re-education through labour. (AI, Human Rights Watch/Asia)

Leading human rights activists Ma Shaohua and Zheng Xuguang were reported missing on 2 December 1993 and are believed to have been arrested. The two men, who had launched a campaign in Xi'an calling for human rights improvements, had also held meetings with members of the Beijing-based Peace Charter group. (AI, *Independent*)

On 22 December 1993 it was announced that Xi Yang, a Beijing correspondent for the Hong Kong daily *Ming Pao*, would be tried in secret and had requested not to be represented by a lawyer. Xi was detained on 27 September 1993 on charges of 'stealing and espionage of state secrets', including unpublished interest rate changes from the People's Bank of China and information on plans for gold transactions. (CPJ)

Representatives of the Xinhua News Agency, China's de facto Hong Kong embassy, visited a private club on 21 January in a bid to prevent the screening of a BBC documentary about the life of Mao Zedong. (*Guardian*)

Xiao Bin, Ding Junze and poet Liao Yiwu, imprisoned for their part in the pro-democracy movement of 1989 were released on 31 January. (*International Herald Tribune*)

In the last week of January, eleven dissidents signed a two-page statement calling for the release of Qin Yongmin (see above). Another petition was signed by 350 people, including intellectuals, artists, journalists and even officials and demanded a fair hearing for an artist's lawsuit against the police, asserting he was illegally detained and beaten. (*International Herald Tribune*)

In February 1,000 copies of the literary magazine *Tendencies*, destined for overseas readers, were seized in Shenzen and destroyed because they contained counter-revolutionary material. (RSF)

Two new measures announced on 7 February forbid foreigners to proselytise or appoint local Chinese as religious workers in an apparent attempt to restrict contact between Chinese Christians and the outside world. The measures also reflect growing concern about

the resurgence of Islam in Xinjiang. (*Daily Telegraph, Times*)

Li Guiren, arrested in 1989 for his involvement in the pro-democracy movement and released on medical parole a year ago, was re-arrested on 16 February in Shaanxi province, apparently in connection with the detention of Ma Shaohua and Zheng Xuguang, who had visited Li's home on several occasions. (PEN, AI)

On 16 February the Ministry of Public Security informed the dissident Wang Dan that his civil and political rights had been officially restored. He was warned, however, that further investigation would be conducted into articles he wrote for foreign media. (CCPJ)

Wei Jingsheng (*Index* 2/1990, 7/1992) disappeared on 6 March, shortly before he was due to talk to foreign journalists about a recent spell in police custody. He reportedly left Beijing voluntarily, possibly on the advice of the police, in the run-up to a state visit by US secretary of state Warren Christopher. He had previously been ordered to cease submitting articles for publication to either the Chinese or foreign press. (*Independent, Guardian*)

Zhai Weimin, who was released in September 1993 after a three-year sentence for his part in the 1989 democracy movement, was arrested by the security police on 6 March. (*Times*)

Recent publications: *Detained in China and Tibet, a Directory of*

Political and Religious Prisoners (Human Rights Watch/Asia, February 1994, 632pp); *China: Dissidents Detained Since 1992 - Political Trials and Administrative Sentences* (Amnesty International, January 1994, 26pp) (see p101)

COLOMBIA

Journalist Arada de San Martín died in Bogota after being stabbed and then hit by a car on 12 January. The assailant has not been identified and the motive appeared to be robbery. (CCPJ, UPI)

Radio journalist Jesús Medina Parra was shot three times in the head on 28 January and later died in a bordertown hospital in Cucuta. The attacker remains unidentified and the motive unknown. (PEN)

Six people charged with the 1991 murders of *El Espectador* journalists Julio Daniel Chaparro and Jorge Torres (*Index* 7/1991) were acquitted on 8 February owing to lack of evidence. Family members and the police believe a paramilitary group is responsible and not drug dealers, as was originally suspected. (IAPA)

Recent publication: *State of War: Political Violence and Counterinsurgency in Colombia* (Human Rights Watch /Americas, December 1993, 149pp)

COSTA RICA

Pilar Isabel Ovares, presenter of the Channel 7 news programme *Telenoticias*, was fired on 7 January after the National

Liberal Party (PNL) allegedly pressured the station over the programme's extensive coverage of a defamation suit brought by PNL leader and president-elect José María Figueres. Figueres brought the suit against the authors of a book which alleged that he had been a member of a death squad involved in the killing of a drug trafficker in the 1970s. The suit, initiated in the run-up to the 6 February presidential elections, was dismissed, and four of Ovares' colleagues have resigned in protest at her dismissal. (RSF, IAPA)

COTE D'IVOIRE

On 24 February Hamed Bakayoko, publisher of *Le Patriote*, was sentenced to one year in prison for insulting the head of state, following the publication of an anonymous article which reportedly questioned the legitimacy of President Bedie's government. (West African Journalists' Association)

Five journalists with *La Voie*, Jacques Prejean, Cesar Etou, Freedom Neruda, Souleymane Sen and Raphael Lakpe, were charged with spreading false news on 3 March as a result of an article which claimed that President Bedie was demanding 10 billion CFA francs from France for the funeral of the late president, Félix Houphouët-Boigny. (West African Journalists' Association)

CROATIA

Viktor Ivancic, editor-in-chief of the only independent weekly *Feral Tribune* was seized by police on 5 January and taken to a military barracks in Split, for reportedly ignoring a conscription notice. After completing military training on 26 January, he was warned that he could be called up by the Croatian army in the near future. His colleagues describe the move as an attempt by the government to intimidate its critics. (PEN)

Veljko Dzakula, a moderate Serbian politician from Krajina, was arrested in Belgrade on 4 February by members of the State Security Service. Dzakula, a prominent critic of the rebel Serbian authorities, is well known as a proponent of reconciliation with Croatia. (AI)

CYPRUS

Salik Askerogul was sentenced by a military court in Lafkosa to three years and three months in prison on 12 November 1993 for failing to obey a conscription notice and for 'making propaganda against the security forces' in a press statement which explained his grounds for conscientious objection to military service. (AI)

CZECH REPUBLIC

In a move widely condemned by opposition parties and human rights groups, President Havel signed an amendment to the criminal code on 23 November 1993 under which persons found guilty of defaming the president, parliament, the constitutional court or the government can be sentenced to two years in jail. (SWB, RFE/RL)

The trial of former federal intelligence agent Václav Wallis began behind closed doors in Plzen military court in December 1993. Wallis was accused of endangering state security by passing documents to Victor Kozeny, president of the Harvard Capital and Consulting Company, the largest investment fund in the Czech Republic (*Index* 10/1993). (SWB)

DJIBOUTI

Mohamed Houmed Soulleh, president of the Association for the Defence of Human Rights (*Index* 10/1993) was sentenced to three months' imprisonment and fined for defamation and spreading false news on 25 October 1993. He was released on 10 November pending appeal. (AI)

On 30 November 1993 Dabaleh Ahmed Kassim, director of the opposition weekly *Combat*, was given a two-year suspended sentence and fined 300,000 Djiboutian francs for defamation and repeating false information (*Index* 10/1993). (RSF)

EGYPT

Salah Bedaiwy, Ali el Gammash, Adel Hussein and Magdi Hussein were charged in October 1993 with distributing terrorist propaganda through their articles in *Al Sha'ab*, the Workers' Party newspaper. Mohammed Helmy Mourad, vice-president of the Workers' Party, was also charged with defamation of the head of state as a result of articles in *Al Sha'ab* about the presidential referendum. Prosecutors also ordered the confiscation of Mourad and Adel Hussein's book, *Why We Say No to Mubarak*. (RSF)

Four men were convicted in military courts in December 1993 of the murder of the writer Farag Fouda in June 1992 (*Index* 8/1992). One was sentenced to death. (CCPJ)

Gunmen fired on a crowd of filmgoers as they left a cinema during the Cairo International Film Festival on 9 December 1993, killing a policeman and injuring seven people. Islamic groups had earlier made verbal threats against the festival in protest at sexually explicit scenes in some foreign films. (*Guardian*, *Times*)

The divorce case brought against Nasr Hamid Abu-Zaid and his wife Ebtehal Younis by a group of Islamist lawyers in June 1993 (*Index* 7/1993) was dismissed by a Cairo court in January. The judge ruled that divorce could only be granted if the petition came from the couple involved. (*Guardian*)

In January the weekly magazine, *Rose al-Youssef*, published extracts from several banned works, including *The Satanic Verses* by Salman Rushdie and *Gablawi's Children* by Naguib Mahfouz. The extracts were accompanied by a statement in defence of freedom of expression. (*Guardian*)

Retired judge Said al-Ashmawi, author of several books which challenge the basis of political Islam, was reported to have been severely criticised for distorting Islamic history in March by the Committee of the Quran and its Sciences, an organ of Al-Azhar. There are serious fears for his safety. (*Guardian*) (see p119)

EL SALVADOR

Around 50 masked men launched incendiary devices at the San Salvador offices of the paper *El Diario de Hoy* on 1 November in protest at the paper's alleged bias toward the FMLN opposition party. (RSF)

The writer, lawyer and *Diario Latino* columnist José María Méndez received several death threats late in 1993 after criticising the government for failure to act on the UN Truth Commission's recommendation that death squad activities be fully investigated. The threats are believed to come from death squads, which have been increasingly active in recent months. (CEPEX)

EQUATORIAL GUINEA

On 27 September 1993 the only opposition paper still circulating, *La Verdad*, was banned for 'issuing untruthful news and information prejudicial to public spiritedness and morality'. (RSF)

ETHIOPIA

Tefera Asmare and Iskander Negga, editors of the weekly *Ethiopis*, were detained in November 1993 and accused of not obtaining proper authorization to distribute the paper. (RSF)

New regulations under the Public Security Ordinance, in force from 20 December 1993, prescribe heavy penalties for sedition and incitement. Offences under these regulations carry prison sentences ranging from three months to 20 years. The offences cover the distribution of material prejudicial to public security, public order or the maintenance of supplies and services essential to the life of the community. (National Peace Council of Norway)

In January and Febuary 16 journalists were arrested, apparently in connection with articles they published either critical of the government or which violate a 1992 press law on defamation and 'incitement of conflict between peoples'. Asrat Damtew and Daniel Kifle of *Fendisha*, Daniel Tafesse of *Wekte*, Atensai Tafesse of *Moged*, Mayik Kassaye of *Beza*, Tesfaye Berehanu, and Yohannes Tefera were arrested in January; and Kinfe Assefa, Girmay Gebre-Tsadik, Mulugeta Jigo, Nesanet Tesfaye, Mesele Haddis, Kibret Mekonnen, Befekadu Moroda, Meleskachew Amha, and Berehane Mewa were detained in February. The detainees are publishers, editors and journalists of independent and mostly Amharic-language magazines such as *Ethiopis, Dewol, Muday, Fendisha, Mogad, Waot, Beza, Aimiro* and *Tomar*. Another editor, Mesfin Shifferaw of *Twaf* magazine, has been missing since 11 Febuary. (RSF, CPJ, AI)

FRANCE

On 1 December 1993 the government banned two Kurdish

groups, the Kurdistan Committee and the Federation of Kurdistan Cultural Associations and Patriotic Workers. Charles Pasqua, minister of the interior, said he believed the groups to be legal fronts for the 'terrorist and criminal' organisation, the Kurdish Workers Party. (*International Herald Tribune*)

On 21 December 1993 a public school sent home a Muslim girl for refusing to remove an Islamic headscarf, the fifth such incident in a month. Teachers at one school argued that the scarves were 'religious symbols that undermine the institution's secular status'. (*Times*)

On 16 February the prime minister, Edouard Balladur, was accused by André Rousselet, former chairman of the television channel Canal Plus, of political meddling in the media by putting his own friends in control of all the large audiovisual media so as to bring them into line in the run-up to the presidential elections. (*Guardian*)

A bill announced by the government on 23 February would ban the use of foreign words in advertising, public announcements and on radio and television. Foreign-language programming would be exempt from the regulation, on which parliament will vote later in the year. (*European*)

GABON

In February it was announced that independent papers and magazines are allowed to publish again after their banning in

September, during the presidential election campaign. (*Index* 10/1993). (RSF)

On 22 February the premises of the opposition-owned Radio Liberté (*Index* 7/1993) were ransacked and the transmitter blown up in a pre-dawn raid. The attack followed the station's backing of a general strike called for 21 February. Prior to the raid their broadcasts were repeatedly being jammed. (*West Africa*)

GAMBIA

Davies Michael Iber, president of the International Society for Human Rights, was detained on 15 February for three days following the publication of his article in the *Daily Observer* in which he criticised the government. The Society's office was also closed, documents were confiscated and telephones disconnected. (*West Africa*)

GEORGIA

All independent newspapers were closed for two weeks in November 1993 and all are reported to face continued pressures from shortages of paper and attacks on journalists. Reports of detentions and disappearances continue to circulate, including the disappearance of Ostankino journalists Igor Tsvetkov and Dmitri Ukhov. At least 12 journalists were detained in October: Gia Agramnashvili, Dodo Chaladze, Zizino Gabiskiria, Mukhran Madzhavariani Gotcha Makhviladze, Tinatin Mgwdlinaschvili, Gala Mchedlishvili, Marab

Ridzhamadze, Mamuka Tsomaia, Levan Uruachadze, Nino Usnadze and Mamana Arabidze were all reported to be free by January. (RSF, SWB, PEN) (see p160)

GERMANY

In early November 1993 Chancellor Helmut Kohl suggested that files compiled by the Stasi should be closed on the grounds that their contents are unreliable. The files are currently open to examination by victims of surveillance or persecution in the former East Germany. So far 670,000 people have applied for access to the files, with another 10,000 applications arriving every month. (*International Herald Tribune*)

On 4 November 1993 German police reportedly ransacked the headquarters of the Kurdistan News Agency in Düsseldorf in search of information about Kurdish attacks on Turkish targets, such as the Turkish newspaper *Hurriyet*, which was raided and occupied by Kurdish militants earlier the same week. (CPJ)

On 26 November 1993 the government banned the Kurdish Workers' Party, (PKK), for its involvement 'with acts of violence in Germany and across the continent'. (*Guardian*)

The film *Profession: Neo-Nazi* was withdrawn by distributors under pressure from public prosecutors on 14 December 1993. Although presentation of the neo-Nazis is far from sympathetic, some have criticised the film for failing fully to denounce them. The uncritical viewer, a Frankfurt court ruled, might not understand that the film was meant as a warning. (*Guardian*).

It was revealed in early January that a high-level security meeting took place between German and Iranian intelligence services a few days before the attempted murder of William Nygaard, Norwegian publisher of *The Satanic Verses* (*Index* 10/93). The meeting was in breach of an undertaking by EU countries not to improve relations with Iran until the death threat against Salman Rushdie has been lifted. (*Times*)

Gerhard Fleische, head of political reporting at the state radio station Deutschlandfunk was arrested on 20 January on suspicion of spying for the former East German state security ministry. (*Independent*)

GREECE

On 7 December 1993 the new socialist-controlled parliament scrapped the media law, passed by the Conservative government in December 1990, which called for jail terms and heavy fines for any media group which published statements made by guerrilla groups. (UPI)

GUATEMALA

The magazine *Crónica* received a letter in November 1993, purportedly from the URNG guerrilla movement, demanding the payment of US$40,000 in return for not declaring the

magazine a military target. URNG leader Miguel Angel Sandoval later said that the movement does not target news media and accused military intelligence of sending the letter to discredit the URNG. (CEPEX)

A van delivering copies of the independent magazine *Tinamit* was hijacked in Guatemala City on 9 December 1993 by six heavily armed men, who were reportedly trying to abduct the magazine's manager. (IAPA)

Victor Manuel Cruz, a reporter for Radio Sonora and *Tinamit*, was shot in Guatemala City on 23 December 1993 and died two days later. The motives for the killing are unclear. (IAPA)

The bodies of the wife and stepdaughter of *Tinamit* columnist Marco Vinicio Mejía Davila (*Index* 5&6/1993, 10/1993) were found in Escuintla department on 26 January. The bodies reportedly showed signs of torture. (IAPA)

Hugo Arce (*Index* 5&6/1993, 10/1993) reported receiving further death threats on 3 February, in connection with his new magazine *Nuestro Tiempo*, which began publication in January with an issue devoted to the press. On 21 February, the magazine's delivery van was intercepted by police who severely beat the driver, Francisco Arce. (PEN, Journalist Safety Service)

Oliverio Muñoz Barrios, director of Radio Nacional de San Marcos, was stabbed to death

in his home on 4 February. (RSF)

Adolfo Barrera Ortiz, director of the news agancy ACEN-SIAG, fled the country early in March after an attempt on his life and a bomb attack on his home on 18 February. The government reportedly refused his requests for protection. (CEPEX)

HAITI

The country's broadcast media continued to come under attack late in 1993: in October, armed members of the pro-military Front for the Advance and Progress of Haiti (FRAPH) took over the national television station and broadcast anti-Aristide material; soldiers closed the stations Radio Provincial and Radio Celestin International in Gonaïve, arresting three members of staff; and armed civilians shot at the home of Radio Television Express journalist Luc François, who was in hiding after receiving threats. In November, Lucner Desir and another, unnamed, technician with Radio Phalanstère International were arrested for 'broadcasting songs by politically committed singers'. (AMARC, PEN)

The Haitian Media Association announced on 19 January that radio stations would have to limit their broadcasting hours because of a fuel shortage caused by the UN embargo. The daily papers *Le Nouvelliste* and *Le Matin* have had to reduce production to three issues per week, and the Creole-language paper *Libeté* has already ceased publication citing 'political and economic constraints'. The private television station Télé-Haiti, which carries national news and foreign programmes, also cut its broadcasting times in January. (RSF)

HONDURAS

In September 1993 Congress amended the Authorship Rights Law to include a provision which prohibits 'the transmission or reproduction of programmes, films or novels which offend culture, morality, family unity and traditions'. The broad and ill-defined terms of the amendment provoked a storm of criticism from all sections of the media, as well as from ex-president Callejas. The Honduran Press Association, however, has supported the new article, saying it does not violate the right to free expression since the material to be prohibited is 'of very poor quality, foreign and contains scenes and phrases which distort the minds of children and adolescents, inciting them to crime, violence, and the adoption of foreign habits'. (*Central America Report*)

The new president, Carlos Roberto Reina, ordered journalists to stop reporting the activities of the presidential office on 31 January. The College of Journalists has provoked criticism from the media by suggesting its affiliates stop all news reporting from Government House in protest at the order. (CCPJ)

HONG KONG

The *Eastern Express*, a new English-language daily, was launched on 1 February by the Oriental Press Group. The launch is seen as part of a battle to preserve the editorial integrity and freedom of Hong Kong's press from self-censorship before 1997. (*Guardian*)

Recent publication: *Urgent Business: Hong Kong, Freedom of Expression and 1997* (Article 19/Hong Kong Journalists' Association, January 1994, 79pp)

HUNGARY

On 25 October 1993 Laszlo Csucs, acting chairman of Hungarian Radio, cancelled the programme *Morning Press Survey* after it cited an article by former television chairman Elemer Hankiss (*Index* 3/1993), criticising the current television leadership. The following day, Andras Bano and three other editors of the liberal Channel 2 news programme *Egyenleg* were suspended over allegations of tampering with video footage of right-wing extremists. Following protests, *Egyenleg* was cancelled permanently and Bano was dismissed in December. (SWB, RFE/RL, IPI, IFJ)

In December 1993 Veszprem County Court overruled an October decision to abandon proceedings against political scientist Laszlo Lengyel for publicly offending the authorities, and imposed a fine of 75,000 forints instead of the verbal warning issued by a lower court. Lengyel's allegations of government corruption, which he said were a matter of public record, were made

during a lecture in June 1993. (SWB)

The Association of Germans in Hungary and the Gypsy organisation Phralipe said in December 1993 that the amended Election Law makes it impossible for ethnic minorities to elect their own deputies to parliament. Under the original law, minorities could elect a deputy with as few as 3,000 votes. (SWB)

State radio dismissed 129 editors and journalists on 4 March, including Istvan Boelcs (editor of *Thought and Sign*), Akos Mester (editor of *168 Hours*), Joszef Barat and Izabella Nagy, reportedly for reasons of economy. Opposition parties, however, believe that the dismissals are part of an ongoing attempt to stifle criticism of the government in the run-up to the general election starting on 8 May. On 5 March the current affairs programme *168 Hours* was not broadcast. The scheduled edition had been compiled by some of the sacked journalists. (*International Herald Tribune*, SWB)

On 8 March parliament passed a law requiring the top officials of various institutions, including universities, national radio, television, and newspapers with a circulation over 30,000, to be vetted before appointment. (SWB)

INDIA

On 30 November 1993 Muslim rebels in Kashmir fired a rocket into the state-owned television complex at Srinagar, killing a senior engineer, in retaliation for 'propaganda' against the Kashmir liberation movement. (Reuter)

Eight staff members at the Punjab daily *Aj Di Awaz*, Jasbir Singh Khalsa, Gurdeep Singh, Malkir Singh, Jasbir Singh Manowan, Devinder Singh, Amrik Singh, Ajab Singh and Kuldeep Singh, appeared in court in late January charged with offences under the Terrorist and Disruptive Activities Act (TADA). They were arrested 10 days after Gurdeep Singh, the paper's managing editor, had been ordered to refrain from criticising government policies and debating issues of interest to Sikhs. The paper had reportedly also been offered inducements to follow a pro-government line. (Sikh Human Rights Internet, PEN)

INDONESIA

In December 1993 the attorney-general's office in Central Java ordered a crackdown on shops selling cassettes by the popular singer Atiek CB because the label has a photograph of men wearing hammer and sickle necklaces. (*Tapol*)

Nuku Sulaiman, chair of the newly formed pro-democracy movement Yayasan Pijar, was sentenced to four years in prison in January for producing a pamphlet which accused President Suharto of being the 'mastermind of all calamities' and denounced human rights abuses in Madura and West Java. Another 21 university students arrested with Sulaiman are awaiting trial. (AI, *Independent*)

Recent publications: *Human Rights Abuses in North Sumatra* (Human Rights Watch/Asia, November 1993, 18pp); *Indonesia: New Developments on Labor Rights* (Human Rights Watch/Asia, January 1994, 8pp)

IRAN

Translator and Christian evangelist Mehdi Dibaji (*Index* 6/1992), sentenced to death for apostasy by the Islamic Revolutionary Court on 3 December 1993, was freed from prison on 16 January, following an appeal and an international campaign for his release. Dibaji, who converted to Christianity 45 years ago, has been detained since 1984. (AI, PEN)

Abbas Abdi (*Index* 10/1993, p 39), editor-in-chief of *Salam* newspaper, was sentenced to one year in prison and given a suspended sentence of 40 lashes in December 1993. The charges against him are still unknown. (CPJ)

Mohammed Hashemi, head of broadcasting services and brother of President Rafsanjani, was replaced by the former culture and Islamic guidance minister, Ali Larijani, in early February after he instituted a third television channel to provide entertainment to Iran's youth and supplement their religious instruction. He has been accused of introducing Western culture into Iran and his successor's brief is to return the service to 'promoting pure Islam'. (*Guardian*)

The government formally re-

iterated the *fatwa* against Salman Rushdie on 13 February, one day before the fifth anniversary of the edict which has forced the British novelist into hiding. (*Guardian*)

IRELAND

The Irish government's decision in January not to renew the broadcasting ban, which dates from 1960 and prevented representatives of Sinn Fein from speaking on television and radio, has increased pressure on the British government to remove its own ban, introduced in 1988 and based on the Irish precedent. A legal challenge to the British ban is currently before the European Commission of Human Rights. (national press) (see p152)

ISRAEL AND OCCUPIED TERRITORIES

Hissaini Hijazi was sacked from *Falastine al-Thawra*, the Cyprus-based publication of the Palestine Liberation Organisation, in December 1993. PLO officials reportedly took exception to an article by Hissaini Hijazi in the London-based *al-Hayat* newspaper which analysed internal PLO politics. (Article 19)

Five journalists were temporarily detained by Israeli military authorities on 26 January while covering protests by Israeli settlers against the new peace accords in Kyriat Arba, near Hebron. The authorities claimed that Menahem Kahana, a photographer with AFP, and four other unnamed journalists had entered a prohibited military area. (RSF)

Palestinian journalist Atta Quessat, of the Israeli news agency Zoom 77, was beaten by undercover Israeli soldiers on 28 January while photographing clashes between Palestinian demonstrators and the Israeli military on the West Bank. (RSF)

ITALY

Indro Montanelli, editor of the Milan-based daily *Il Giornale Nuovo*, resigned on 12 January, citing editorial interference, after demands by media tycoon Silvio Berlusconi that the paper support his election campaign in return for rescuing it from its current financial crisis. Berlusconi's critics say that his right-wing Forza Italia movement has 'the biggest information monopoly in Europe' and are concerned at his ability to influence voters in the run-up to the elections in late March. (*Independent*)

KAZAKHSTAN

Charges against journalist Karishal Azanov (*Index* 10/1993) were dropped in December 1993 following the repeal of the law against slander

under which he was due to be prosecuted. (RSF)

The private television and radio station Max was closed down on 14 February after airing charges that the authorites had violated the election laws. (RFE/RL)

KENYA

On 14 January the government banned the book *Kenya: Return to Reason*, by opposition leader Kenneth Matiba, for contravention of the Prohibited Publication Act. The book is highly critical of President Daniel arap Moi and his government. The ban follows a raid on a printing press by 200 armed policemen who seized 15,000 copies of the book. (PEN)

Koigi wa Wamere (*Index* 10/1993) was re-arrested on 10 November 1993, along with five others, and formally charged with attempted theft of guns with violence and possession of arms without a certificate for which he could be sentenced to death. His arrest is apparently connected with attempts by himself and others to investigate ethnic violence in the Rift Valley. The government, which has been accused of inciting the violence, has closed parts of the region and it is believed that members of the Kalenjin ethnic group, who make up the majority of the government, have embarked on a policy of ethnic cleansing of other groups in the region. (AI, PEN)

Recent publication: *Divide and Rule: State-Sponsored Ethnic*

Violence in Kenya (Human Rights Watch/Africa, November 1993, 97pp)

LITHUANIA

In December 1993 a man was charged with the assassination of Vitas Lingis, deputy editor and co-owner of the newspaper *Respublika*, who was shot in the street on his way to work in October 1993. Lingis was well known for his investigations into organised crime. (Center for Foreign Journalists, *Baltic Observer*)

MALAWI

The Dress Act, in force for two decades, was repealed on 16 November 1993. The law compelled women to wear dresses which completely covered their knees and forbade them to wear trousers. Men were not allowed to grow their hair beyond a certain length. (*Southern Africa Political & Economic Monthly*)

Recent publications: *Censorship News*, issue 29 *Malawi's Past: The Right to Truth* (Article 19, November 1993, 18pp); *Censorship News*, issue 32 *Freedom of Expression in Malawi: More Change Needed* (Article 19, February 1994, 22pp)

MALAYSIA

The deputy home minister, Megat Junid, threatened to bar foreign journalists who 'libelled' the country on 6 March after further revelations in the British press about the Pergau dam affair. Junid also threatened to pursue 'traitors' who had acted as sources for

British journalists. (*Guardian*)

MALI

On 17 February the opposition station Radio Kayira was closed following a broadcast on 3 February in which opposition leader Mamadou Maribatrou Diaby accused the government of incompetence and called for the military to 'intervene'. The authorities said the closure was necessary to maintain public order. (RSF)

MAURITIUS

The prime minister, Aneerood Jugnauth, ordered the banning of Lindsey Collen's novel, *The Rape of Sita*, in December 1993. Sita is a Hindu deity and it is claimed that the book's title is an outrage against religion. Under Mauritian law, those who sell or distribute such material can be imprisoned for up to a year. Graffiti appearing on walls in December called for Collen to be publicly raped and attacked with acid. Anonymous telephone callers have reportedly repeated the threats. (PEN)

MEXICO

Brigadier General José Francisco Galiardo has been in prison since 9 November 1993 on charges including defamation of the army, because of his article in the magazine *Forum*, in which he accused army members of corruption, human rights abuses and drug trafficking. (*Latinamerica Press*)

The broadcasting licencing body RTC investigated two television stations in northern Mexico during December in an attemp to revoke their licences on the grounds that they occasionally broadcast in English, contravening the licence obligation to 'exalt Mexican national values'. Both stations had recently aired positive reports about the opposition National Action Party (PAN). (*Latinamerica Press*)

Ismael Romero of the Mexico City daily *La Jornada* was shot several times on 3 January while covering clashes between the rebel Zapatista National Liberation Army (EZLN) and the army in Chiapas. Government officials strongly denied responsibility for the attack but, two days later, Gerardo Tena of AFP, Elia Baltazar of the magazine *Mira*, and several members of a Univisión television crew reported being fired on by the Mexican air force although their van was clearly marked as a press vehicle. In late January, *La Jornada* received several threats from the Mexican Anticommunist Front (FAM), accusing the paper of bias towards the EZLN. Amado Avendano and Gaspar Morquecho of *El Tiempo* and Leticia Hernández Montoya and Antonio Reyes Zurita of *Excelsior*, were reportedly abducted by EZLN members on 3 January and releasedlater on payment of a ransom. (PEN, RSF, IAPA) (see p162)

Carlos Ramírez, political commentator for *El Financiero*, claimed on 28 January that his telephone is under surveillance and that the line often breaks down for several days after has been critical of the govern-ment. Ramírez has criticised José Cordoba, head of national security, for his handling of the events in Chiapas, and believes that he may have ordered the surveillance. (CCPJ)

MOLDOVA

The state broadcasting committee of the breakaway region of Trans-Dnistria withdrew accreditation from *Ekspress-Khronika* reporter Lev Rozenberg on 3 January, in connection with an article he wrote alleging that authorities in Tiraspol sent forces to defend the Moscow White House in October 1993. (SWB)

Two radio journalists with Romanian radio, Anca Florea and Mircea Dascaliuc, were beaten up on 2 February in Chisinau after covering a story on Ilie Ilascu, a political activist who seeks the reunification of Moldova with Romania and who was sentenced to death in December 1993 in Trans-Dnistria. (CCPJ)

MYANMAR

Short story writer and National League for Democracy (NLD) member, Ma Thida, and 10 other political activists, were sentenced to 20 years in prison on 15 October 1993. They were charged under the Emergency Powers Act for 'endangering public tranquillity, for having contact with illegal organisations and distributing political literature'. (PEN)

Aung San Suu Kyi (*Index* 10/1993) will be kept under

house arrest for another year, it was announced in February. Her five-year detention was due to end in July. (*Telegraph*)

NEPAL

The body of Lokendra Kumar Burathoki, local correspondent for the Communist Party (CPN) daily *Dristhi*, was found on 11 January at his home in Rajbiraj. Colleagues say the circumstances of his death suggest he committed suicide but some CPN members believe that politicians criticised in Burathoki's articles may have ordered his death. (RSF)

NIGERIA

On 2 January government agents raided the Academy Press, printers of *Tell*, and seized 50,000 copies of the magazine because of its headline 'The Return of Tyranny: Abacha Bears His Fangs'. (*Nigeria Now*)

Two *Razor* journalists, Moshood Fayewimo and Tony Drilade, were charged with sedition on 12 January, following publication of an article predicting a violent coup against General Abacha. (*West Africa*)

The private radio station, Ray Power 100, was closed down on 13 January after being on air for 10 days. Officials say the station was broadcasting illegally by refusing to wait for its licence to be issued. The licence is reportedly complete but has remained unreleased for six months. (*Newswatch*)

On 12 February Major-General

Shehu Musa Yar'Adua was arrested by officers of the state security service after he gave a press conference in which he called for General Abacha's Ruling Provisional Council to stand down by 31 December, and for a lifting of the ban on party politics. (*West Africa*)

PAKISTAN

Sailab Mahsud, correspondent for the Urdu daily *Jang* and *The News*, was released on 22 November 1993, reportedly after presidential intervention in his case. He had been sentenced to 10 years in prison on 13 October, with no right of appeal, after interviewing Amanullah Khan, a prominent man wanted on drugs charges. (PEN)

PARAGUAY

In late December 1993 there was a wave of death threats against journalists, mainly in the interior of the country, where many are investigating the activities of local government officials. Those threatened include Juan Pelayo, Blanca Mino, Heriberto Arguello and Francisco Servía of the paper *Tiempo 14* and the station Radio Mburucuya; and Candida Benítez of the Asunción paper *Hoy*. (Paraguayan Journalists' Union)

PERU

Congress restored habeas corpus rights for those charged with terrorist offences on 12 November 1993. It also restored the right to review sentences passed by military courts and prohibited the trial

in absentia of persons accused of terrorism and treason. (IAPA)

Five people were injured when a bomb, believed to have been planted by Shining Path guerrillas, exploded outside the headquarters of the official government paper of record, *El Peruano*, in Lima on 2 December 1993. (Instituto Prensa y Sociedad)

María Carlin Fernández, a reporter for the station Radio Televisión Peruana, was shot dead on 10 December 1993 at a restaurant in Chimbote. Two other people were seriously injured in the attack which the police believe is linked to Carlin's ongoing investigation into the murder of her brother some months earlier. (RSF)

A report in *Sí* magazine in January claimed that missing *Punto Final* journalist Pedro Yauri Bustamente (*Index* 9/1992, 3/1993) was killed by a special military unit linked to the intelligence services because of his alleged sympathies with the Tupac Amaru Revolutionary Movement. (PEN)

In February a civil suit for defamation was brought by a former Supreme Court judge against Nicolas Lucar and Rosana Cueva, director and reporter with the popular current affairs programme *La Revista Dominical*. The case is the first test of the controversial new 'Habeas Data' law which limits the publication of personal information and allows aggrieved parties to seek restitution. (PEN)

Congress passed a law changing the Supreme Court's appeals procedure on 8 February, so as to allow the 10 soldiers accused of carrying out the La Cantuta massacre (*Index* 8&9/1993) to be tried by a military court. Prime minister Alfonso Bustamente resigned in protest at the move. (*Guardian*)

On 18 February hearings began in the cases of several journalists accused of supporting terrorism because they have worked for the Shining Path paper *El Diario*. Carlos Alberto Guerrero Gamarra, Fernando Avila Rosales, José Herrera Mendoza, Monica Palomo Malaga, Juan Antonio Morales Rossi, Alex Ramón Morales, Jhonny Navarro Ipanque and Luís Becerra Mori all worked for *El Diario* prior to 1990, when the paper was circulated legally. In late February the Supreme Court ordered new trials for several other journalists who had recently been acquitted of having worked for *El Diario*, including Gisela Gutarra Sedano (*Index* 8&9/1993) and Juan Huamancusi Quispe. (IFJ)

PHILIPPINES

Two reporters for *Cotabato Ngayon*, Rosauro Lao and Ding Sade, were shot dead on 22 November 1993 in Cotabato city. No motive for the killings has been established. (*Philippine Press Freedom Advocate*)

Station DXIF Radyo Bombo in Cagayan de Oro was fired on by gunmen with M-16 rifles in December 1993. The station

has antagonised many with its critical investigations into official corruption. (*Philippine Press Freedom Advocate*)

ROMANIA

In November 1993 the Romanian Journalists' Association criticised proposed amendments to the criminal code which would allow journalists who print 'insults and calumnies' to be sentenced to two years in prison. Libel by a non-journalist would carry a maximum penalty of one year. (SWB)

The prosecutor-general lifted President Iliescu's ban on *Mein Kampf* in November 1993 because the far-right groups which the ban was intended to affect are legally registered. (SWB)

On 11 January television director-general Paul Everac resigned after criticism of a television documentary on the 1946 execution of wartime leader Marshall Antonescu, which reportedly implied the involvement of ex-King Mihaithe. The film had been recommended by Corneliu Tudor Vadim, chairman of the Greater Romania Party, who alleged that at least seven ministers had supported the broadcast. The government has denied any involvement in the broadcast. (SWB)

Nicolae Andrei was arrested on 14 February for writing satirical articles in *Conflict* which were deemed insulting to President Iliescu. Denigrating the country or the Romanian nation is an offence under the penal

code which carries a sentence of up to three years. (RSF)

RUSSIAN FEDERATION

Russia: Two of Russia's most-prominent news agencies were brought back under government control by decree of President Yeltsin on 22 December 1993. Itar-Tass and Ria-Novosti were proclaimed independent in the aftermath of the August 1991 coup, but their extensive coverage of December's parliamentary election campaign appears to have caused official displeasure. (*Baltic Observer*)

According to the Glasnost Defence Foundation, a total of 24 journalists, including three foreign correspondents, were killed in 1993 in the former Soviet Union; and seven journalists were killed, 14 wounded and 36 assaulted during the constitutional crisis in Moscow in October 1993. (Glasnost Defence Foundation)

The trial of Vil Mirzayanov, who published an article claiming that chemical weapons testing has continued in Russia in violation of international agreements, opened in camera on 24 January. On 26 January Mirzayanov was taken into police custody for contempt of court after refusing to attend the hearings on the grounds that the trial was unconstitutional. He was released on 22 February, pending further hearings. (RFE/RL)

Journalists were barred from attending meetings of the cabinet from 3 February. Previously, officials and journalists were allowed to attend but this permission has now been restricted to one reporter from the government-owned paper *Rossiiskaya Gazeta*. (Itar-Tass)

Sergei Doubov, an editor for several publications, was shot dead outside his home in Moscow on 1 February. He had frequently been threatened by organised crime syndicates. (AFP)

Zufar Gareev reports: On 4 February Alexei Kostin, the publisher of the popular erotic journal *Yeshcho* was arrested and charged under Article 228 of the Legal Code of the Russian Federal Republic with 'manufacturing pornography'. The affair began during the October putsch when the militia closed down the paper, tied up Alexei Kostin and hand-cuffed him for three days in an 'isolator' (a special prison for political detainees and those suspected of espionage). Shortly after this, he was re-arrested and deposited in the Byutirski prison in a communal cell. Each prisoner is allocated one square metre of floor space in which they sleep and sit in rows on stools. The insult to the man was intended to crush the paper, and was the culmination of a series of legal harassments by the authorities. *Yeshcho* is the only erotic journal in Russia with an anti-Communist line. Its Rigan editor, Vladimir Linderman, is a veteran independent journalist from Soviet times. During *perestroika* he published a journal of the literary underground in Riga, *Tretya Modernizatsia*, for which he was hounded by the authorities and the KGB. He produced the first independent political journal, *Atmoda*, and two years ago began to publish *Yeshcho*. Despite its popularity with intellectuals, the Moscow authorities took an immediate dislike to it and attempted to close it down by bringing a criminal action against it for 'insulting the honour and dignity' of President Mikhail Gorbachev. The persecution of the paper has continued ever since, currently with the help of experts specially selected to fabricate evidence of the paper's pornographic nature. They argue that, since the signing of the new constitution, it has no constitutional, legal or moral guarantee. It does however conform with Article 29 of the constitution, which forbids only the publication of anything which aims to incite national, social, racial or religious dissent. However, the MVD (Interior Ministry) and the public prosecutor's office are openly contemptuous of the constitution. The trial of strength with *Yeshcho* is the first serious confrontation with the press.

Chechnia: Four armed policemen broke into the offices of *Justice*, the only opposition paper, on 3 December 1993 and removed papers and computer equipment. The paper's previous issue had dealt with opposition leader Yragi Mamodayev's plans for a 'government of people's trust'. (SWB)

Tatarstan: A Kazan correspondent of the newspaper *Vesti* was reportedly beaten to death by three unknown assailants on 21 December 1993. There have previously been numerous threats against *Vesti* correspondents in Kazan. (SWB)

RWANDA

On 11 January an unidentified man threw a grenade at André Katabarwa, a human rights activist working for the Association of Peace Volunteers (AVP). Witnesses claim that members of the gendarmerie close to the scene made no attempt to apprehend the assailant. (AI)

Recent publication: *Arming Rwanda: The Arms Trade and Human Rights Abuses in the Rwandan War* (Human Rights Watch Arms Project, January 1994, 64pp)

SAO TOMÉ & PRINCIPE

Sao Tomean television director Carlos Teixera was dismissed on 27 January by the state secretary for social communication and culture, reportedly for refusing to mix propaganda with public sevice broadcasting. (RSF)

SAUDI ARABIA

The government was reported in November 1993 to be negotiating for control of at least three Arabic-language papers in Europe, *Al-Arab, Muharar* and *Sourakia*, raising fears that it is trying to gag them following the printing of anti-Saudi material. The London-based *Al-Arab* has been serialising an Amnesty International report detailing oppression of Shia Muslims and Christians in Saudi Arabia. (*Independent,*

Middle East Dialogue)

SERBIA-MONTENEGRO

On 31 January a memorial gathering was held at a house in Ferizaj in honour of young Albanians shot dead by Serbian police between 1981 and 1993. Serbian police broke up the gathering, detaining 35 participants, several of whom were severely beaten. (*Kosova Communication*)

On 10 February Kosovo Information Centre reported that Serbian police had arrested the leadership of the Parliamentary Party of Kosovo in Lipjan and that of the Democratic League of Kosovo in the same area. (SWB)

After a long campaign of threatened closure against the Kosovo Academy of Sciences and Arts, Serbian officials took over the building on the evening of 22 February and members of the Albanian staff found themselves locked out of the building the following morning. The move has been condemned as 'an act of violence aimed at a physical and cultural annihilation of the Kosovo Albanians'. (ATA Tirana, SWB)

Recent publication: *Yugoslavia: Ethnic Albanians - Trial By Truncheon* (Amnesty International, February 1994, 15pp)

SIERRA LEONE

New press guidelines, in force from 30 March, require annual registration of newspapers with the department of information and stipulate that editors must have a university degree or an advanced certificate in journalism and at least five years' experience as a staff reporter. Newspapers are also required to show evidence of having paid business and income taxes (*Index* 4/1993). (*West Africa*)

SINGAPORE

The Ministry of Information and the Arts said that from 15 January the *Economist* (*Index* 10/1993) would again be allowed to circulate freely, lifting distribution curbs imposed last year. The statement said the magazine would not be required to appoint a local distributor nor to have its copies marked with stickers stating it was approved for sale. (*Independent*)

Charges against Tharman Shanmugaratnam, the director of the Singapore Monetary Authority's economics section, accused of leaking a statistic a few days before its official publication, have been reduced from communicating classified information to negligence. In the same case Patrick Daniel, editor of *Business Times*, and an unnamed staff reporter also face charges of misusing state secrets. (*Guardian, International Herald Tribune*)

SLOVAKIA

Parliament dismissed television council chairman Igor Ciel and council member Marain Lesko on 26 October 1993 and elected seven new members, all reportedly ruling-coalition (MFDS and SNP) supporters. On 11 December central director of television Peter Malec resigned because the new council chairman had effectively removed his authority to sign documents. Maria Hluchnova, *Radiozurnal* editor, resigned in protest at the allegedly political dismissal of radio news and current affairs editor Lubomir Litner. Radio and television staff, including Litner, had reportedly protested against the government's suspension of television and radio funding. Slovak Radio is believed to be on the verge of financial collapse and, in December, radio director Vladimir Stefko warned of staff cuts and programme cancellations in 1994. (SWB)

In December 1993 the government approved a recommendation that female surnames could be registered, on request, without the Slovak 'ova' suffix. (SWB)

Police seized state secretary for privatisation Ivan Lexa's travel documents in January in connection with charges against him of defaming the president in the papers *Sme* and *Republika*. On 25 January Andrej Hrico, editor-in-chief of *Domino Efekt* was also charged with defaming the president. The criminal code allows imprisonment of up to two years for defamation. (SWB, AI)

On 8 January Slovak police reportedly attempted to prevent ethnic Hungarians attending a meeting at Komarno held to organise a campaign for greater autonomy for the Hungarian minority. Ethnic Hungarian parties fear that the proposed redrawing of regional boundaries would artificially divide regions inhabited by ethnic minorities ensuring a Slovak majority in each region. If the minority population in any region falls below 20 per cent of the total it risks losing rights to mother-tongue use in education and administration. (SWB)

On 28 January the Telecommunications Ministry reversed its decision to cancel Radio Free Europe's right to broadcast in Slovakia. Officials have criticised RFE's Slovakian coverage for having a 'one track orientation'. (SWB)

SOMALIA

Car thieves shot dead a Somali driver working for Cable News Network television in Mogadishu on 28 November 1993. He was the fifth CNN Somali employee to be killed in Mogadishu since October. (AFP)

SOUTH AFRICA

A public inquiry into surveillance at the South African Broadcasting Corporation began on 2 December 1993 after freelance producer Helena Norgueira claimed that she had been spied upon by a hidden camera after her managers had reportedly accused her of holding 'leftist views'. The SABC is reported to have confirmed that Norgueira was secretly filmed while using an editing suite because there were suspicions that she was doing unauthorised freelance work. (*Southern African Report*)

All charges against Bush Radio (*Index* 7/1993) were dropped on 10 December 1993. The station had been broadcasting without a licence in an attempt to end the broadcasting monopoly of the SABC. An Independent Broadcasting Authority, to license private stations, is to be established soon and it is thought that this is the reason the charges were dropped. (AMARC)

Several hundred people, including members of the neo-Nazi Afrikaner Resistance Movement (AWB), responded to a Radio Pretoria appeal to gather at the station's premises on 13 December 1993 to resist any police attempt to stop broadcasts. The right-wing station's licence expired on 4 January but broadcasts have continued since then. (*Guardian, International Herald Tribune*)

Abdul Shariff, a freelance photographer with Associated Press, was shot dead on 8 January at Katlehong township, when gunmen opened fire on a party including ANC general secretary Cyril Ramaphosa and Communist Party chairman Joe Slovo. Two SABC reporters, Charles Moikanyang and Anthea Warner, were also wounded. (CPJ, Associated Press)

Journalism student Mohseen Jeenah was shot dead at a police station in Durban on 17 January. Police claim he was taking part in an armed raid on the station by members of the Azanian People's Liberation Army (APLA), but his family say he was not a member of APLA and had gone to the sta-

tion to research a story. (MISA)

The anti-establishment Afrikaans-language weekly *Vrye Weekblad* closed on 2 February owing to financial problems. Editor Max du Preez blamed the reluctance of Afrikaner businesses to advertise in the paper and the ongoing costs of judicial proceedings against it.

Television crews from the SABC and Sky News were severly harassed while covering violent unrest in Bophuthatswana on 9 March. The following day members of a Reuter television crew were badly beaten by police and BBC correspondent James Harrison was killed in a road accident between Mmabatho and Zeerust. A crew from the agency WTN was also beaten in Mafikeng. (MISA, IFJ)

Recent publication: *South Africa's Transition: Testing the pieties* (Richard Steyn, World Press Freedom Committee, December 1993, 40pp)

SOUTH KOREA

On 23 December 1993, Masato Shinohara, a Japanese journalist, was sentenced to two years in prison for illegally obtaining and leaking classified military documents between 1989 and 1992, when he was the Seoul bureau chief of Japan's Fuji Television Company. Ko Young Chui, a lieutenant commander in the South Korean army who provided him with the information, was jailed for two years for passing on secrets. (CCPJ)

Publisher Choi Il-bung (*Index*

4/1993) was reportedly released from prison on 24 December 1993, around one year early. (PEN)

Fourteen people were arrested on 21 and 22 February after allegedly distributing leaflets at a public rally, in workplaces and in bookshops. The fourteen are accused of belonging to the group Socialists for Workers' Liberation and face charges under the National Security Law. In addition, five members of the Bird of Hope singing troupe were detained on charges of planning a musical which contained 'anti-state' elements and praised North Korea. (AI)

Warner Brothers withheld the film *Falling Down* from circulation in March after threats of a boycott over a scene in which a Korean grocer in the United States is beaten with a baseball bat. (*International Herald Tribune*)

SPAIN

On 15 November 1993 police dismantled a network of telephone taps placed around the office of *La Vanguardia*, the Barcelona daily paper. According to *El Pais*, Spain's military intelligence service, Cesid, was directly involved in the illegal surveillance. (*Guardian*)

SRI LANKA

The government instituted a series of emergency regulations in late December 1993 prescribing penalties of up to 20 years in prison for offences of sedition and incitement. The

regulations make it a crime to display posters or distribute leaflets 'the contents of which are prejudicial to public security' and specifically proscribe acts of civil disobedience. (Article 19)

Journalists who reported on the discovery of clandestine mass graves at Suriyakanda on 3 January have been pressured by police to reveal their sources. Daya Lankapura and Edmund Ranasinghe of *Divaina* and Niresh Eliyathamby, MLZ Hussain and Sharmindra Ferdinando of the *Island* were interviewed by police investigators on 6 and 10 January. Officials of the Sri Lanka Freedom Party are also reported to have received threats in connection with their interest in the graves, which are believed to contain the remains of students at Embilipitiya Central College, abducted four years ago by army soldiers during a purge of suspected Communists. (*Independent*, Article 19)

Recent publications: *The Human Rights Situation in Sri Lanka 1993: A Brief Overview* (Sri Lanka Information Monitor, January 1994, 19pp); *Sri Lanka: Summary of Human Rights Concerns* (Amnesty International, February 1994, 17pp); *Balancing Human Rights and Security: Abuse of Arrest and Detention Powers in Colombo* (Amnesty International, February 1994, 25pp)

SWAZILAND

Three journalists working for the *Swazi Observer*, a state-controlled newspaper, received

anonymous death threats on 3 January after the publication of opposition criticism of the prime minister's plans to buy a fleet of luxury cars. One of the journalists was accused by an anonymous caller of 'promoting opposition parties'. It is illegal to form political parties in the kingdom. (MISA)

Jan Sithole, secretary-general of the Swaziland Federation of Trade Unions, claimed that the government instructed the state-run television and radio networks to give no coverage to the general strike of 21 and 22 February or to the strikers' demands. The government has denied the claims. Some observers believe officials within the broadcasting corporation acted on their own initiative and chose to ignore the strike. (MISA)

SYRIA

The continued detention of a number of writers and journalists was reported in January, including: Khalil Brayez, arrested in Beirut in 1970; Tadrus Trad, a writer, poet and teacher, arrested in March 1980; Abdallah Muqdad, arrested in 1980; Rada Haddad, journalist at the Ba'ath Party paper, *Tishrin*, arrested in October 1980; Ahmad Swaidan, journalist for *al-Kifah al-Ummal*, arrested in January 1982; Isma'il al-Hajje, arrested in January 1982; Samir al-Hassan, Palestinian editor of *Fatah al-Intifada*, arrested in April 1986; Anwar Bader, a radio and television reporter, arrested in December 1986; Faraj Beraqdar, a poet, arrested in March 1987 (*Index* 3/1993);

Editorial annexe, Ozgür Gündem.
'They should install a coffee machine here.'

and Ahmed Hasso, a Kurdish writer, and Salama George Kila, a Palestinian writer, both arrested in March 1992. (PEN, Human Rights Watch)

Recent publication: *Syria: European Parliament Should Condition EC Aid on Human Rights Improvements* (Human Rights Watch/Middle East, November 1993, 13pp)

TAJIKISTAN

Adzhik Aliyev (*Index* 10/1993) was not executed as had been feared in October 1993, but remains alive under threat of execution. People present at Aliyev's trial, including relatives of those killed in the civil war, reportedly placed pressure on the judge by threatening to burn down the courthouse unless the death sentence was passed. (AI)

Poet and opposition activist Bozor Sobir (*Index* 7/1993), was released from prison on 29 December 1993 after being given a two-year suspended sentence on charges stemming from an incident in April 1992, in which demonstrators took MPs and government officials hostage for a day; and from criticism of Russian influence in Tajikistan in his poetry and articles, for which he was accused of inciting ethnic hatred. (CCPJ, PEN)

Recent publication: *Human Rights in Tajikistan in the Wake of Civil War.* (Human Rights Watch/Memorial, December 1993, 64pp) (see p103)

TANZANIA

On 21 January the weekly paper *Baraza* was closed down for breaching the 1976 Newspaper Act by not informing the government that the newspaper had moved to a new printing firm, by publishing 'malicious news' and because the editor, Hassan Yahya, was not qualified according to the provisions of the act. The closure followed the publication of an article accusing the authorities of complicity in the death of prominent Muslim leader Kassim Juna, who died in police detention. The paper appeared again on 21 February amid reports that it had since appointed a qualified editor. (MISA)

TIBET

Gendun Rinchen and Lobsang Yonten, two Tibetan human rights monitors arrested in May 1993 in Lhasa, were unexpectedly released on 10 and 11 January. Chinese authorities have so far not issued any statement regarding the conditions of the two men's release. (Tibet Information Network)

Jail terms imposed on 14 Buddhist nuns have been increased because they recorded pro-independence songs from their jail cells, it was reported on 22 February. The nuns, originally sentenced to five years for taking part in peaceful demonstrations against Chinese rule, had their sentences increased to between nine and 17 years. (Tibet Information Network)

TUNISIA

The offices of the official Kuwaiti agency KUNA were closed by the government for three days in February following the broadcast of a statement by the leader of the banned Islamist group An-Nadha. (AFP)

Alfred Hermida, correspondent for the BBC, was expelled from the country on 18 February for spreading 'disinformation' and 'false, fantastic and tendentious news'. (RSF)

Recent publications: *The Press in Tunisia: Plus Ça Change* (Article 19, November 1993, 12pp); *Tunisia: Rhetoric versus Reality: the Failure of a Human Rights Bureaucracy* (Amnesty International, January 1994, 42pp)

TURKEY

Recep Marasli, a publisher with the Komal publishing house, was sentenced to two years in prison on 25 November 1993 for disseminating separatist propaganda. He is currently free, pending appeal. (PEN)

Writer Omer Agin was sentenced to 20 months in prison and fined 42 million lira after an article appeared in the weekly *Demokrat* debating the possibility of a separate Kurdish state. Engin Gunay (*Index* 7/1993), chief editor of the magazine which is now banned, was sentenced to six months and fined 50 million lira. (PEN)

Two journalists with the HBB network, an independent Istanbul television company, are appealing against a two-month sentence for encouraging draft-dodging. Ali Tevfik Berber and Erhan Akyildiz were arrested after interviews with peace activists opposed to military service were included in their programme *Anten*. (CCPJ)

In December 1993, police raided the offices of *Ozgür Gündem* in Istanbul and other cities,

detaining over 150 employees and seizing equipment. Over 20 staff still remain in police custody, while others report police intimidation. On 24 December the Istanbul State Security Court banned the paper for two months and sentenced former editor Isik Yurtcu to four years' imprisonment. Current editor Davut Karadag was also sentenced to one year in prison on 30 December. The banning order was extended for one month on 18 February. An appeal has been lodged and meanwhile the paper continues to publish. (AFP, AI, CPJ, INFO-TURK, PEN) (see p164)

Ruhi Can Tul, a translator and reporter for the *Turkish Daily News*, was killed in a PKK bomb attack on a bus on 14 January. (PEN)

On 20 January the well known Kurdish writer Ismail Besikci (*Index* 7/1993), was sentenced to two years in prison and fined 250 million lira under the Anti-Terror Law in connection with his book *Nation That Discovered Itself: The Kurds*. (PEN)

Hale Soysu, editor of the left-wing paper *Aydinlik*, was sentenced to 10 months on 20 January for two articles written by news manager Ferit Ilsever, who was given the same sentence. (PEN)

Kutlu Esendemir and Recep Ozturk, two journalists working for the private TGRT television station were abducted by the PKK on 29 January. Since the PKK banned journalists from the south-east region in October 1993, all reporters

must get permission before entering. (AFP)

Mehmet Ali Baris Besli, owner and editor of *Ogni* magazine which is partly published in the Laz dialect, was reported to be awaiting trial on charges of separatism in February, after publishing an article which said that there is a culturally distinct Laz nation within Turkey, which should be granted official recognition. (*Turkish Daily News*)

Recent publication: *Turkey: Twenty-one Deaths in Detention in 1993* (Human Rights Watch/Helsinki, January 1994, 6pp)

UKRAINE

Captain Andriy Lazebnikov, head of the Black Sea Fleet press centre, was shot dead in the entrance to his office on 15 December 1993. The Ukrainian armed forces have strongly denied responsibility for the killing. (SWB)

On 22 February Valeriy Ashtakov, president of Crimean Television and Radio Broadcasting, reported that he had refused the request of Crimean president Yuri Meshkov for his resignation. Several radio and television journalists in Crimea, including Tatyana Korobova, Lilya Budzhurova and Leonid Pilunsky, were reportedly harassed in February by pro-Russian groups. (*Holos Ukrayiny*)

USA

This winter, the California

Board of Education removed two stories by Alice Walker from a standardised English test given to high school students statewide. One story, 'Roselily', was removed on the grounds that it is 'anti-religious', the other 'Am I Blue', because it is 'anti-meat-eating'. An excerpt from An American Childhood, by Annie Dillard, was also banned from the test because Board members found a description of a snowball fight too violent. (*New York Times*)

A draft report of a new policy on government classification, released in January, proposed that secret documents be declassified automatically after 40 years. President Clinton, who controls classification policy, has promised greater openness than his two predecessors but critics of the proposals say 40 years is still too long. (*New York Times*)

The Supreme Court ruled unanimously on 24 January that the Racketeer Influenced and Corrupt Organisations Act (RICO) can be invoked to sue anti-abortion protesters who block access to clinics (*Index* 1/1991, 2/1990). This latest extension of the act is the first to go beyond the definition of racketeering as an enterprise motivated by economic gain. Civil libertarians fear that after this ruling, an ideological motive may suffice. (*Boston Globe, New York Times*)

After a nine-month review, the Commerce Department announced in February that it will continue its policy on encryption, which enables the government to intercept and decode messages sent over private computer or telephone lines (*Index* 1/1990 p12). Opponents of the policy charge that it favours national security and law enforcement agencies and constitutes invasion of privacy. (*Washington Post*)

Gerry Adams, leader of Northern Ireland's Sinn Fein, was granted a limited visa to visit the US in February. Adams has been denied entry eight times in the past 10 years on the grounds that he supported terrorism (*Index* 7/1993). During the visit, the Cable News Network's satellite service to Europe and the Middle East withheld a live interview with Adams so as to comply with the British broadcasting ban. (States News Service, IFJ)

Oral arguments on the remaining issue in Finley v NEA began on 3 February. The issue concerns a 1990 law requiring recipients of National Endowment for the Arts grants to comply with 'general standards of decency and respect for the diverse beliefs and values of the American public' (*Index* 7&8/1993, 9/1993). These content restrictions were ruled unconstitutional in 1992, but the Justice Department appealed. (National Association of Artists' Organizations)

In response to threats of governmental regulation, the network and cable television industries announced in February that they will set up independent systems to monitor television violence. Cable operators also endorsed a rating system and the 'V chip', a tech-nological device that allows viewers to block programmes with a 'violence' rating. Ten bills aimed at restricting or banning violent programming have been introduced in Congress this year. (national press)

Congress held hearings about instituting mandatory rating systems for rap music in February and for video games in December 1993. On 4 March the video game industry announced that it would have its own labelling system indicating the level of sex and violence in its products in place by the end of this year. Nonetheless, Congress continues to consider a system of compulsory labelling. (Associated Press, *Washington Post, Boston Globe*)

In November1993 federal regulations restricting 'indecent' broadcasts to the hours of midnight to 6am were ruled unconstitutional (*Index* 5/1992, 9/1992). The Federal Communications Commission (FCC) responded by lengthening the period in which such programmmes can be aired. In a separate ruling, a federal court found that the FCC regulation allowing cable television stations to ban 'indecent' programming from public access channels was also unconstitutional. (*Boston Globe, Media Law Reporter*)

On 7 March the Supreme Court ruled that artists who use copyrighted work as a basis for parody are protected by the First Amendment. The case involved the rap group 2 Live Crew and their satirical version of the song 'Oh Pretty

Woman'. (*Boston Globe*)

Recent publications: *Human Rights Violations in the United States* (Human Rights Watch/ACLU, 1994, 216pp); *Media Studies Journal: The Race for Content* (Freedom Forum Media Studies Center at Columbia University, Winter 1994, 182pp). *Sex, Sin, and Blasphemy: A Guide to America's Censorship Wars* (Marjorie Heins, The New Press 1993, 210 pp)

UZBEKISTAN

Two dissident Uzbek journalists, Albert Musin, and Abdurashid Sharipov, and poet Yadgar Abid, were beaten and threatened at gun-point in their Moscow apartment in November 1993. The attackers reportedly stole their passports and some anti-government literature. The three believe their assailants were members of the Uzbek secret service, and observers suggest the attack represents a pattern in which Central Asian authorities are reaching beyond their own borders to harass government opponents seeking refuge in other republics. (*International Herald Tribune*)

On 23 November 1993, four staff members of the opposition IRK Party newspaper, editor-in-chief, I Khakulov, deputy editor I Nazachov, and staff members K Safanov and S Sukurov, were sentenced to two-year conditional prison terms for embezzlement and abuse of public office. The newspaper's opposition to the government is thought to be the real reason behind the sen-

tences. The newspaper itself was forcibly closed on 13 November 1993. (AI, *Ekspress-Khronika*)

It was reported in late February that IRK Party activist Safar Bekjan had been sentenced to three years in prison in July 1993. He was found guilty of stealing a gold coin from a museum but observers believe he was framed on account of his political activities. (RFE/RL)

VIETNAM

In November 1993 new regulations were set, restricting the amount of advertising allowed in newspapers and magazines to no more than 10 per cent of total page space; and to no more than five per cent of air time on television. It is believed that this is intended to secure government control over the booming media sector. (AFP)

YEMEN

Two unnamed French journalists were deported from Yemen in January after being accused of writing provocative news reports. The expulsions follow the arrest and subsequent deportation of British television journalist Ray Shillito in October 1993. (CPJ)

ZAIRE

Between 27 October and 9 November 1993 five newspapers were suspended for several days following criticism of the Birindwa government's monetary policy. The five papers, *La Renaissance* (daily and weekly),

Umoja, Salongo, and *Elima*, are all linked to the opposition. (RSF)

Belgian journalist and film maker Thierry Michel was arrested and expelled from the country on 4 March for 'suspicious activities and intelligence work for a foreign power'. He was trying to obtain authorisation for a documentary on expatriate Europeans living in Zaire. (IFJ)

Recent publication: *Prison Conditions in Zaire* (Human Rights Watch/Prison Project, January 1994, 62pp)

ZAMBIA

On 29 January *Weekly Post* photographer Sheik Chifuwe was detained in Lusaka after photographing police officers beating a suspect. He was released soon afterwards but the film in his camera was only returned to the *Weekly Post* some days later, after the paper's lawyers intervened. On 2 February another *Weekly Post* journalist, Bright Mwape, was threatened with detention at Kafue police station, where he had gone to follow up a story about the shooting of a suspect in police custody. (MISA)

Compiled by: Laura Bruni, Juliet Dryden, Anna Feldman, Jason Garner, Oren Gruenbaum, Robin Jones, Annie Knibb, Nan Levinson, George McDonald, Robert Maharajh, Heather Nielsen, Philippa Nugent, Natasha Pairaudeau, Vera Rich, Amy Sjoberg and Han Shih Toh.

CONTRIBUTORS

ANTHONY BURTON is senior partner at Simons, Muirhead and Burton.

PETER CALVERT is Professor of Comparative and International Politics at the University of Southampton

MATTHEW D'ANCONA is special writer at *The Times*.

RONALD DWORKIN is Professor of Jurisprudence at the University of Oxford.

UMBERTO ECO, linguist, semiologist and professor at Bologna University, is best known for his novels *The Name of the Rose* and *Foucault's Pendulum*. An English translation of *Secundo Diario Minimo: Selected Stories* will be published by Secker in 1994.

MICHAEL FARRELL is a lawyer and vice-chair of the Irish Council for Civil Liberties, which campaigned against the broadcasting ban.

JAMES FENTON's latest book of poems is *Out of Danger* (Penguin, 1993).

SUZANNE GIBSON is Fellow in Law at New College, Oxford.

JOHN GITTINGS is China specialist at the *Guardian*, London.

SABINE GOODWIN is working with the Arab Association for Human Rights in Nazareth, Israel.

MICHAEL GRADE is chief executive, Channel Four Television UK.

RONALD HARWOOD is a playwright and novelist, and president of International PEN.

ANDREW KELLY is a lawyer and works at Amnesty International, London.

DORIS LESSING's best-known works are *The Golden Notebook* and the two-novel series *Children of Violence* and *Canopus in Argus*. Her latest book is *African Laughter*. The first volume of her autobiography will be published this year.

ROBERT McCRUM is a writer and journalist. He is a member of *Index's* Council.

ADEWALE MAJA-PEARCE represents *Index* in Africa. He is based in Lagos, Nigeria.

ALBERTO MANGUEL is a Canadian writer and anthologist. He has edited several collections including *The Gates of Paradise: the Flamingo Anthology of Erotic Short Fiction*. In *Another Part of the Forest* will be published by Harper Collins in May.

CAROLINE MOOREHEAD is a writer and also a film-maker specialising in human rights. Her latest book, *Bertrand Russell: a Life*, was published by Sinclair Stevenson in 1992.

ANNE NELSON is a writer and journalist active in the field of human rights and free expression.

JEFF RIGSBY is a freelance journalist based in Berkeley, California. He was in Belarus at the end of 1993.

SALMAN RUSHDIE is the author of five novels. *Midnight's Children* was awarded the Booker of Booker's Prize in 1993. *The Satanic Verses* won the Whitbread Prize for the Best Novel, the German Author of the Year Award and the Italian Premio Pedrocchi. In 1994 he became first president of the Strasbourg-based International Parliament of Writers.

POSY SIMMONDS is a cartoonist and author. Her latest book, *Mustn't Grumble*, was published by Jonathan Cape in 1993.

STEPHEN SPENDER, poet, author and critic, was a founder of *Index*.

DUBRAVKA UGRESIC is an author and journalist. Her most recent book, *Have a Nice Day,* is due to be published by Jonathan Cape in November 1994.

ALEKSEI VENEDIKTOV is a radio journalist with *Ekho Moskva (Moscow Echo)*

VLADIMIR ZHIRINOVSKY is leader of the Liberal Democratic Party and a member of the Russian parliament.

EGYPT REPORT:

KARIM ALRAWI is an Egyptian writer living in Cairo. He is deputy secretary general of the Egyptian Organisation for Human Rights.

SAID AL-ASHMAWI is an author and former head of the State Security and Higher Criminal Courts. He has written widely on the rise of militant Islam, including his recent *Islam and the Political Order.*

FARAG FOUDA, writer and academic, was murdered by Islamic extremists in 1992

GAMAL EL-GHITANI is editor of *Akhbar el-Adab*, a weekly cultural magazine published in Cairo. His novel, *Zayni Barakat,* is published in English by Penguin.

MAHMOUD EL-LOZY is assistant professor of English at the American University of Cairo.

NAGUIB MAHFOUZ is a novelist and won the Nobel Prize for Literature in 1988. His works include *Gablawi's Children, Wedding Song, Palace Walk, the Beggar, Autumn Quail, Palace of Desire, The Search,* and *Sugar Street,* published by Doubleday.

MARIAM MUHAMAD is a regular contributor to *Egypt Today*, a monthly magazine published in Cairo.

MOHAMED MUSTAGEB was born in 1938 in Dairout. He is the author of a novella and two volumes of short stories. He now works in the Arabic Language Academy.

LATIFA AL-ZAYYAT is a critic, author and translator.

AIM:

VESNA BJEKIC, OZRENKA RADULOVIC and **VESNA ROLLER** are journalists with the Belgrade-based Association of Independent Media.

REPORTERS SANS FRONTIÈRES:

ROBERT MÉNARD is the founding director of *Reporters sans frontières* (RSF). **ALEXANDRINE CIVARD, NATHALIE NOUGAYREDE, HENRI FRASQUE** and **BORIS ADAM** are journalists with *La Lettre*, published by RSF.

THANK YOU

Index on Censorship and Writers and Scholars Educational Trust would like to thank all those whose generosity over the years has helped us to maintain our quality and independence, and now enables us to relaunch. In the past three years our supporters include:

Arts Council of Great Britain
Bromley Trust
Carlton Communications plc
Channel Four Television
Charity Know How
John S Cohen Foundation
DANIDA
European Commission
European Human Rights Foundation
Finland, Ministry of Education
Finnish PEN
Ford Foundation
Freedom Forum
Fritt Ord Foundation
Fund for Democracy, Denmark
Gatsby Charitable Foundation
Robert Gavron
Goldberg Charitable Trust

David Hockney
ITN
Lyndhurst Settlement
MAI plc
NORAD
Norway, Ministry of Foreign Affairs
Onaway Trust
Open Society Fund Inc
Lord Palumbo
Penguin Books
Rayne Foundation
E J B Rose Charitable Trust
Joseph Rowntree Charitable Trust
Alan and Babette Sainsbury Charitable Fund
SIDA
Anthony Smith
Umverteilen!
UNESCO

and the *Index* Committees in Australia, Denmark, the Netherlands, Norway and Sweden. Also, special thanks for this relaunch issue to: Sara Marafini and David Eldridge of Senate Design; Camera Press; Caroline Michel; Gara La Marche; Martin Neild; John Scanlon and especially to all our volunteer assistants.

Coming in the July issue of *Index on Censorship*. . .

CHRISTOPHER HIRD   Satellite TV and sky wars
YELENA BONNER   Jewish in Moscow
BURMA   Country file
SOUTH AFRICA   **Adewale Maja-Pearce:** After the elections
TIAN ZHUANGZHUANG   New wave Chinese cinema
ROBERT SUTCLIFFE   Borders, boundaries and refugees
ANDREW GRAHAM-YOOLL   New writing from Latin America
SHERE HITE   Me and the censors
FATIMA MERNISSI   Islam and Democracy